Deep Learning with Python

A Hands-on Introduction

Nikhil Ketkar

Apress®

Deep Learning with Python: A Hands-on Introduction

Nikhil Ketkar
Bangalore, Karnataka, India

ISBN-13 (pbk): 978-1-4842-2765-7   ISBN-13 (electronic): 978-1-4842-2766-4
DOI 10.1007/978-1-4842-2766-4

Library of Congress Control Number: 2017939734

Copyright © 2017 by Nikhil Ketkar

This work is subject to copyright. All rights are reserved by the Publisher, whether the whole or part of the material is concerned, specifically the rights of translation, reprinting, reuse of illustrations, recitation, broadcasting, reproduction on microfilms or in any other physical way, and transmission or information storage and retrieval, electronic adaptation, computer software, or by similar or dissimilar methodology now known or hereafter developed.

Trademarked names, logos, and images may appear in this book. Rather than use a trademark symbol with every occurrence of a trademarked name, logo, or image we use the names, logos, and images only in an editorial fashion and to the benefit of the trademark owner, with no intention of infringement of the trademark.

The use in this publication of trade names, trademarks, service marks, and similar terms, even if they are not identified as such, is not to be taken as an expression of opinion as to whether or not they are subject to proprietary rights.

While the advice and information in this book are believed to be true and accurate at the date of publication, neither the authors nor the editors nor the publisher can accept any legal responsibility for any errors or omissions that may be made. The publisher makes no warranty, express or implied, with respect to the material contained herein.

> Managing Director: Welmoed Spahr
> Editorial Director: Todd Green
> Acquisitions Editor: Celestin Suresh John
> Development Editor: Matthew Moodie and Anila Vincent
> Technical Reviewer: Jojo Moolayail
> Coordinating Editor: Prachi Mehta
> Copy Editor: Larissa Shmailo
> Compositor: SPi Global
> Indexer: SPi Global
> Artist: SPi Global
> Cover image designed by Freepik

Distributed to the book trade worldwide by Springer Science+Business Media New York, 233 Spring Street, 6th Floor, New York, NY 10013. Phone 1-800-SPRINGER, fax (201) 348-4505, e-mail orders-ny@springer-sbm.com, or visit www.springeronline.com. Apress Media, LLC is a California LLC and the sole member (owner) is Springer Science + Business Media Finance Inc (SSBM Finance Inc). SSBM Finance Inc is a **Delaware** corporation.

For information on translations, please e-mail rights@apress.com, or visit http://www.apress.com/rights-permissions.

Apress titles may be purchased in bulk for academic, corporate, or promotional use. eBook versions and licenses are also available for most titles. For more information, reference our Print and eBook Bulk Sales web page at http://www.apress.com/bulk-sales.

Any source code or other supplementary material referenced by the author in this book is available to readers on GitHub via the book's product page, located at www.apress.com/9781484227657. For more detailed information, please visit http://www.apress.com/source-code.

Printed on acid-free paper

To Aditi.

Contents at a Glance

About the Author xiii

About the Technical Reviewer xv

Acknowledgments xvii

■Chapter 1: Introduction to Deep Learning 1

■Chapter 2: Machine Learning Fundamentals 7

■Chapter 3: Feed Forward Neural Networks 17

■Chapter 4: Introduction to Theano 35

■Chapter 5: Convolutional Neural Networks 63

■Chapter 6: Recurrent Neural Networks 79

■Chapter 7: Introduction to Keras 97

■Chapter 8: Stochastic Gradient Descent 113

■Chapter 9: Automatic Differentiation 133

■Chapter 10: Introduction to GPUs 149

■Chapter 11: Introduction to Tensorflow 159

■Chapter 12: Introduction to PyTorch 195

■Chapter 13: Regularization Techniques 209

■Chapter 14: Training Deep Learning Models 215

Index 223

Contents

About the Author xiii

About the Technical Reviewer xv

Acknowledgments xvii

■Chapter 1: Introduction to Deep Learning 1
Historical Context 1
Advances in Related Fields 3
Prerequisites 3
Overview of Subsequent Chapters 4
Installing the Required Libraries 5

■Chapter 2: Machine Learning Fundamentals 7
Intuition 7
Binary Classification 7
Regression 8
Generalization 9
Regularization 14
Summary 16

■Chapter 3: Feed Forward Neural Networks 17
Unit 17
    Overall Structure of a Neural Network 19
    Expressing the Neural Network in Vector Form 20
    Evaluating the output of the Neural Network 21
    Training the Neural Network 23

vii

CONTENTS

Deriving Cost Functions using Maximum Likelihood 24
    Binary Cross Entropy 25
    Cross Entropy 25
    Squared Error 26
    Summary of Loss Functions 27

Types of Units/Activation Functions/Layers 27
    Linear Unit 28
    Sigmoid Unit 28
    Softmax Layer 29
    Rectified Linear Unit (ReLU) 29
    Hyperbolic Tangent 30

Neural Network Hands-on with AutoGrad 33

Summary 33

■Chapter 4: Introduction to Theano 35

What is Theano 35

Theano Hands-On 36

Summary 61

■Chapter 5: Convolutional Neural Networks 63

Convolution Operation 63

Pooling Operation 70

Convolution-Detector-Pooling Building Block 72

Convolution Variants 76

Intuition behind CNNs 77

Summary 78

■Chapter 6: Recurrent Neural Networks 79

RNN Basics 79

Training RNNs 84

Bidirectional RNNs 91

Gradient Explosion and Vanishing 92

Gradient Clipping	93
Long Short Term Memory	95
Summary	96

Chapter 7: Introduction to Keras 97

Summary	111

Chapter 8: Stochastic Gradient Descent 113

Optimization Problems	113
Method of Steepest Descent	114
Batch, Stochastic (Single and Mini-batch) Descent	115
Batch	116
Stochastic Single Example	116
Stochastic Mini-batch	116
Batch vs. Stochastic	116
Challenges with SGD	116
Local Minima	116
Saddle Points	117
Selecting the Learning Rate	118
Slow Progress in Narrow Valleys	119
Algorithmic Variations on SGD	119
Momentum	120
Nesterov Accelerated Gradient (NAS)	121
Annealing and Learning Rate Schedules	121
Adagrad	121
RMSProp	122
Adadelta	123
Adam	123
Resilient Backpropagation	123
Equilibrated SGD	124

CONTENTS

Tricks and Tips for using SGD 124
- Preprocessing Input Data 124
- Choice of Activation Function 124
- Preprocessing Target Value 125
- Initializing Parameters 125
- Shuffling Data 125
- Batch Normalization 125
- Early Stopping 125
- Gradient Noise 125

Parallel and Distributed SGD 126
- Hogwild 126
- Downpour 126

Hands-on SGD with Downhill 127

Summary 132

Chapter 9: Automatic Differentiation 133

Numerical Differentiation 133

Symbolic Differentiation 134

Automatic Differentiation Fundamentals 135
- Forward/Tangent Linear Mode 136
- Reverse/Cotangent/Adjoint Linear Mode 140
- Implementation of Automatic Differentiation 143

Hands-on Automatic Differentiation with Autograd 145

Summary 148

Chapter 10: Introduction to GPUs 149

Summary 158

Chapter 11: Introduction to Tensorflow 159

Summary 194

Chapter 12: Introduction to PyTorch 195

Summary 208

Chapter 13: Regularization Techniques 209

Model Capacity, Overfitting, and Underfitting 209

Regularizing the Model 210

Early Stopping 210

Norm Penalties 212

Dropout 213

Summary 214

Chapter 14: Training Deep Learning Models 215

Performance Metrics 215

Data Procurement 218

Splitting Data for Training/Validation/Test 219

Establishing Achievable Limits on the Error Rate 219

Establishing the Baseline with Standard Choices 220

Building an Automated, End-to-End Pipeline 220

    Orchestration for Visibility 220

Analysis of Overfitting and Underfitting 220

Hyper-Parameter Tuning 222

Summary 222

Index 223

About the Author

Nikhil Ketkar currently leads the Machine Learning Platform team at Flipkart, India's largest e-commerce company. He received his PhD from Washington State University. Following that, he conducted postdoctoral research at University of North Carolina at Charotte, which was followed by a brief stint in high frequency trading at TransMarket in Chicago. More recently, he led the data mining team in Guavus, a startup doing big data analytics in the telecom domain and Indix, a startup doing data science in the e-commerce domain. His research interests include machine learning and graph theory.

About the Technical Reviewer

Jojo Moolayil is a data scientist and author of *Smarter Decisions—The Intersection of Internet of Things and Decision Science*. With over four years of industrial experience in data science, decision science, and IoT, he has worked with industry leaders on high-impact and critical projects across multiple verticals. He is currently associated with General Electric, a pioneer and leader in data science for industrial IoT, and lives in Bengaluru, the Silicon Valley of India.

He was born and raised in Pune, India and graduated from the University of Pune with a major in information technology engineering. He started his career with Mu Sigma, the world's largest pure play analytics provider, and worked with the leaders of many Fortune 50 clients. One of the early enthusiasts to venture into IoT analytics, he now focuses on solving decision science problems for industrial IoT use cases. As a part of his role at GE, he also develops data science and decision science products and platforms for industrial IoT.

Acknowledgments

I would like to thank my colleagues at Flipkart and Indix, and the technical reviewers for their feedback and comments. I will also like to thank Charu Mudholkar for proofreading in the final stages.

CHAPTER 1

Introduction to Deep Learning

This chapter provides a broad overview and an historical context on the subject of deep learning. It also gives the reader a roadmap for navigating the book, its prerequisites, and further reading to dive deeper into the subject matter.

Historical Context

The field of Artificial Intelligence (AI), which can definitely be considered to be the parent field of deep learning, has a rich history going back to 1950. While we will not cover this history in much detail, we will go over some of the key turning points in the field which will lead us to deep learning.

Tasks that AI focused on in its early days were tasks that could be easily described formally, like the games of checkers and chess. This notion of *being able to easily describe the task formally* is at the heart of what a computer program can or cannot do easily. For instance, consider the game of chess. The formal description of the game of chess would be the representation of the board, a description of how each of the pieces moves, the starting configuration, and a description of the configuration wherein the game terminates.

With these notions formalized, it's relatively easy to model a chess-playing AI program as a search, and given sufficient computational resources, it's possible to produce a relatively good chess-playing AI.

The first era of AI focused on such tasks with a fair amount of success. At the heart of the methodology was a symbolic representation of the domain and the manipulation of symbols based on given rules (with increasingly sophisticated algorithms for searching the solution space to arrive at a solution).

It must be noted that the formal definitions of such rules were done manually. However, such early AI systems were fairly general purpose task/problem solvers in the sense that any problem that could be described formally could be solved using the generic approach.

The key limitation of such systems is that the game of chess is a relatively easy problem for AI simply because the problem setting is relatively simple and can be easily formalized. This is not the case with many of the problems human beings solve on a day-to-day basis (natural intelligence). For instance, consider diagnosing a disease as a physician does or transcribing human speech to text. These tasks, like most other tasks human beings master easily, are hard to describe formally and thus presented a challenge in the early days of AI.

Human beings address such tasks by leveraging a large amount of knowledge about the task/problem domain. Given this observation, subsequent AI systems relied on a large knowledge base which captured the knowledge about the problem/task domain. One point to be noted is the term used here is "knowledge" not "information" or "data." By knowledge we simply mean data/information that a program/algorithm can reason about. An example of this could be a graphic representation of a map with edges labeled with distances and or one of traffic (which is being constantly updated) which allows a program to reason about the shortest path between points.

© Nikhil Ketkar 2017
N. Ketkar, *Deep Learning with Python*, DOI 10.1007/978-1-4842-2766-4_1

Such knowledge-based systems wherein the knowledge was compiled by experts and represented in a way that allowed algorithms/programs to reason about it represent the second generation of AI. At the heart of such approaches were increasingly sophisticated methods for representing and reasoning about knowledge to solve tasks/problems that required such knowledge. Examples of such sophistication include the use of first-order logic to encode knowledge and probabilistic representations to capture and reason where uncertainty is inherent to the domain.

One of the key challenges that such systems faced and addressed to some extent was the uncertainty inherent in many domains. Human beings are relatively good at reasoning in environments with unknowns and uncertainty. One key observation here is that even the knowledge we hold about a domain is not black or white but gray. A lot of progress was made in this era on representing and reasoning about unknowns and uncertainty. There were some limited successes in tasks like diagnosing a disease, which relied on leveraging and reasoning using a knowledge base in the presence of unknowns and uncertainty.

The key limitation of such systems was the need to hand-compile the knowledge about the domain from experts. Collecting, compiling, and maintaining such knowledge bases rendered such systems impractical. In certain domains, it was extremely hard even to collect and compile such knowledge—for instance, transcribing speech to text or translating documents from one language to another. While human beings can easily learn to do such tasks it's extremely challenging to hand-compile and encode the knowledge related to the tasks—for instance, the knowledge of the English language and grammar, accents, and subject matter.

Human beings address such tasks by acquiring knowledge about a task/problem domain, a process referred to as learning. Given this observation, the focus of subsequent work in AI shifted over a decade or two to algorithms that improved their performance based on data provided to them. The focus of this subfield was to develop algorithms that acquired relevant knowledge for a task/problem domain given data. It is important to note that this knowledge acquisition relied on labeled data and a suitable representation of labeled data as defined by a human being.

For instance, consider the problem of diagnosing a disease. For such a task, a human expert would collect a lot of cases where a patient had and did not have the disease in question. Then, the human expert would identify a number of features that would aid in making the prediction, like, say, the age of the patient, the gender, and results from a number of diagnostic tests such as blood pressure, blood sugar, and so on. The human expert would compile all this data and represent it in a suitable format (e.g., scaling/normalizing the data). Once this data was prepared, a Machine Learning (ML) algorithm could identify how to infer whether the patient has the disease or not by generalizing from the labeled data. Note that the labeled data consisted of patients who both have and do not have the disease. So, in essence the underlying ML algorithm is essentially doing the job of finding a mathematical function that can produce the right outcome (disease or no disease) given the inputs (features like age, gender, data from diagnostic tests, etc.). Finding the simplest mathematical function that predicts the outputs with required level of accuracy is the heart of ML. Specific questions like how many examples are required to learn a task or the time complexity of the algorithm, for example, are specific questions on which the field of ML has provided answers with theoretical justification. The field has matured to a point where, given enough data, computer resources, and human resources to engineer features, a large class of problems are solvable.

The key limitation of mainstream ML algorithms is that applying them to a new problem domain requires a massive amount of feature engineering. For instance, consider the problem of recognizing objects in images. Using traditional ML techniques, such a problem will require a massive feature engineering effort wherein experts would identify and generate features that would be used by the ML algorithm. In a sense, the true intelligence is in the identification of features and what the ML algorithm is doing is simply learning how to combine these features to arrive at the correct answer. This identification of features or the representation of data, which domain experts do before they apply ML algorithms, is both a conceptual and practical bottleneck in AI.

It's a conceptual bottleneck because if features are being identified by domain experts, and the ML algorithm is simply learning to combine and draw a conclusion from this, is it really AI? It's a practical bottleneck because the process of building models via traditional ML is bottlenecked by the amount of feature engineering required; there are limits to how much human effort can be thrown at the problem.

Human beings learn concepts starting from raw data. For instance, a child shown a few examples/instances of a particular animal (like, say, cats) will soon learn to identify cats. The learning process does not involve a parent identifying features (e.g., look at the whiskers or see the fur or the tail). Human learning goes from raw data to a conclusion without the explicit step where features are identified and provided to the learner. In a sense, human beings learn the appropriate representation of data from the data itself. Furthermore, they organize concepts as a hierarchy where complicated concepts are expressed using primitive concepts.

The field of deep learning has its primary focus on learning appropriate representations of data such that these could be used to draw conclusions. The word "deep" in deep learning refers to the idea of learning the hierarchy of concepts directly from raw data. A more technically appropriate term for deep learning would be "representation learning" and a more practical term for the same would be "automated feature engineering."

Advances in Related Fields

It is important to make a note of advances in other fields that have played a key role in the recent interest and success of deep learning. The following points are to be noted:

1. The ability to collect, store, and operate over large amounts of data has greatly advanced over the last decade (for instance, the Apache Hadoop Ecosystem).

2. The ability to generate supervised training data (which is basically data with labels, an example of this would be pictures annotated with the objects in the picture) has improved a lot with the availability of crowd-sourcing services (like Amazon Mechanical Turk).

3. The massive improvements in computational horsepower brought about by Graphical Processing Units (GPUs).

4. The advances in both theory and software implementation of automatic differentiation (like Theano).

While these advancements are peripheral to deep learning, they have played a big role in enabling advances in deep learning.

Prerequisites

The key prerequisites for reading this book are a working knowledge of Python and some coursework on linear algebra, calculus, and probability. It is recommended that readers refer to the following in case they need to cover these prerequisites:

1. *Dive Into Python* by Mark Pilgrim for Python.

2. *Linear Algebra* by Gilbert Strang for linear algebra.

3. *Calculus* by Gilbert Strang for calculus.

4. *All of Statistics* by Larry Wasserman for probability (Section 1, chapters 1–5).

CHAPTER 1 ■ INTRODUCTION TO DEEP LEARNING

Overview of Subsequent Chapters

We now provide an overall outline of the subsequent chapters for the reader. It is important to note that each of the chapters covers either the concepts or the skills (or in certain cases both) with respect to deep learning. We highlight these next so that the readers can ensure that they have internalized these concepts and skills. It is highly recommended that the reader not only read the chapters but also work out the mathematical details (using pen and paper) and play with the source code provided in each of the chapters.

1. Chapter 2 covers the basics of Machine Learning. The key take-home point for this chapter is the concept of generalizing over unseen examples, the ideas of overfitting and underfitting the training data, the capacity of the model, and the notion of regularization.

2. Chapter 3 covers Feed Forward Neural Networks and serves as the conceptual foundation for the entire book. Concepts like the overall structure of the neural network, the input, hidden and output layers, cost functions, and their basis on the principle of Maximum Likelihood are the important concepts in this chapter.

3. Chapter 4 provides a hands-on introduction to the Theano library. It covers how to define networks as computational graphs, automatically derive gradients for complicated networks, and train neural networks.

4. Chapter 5 covers Convolutional Neural Networks, which are perhaps the most successful application of deep learning.

5. Chapter 6 covers Recurrent Neural Networks and Long Short Term Memory (LSTM) networks which are another successful application of deep learning.

6. Chapter 7 provides a hands-on introduction to the Keras library. The Keras library provides a number of high level abstractions over the Theano library and is probably the ideal go-to tool when it comes to building deep learning applications.

7. Chapter 8 introduces the reader to Stochastic Gradient Descent (SGD) which is the most common procedure used to train neural networks. This chapter also covers the shortcomings of SGD and a number of variations to SGD that address these shortcomings.

8. Chapter 9 introduces the reader to Automatic Differentiation (commonly referred to as back propagation) which is a standard technique used to derive gradients (required for SGD) for arbitrarily complicated networks.

9. Chapter 10 introduces the reader to GPUs and GPU-based computation, which has acted as a key enabling technology for deep learning.

10. Chapter 11 introduces the reader to the Tensorflow library. It covers how to define networks as computational graphs, automatically derive gradients for complicated networks, and train neural networks.

11. Chapter 12 introduces the reader to the PyTorch library which provides the ability to define mathematical functions and compute their gradients.

12. Chapter 13 introduces the reader to regularization techniques in deep learning.

13. Chapter 14 introduces the reader to the process and practice of developing deep learning models.

Installing the Required Libraries

There are a number of libraries that the reader will need to install in order to run the source code for the examples in the chapters. We recommend that the reader install Anaconda Python Distribution https://www.continuum.io/downloads, which would make the process of installing the required packages significantly easy (using either conda or pip). The list of packages the reader would need include Scikit-learn, Theano, Autograd, Keras, and PyOpenCL.

CHAPTER 2

Machine Learning Fundamentals

Deep Learning is a branch of Machine Learning and in this chapter we will cover the fundamentals of Machine Learning. While machine learning as a subject is inherently mathematical in nature, we will keep mathematics to the basic minimum required to develop intuition about the subject. Prerequisites for the subject matter covered in this chapter would be linear algebra, multivariable calculus, and basic probability theory.

Intuition

As human beings we are intuitively aware of the concept of learning: it simply means to get better at a task over a period of time. The task could be physical (like learning to drive a car) or intellectual (like learning a new language). The subject of machine learning focuses on development of algorithms that can learn as humans do; that is, they get better at a task over a period over time, with experience.

The first question to ask is why we would be interested in development of algorithms that improve their performance over time with experience. After all there are many algorithms that are developed and implemented to solve real world problems that don't improve over time, they simply are developed by humans and implemented in software and they get the job done. From banking to e-commerce and from navigation systems in our cars to landing a spacecraft on the moon algorithms are everywhere and a majority of them do not improve over time. These algorithms simply perform the task they are intended to perform, with some maintenance required from time to time. Why do we need machine learning?

The answer to this question is that for certain tasks it is easier to develop an algorithm that learns/improves its performance with experience than to develop an algorithm manually. While this might seem unintuitive to the reader at this point, we will build intuition for this during the course of this chapter.

Binary Classification

In order to further discuss the matter at hand, we need to be precise about some of the terms we have been intuitively using, like task, learning, experience, and improvement. We will start with the task of binary classification.

Consider an abstract problem domain where we have data of the form

$$D = \{(x_1, y_1), (x_2, y_2), \ldots (x_n, y_n)\}$$

where $x \in \mathbb{R}^n$ and $y = \pm 1$. We do not have access to all such data but only a subset $S \in D$. Using S, our task is to generate a computational procedure that implements the function $f : x \to y$ such that we can use f to make predictions over unseen data $(x_i, y_i) \notin S$ that are correct, $f(x_i) = y_i$. Let us denote $U \in D$ as the set of unseen data, that is, $(x_i, y_i) \notin S$ and $(x_i, y_i) \in U$. We measure performance over this task as the error over unseen data,

$$E(f, D, U) = \frac{\sum_{(x_i, y_i) \in U} [f(x_i) \neq y_i]}{|U|}.$$

We now have a precise definition of the task, which is to categorize data into one of two categories ($y = \pm 1$) based on some seen data S by generating f. We measure performance (and improvement in performance) using the error $E(f, D, U)$ over unseen data U. The size of the seen data $|S|$ is the conceptual equivalent of experience. In this context, we want to develop algorithms that generate such functions f (which are commonly referred to as a model). In general, the field of machine learning studies the development of such algorithms that produce models that make predictions over unseen data for such algorithms, and other formal tasks (we will be introducing multiple such tasks later in the chapter). Note that the x is commonly referred to as the input/input variable and y is referred to as the output/output variable.

As with any other discipline in computer science, the computational characteristics of such algorithms is an important facet, but in addition to that we also would like to have a model f that achieves a lower error $E(f, D, U)$ with as small a $|S|$ as possible.

Let us now relate this abstract but precise definition to a real world problem so that our abstractions are grounded. Let us say an e-commerce web site wants to customize the landing page for registered users to show them the products the users might be interested in buying. The web site has historical data on users and would like to implement this as a feature so as to increase sales. Let us now see how this real world problem maps onto the abstract problem of binary classification we described earlier.

The first thing that one might notice is that given a particular user and a particular product, one wants to predict whether the user will buy the product. Since this is the value to be predicted, it maps onto $y = \pm 1$, where we will let the value of $y = +1$ denote the prediction that the user will buy the product and we will denote $y = -1$ as the prediction that the user does not buy the product. Note that that there is no particular reason for picking these values; we could have swapped this (let $y = +1$ denote the does not buy case and $y = -1$ denote the buy case) and there would be no difference. We just use $y = \pm 1$ to denote the two classes of interest to categorize data. Next, let us assume that we can somehow represent the attributes of the product and the user's buying and browsing history as $x \in \mathbb{R}^n$. This step is referred to as feature engineering in machine learning and we will cover it later in the chapter. For now, it suffices to say that we are able to generate such a mapping. Thus, we have historical data of what the users browsed and bought, attributes of a product and whether the user bought the product or not mapped onto $\{(x_1, y_1), (x_2, y_2), \ldots (x_n, y_n)\}$. Now, based on this data, we would like to generate a function or a model $f : x \to y$ which we can use to determine which products a particular user will buy and use this to populate the landing page for users. We can measure how well the model is doing on unseen data by populating the landing page for users and see whether they buy the products or not and evaluate the error $E(f, D, U)$.

Regression

Let us introduce another task, namely regression. Here, we have data of the form $D = \{(x_1, y_1), (x_2, y_2), \ldots (x_n, y_n)\}$ where $x \in \mathbb{R}^n$ and $y \in \mathbb{R}$ and our task is to generate a computational procedure that implements the function $f : x \to y$. Note that instead of the prediction being a binary class label $y = \pm 1$ like in binary classification, we have real valued prediction. We measure performance over this task as the root mean squared error (RMSE) over unseen data,

$$E(f,D,U) = \left(\frac{\sum_{(x_i,y_i) \in U} (y_i - f(x_i))^2}{|U|} \right)^{\frac{1}{2}}.$$

> **Note** That the RMSE is simply taking the difference between the predicted and actual value, squaring it so as to account for both positive and negative differences, taking the mean so as to aggregate over all the unseen data and, finally, taking the square root so as to counterbalance the square operation.

A real world problem that corresponds to the abstract task of regression is to predict the credit score for an individual based on their financial history, which can be used by a credit card company to extend the line of credit.

Generalization

Let us now cover what is the single most important intuition in Machine Learning, which is that we want to develop/generate models that have good performance over unseen data. In order to do that, let us introduce a toy data set for a regression task first.

We generate the toy dataset by generating 100 values equidistantly between -1 and 1 as the input variable (x). We generate the output variable (y) based on $y = 2 + x + 2x^2 + \epsilon$ where $\epsilon \sim \mathcal{N}(0, 0.1)$ is noise (random variation) from a normal distribution with 0 mean and 0.1 being the standard deviation. Code for this is presented in Listing 2-1 and the data is plotted in Figure 2-1.

Listing 2-1. Generalization vs. Rote Learning

```
#Generate Toy Dataset
import pylab
import numpy
x = numpy.linspace(-1,1,100)
signal = 2 + x + 2 * x * x
noise = numpy.random.normal(0, 0.1, 100)
y = signal + noise
pylab.plot(signal,'b');
pylab.plot(y,'g')
pylab.plot(noise, 'r')
pylab.xlabel("x")
pylab.ylabel("y")
pylab.legend(["Without Noise", "With Noise", "Noise"], loc = 2)
x_train = x[0:80]
y_train = y[0:80]

# Model with degree 1
pylab.figure()
degree = 2
X_train = numpy.column_stack([numpy.power(x_train,i) for i in xrange(0,degree)])
```

CHAPTER 2 ■ MACHINE LEARNING FUNDAMENTALS

```
model = numpy.dot(numpy.dot(numpy.linalg.inv(numpy.dot(X_train.transpose(),X_train)),
X_train.transpose()),y_train)
pylab.plot(x,y,'g')
pylab.xlabel("x")
pylab.ylabel("y")
predicted = numpy.dot(model, [numpy.power(x,i) for i in xrange(0,degree)])
pylab.plot(x, predicted,'r')
pylab.legend(["Actual", "Predicted"], loc = 2)
train_rmse1 = numpy.sqrt(numpy.sum(numpy.dot(y[0:80] - predicted[0:80],
y_train - predicted[0:80])))
test_rmse1 = numpy.sqrt(numpy.sum(numpy.dot(y[80:] - predicted[80:],
y[80:] - predicted[80:])))
print("Train RMSE (Degree = 1)", train_rmse1)
print("Test RMSE (Degree = 1)", test_rmse1)

# Model with degree 2
pylab.figure()
degree = 3
X_train = numpy.column_stack([numpy.power(x_train,i) for i in xrange(0,degree)])
model = numpy.dot(numpy.dot(numpy.linalg.inv(numpy.dot(X_train.transpose(),X_train)),
X_train.transpose()),y_train)
pylab.plot(x,y,'g')
pylab.xlabel("x")
pylab.ylabel("y")
predicted = numpy.dot(model, [numpy.power(x,i) for i in xrange(0,degree)])
pylab.plot(x, predicted,'r')
pylab.legend(["Actual", "Predicted"], loc = 2)
train_rmse1 = numpy.sqrt(numpy.sum(numpy.dot(y[0:80] - predicted[0:80],
y_train - predicted[0:80])))
test_rmse1 = numpy.sqrt(numpy.sum(numpy.dot(y[80:] - predicted[80:],
y[80:] - predicted[80:])))
print("Train RMSE (Degree = 2)", train_rmse1)
print("Test RMSE (Degree = 2)", test_rmse1)

# Model with degree 8
pylab.figure()
degree = 9
X_train = numpy.column_stack([numpy.power(x_train,i) for i in xrange(0,degree)])
model = numpy.dot(numpy.dot(numpy.linalg.inv(numpy.dot(X_train.transpose(),X_train)),
X_train.transpose()), y_train)
pylab.plot(x, y,'g')
pylab.xlabel("x")
pylab.ylabel("y")
predicted = numpy.dot(model, [numpy.power(x,i) for i in xrange(0,degree)])
pylab.plot(x, predicted,'r')
pylab.legend(["Actual", "Predicted"], loc = 3)
train_rmse2 = numpy.sqrt(numpy.sum(numpy.dot(y[0:80] - predicted[0:80],
y_train - predicted[0:80])))
test_rmse2 = numpy.sqrt(numpy.sum(numpy.dot(y[80:] - predicted[80:],
y[80:] - predicted[80:])))
print("Train RMSE (Degree = 8)", train_rmse2)
print("Test RMSE (Degree = 8)", test_rmse2)
```

```
# Output
Train RMSE (Degree = 1) 3.50756834691
Test RMSE (Degree = 1) 7.69514326946
Train RMSE (Degree = 2) 0.91896252959
Test RMSE (Degree = 2) 0.446173435392
Train RMSE (Degree = 8) 0.897346255079
Test RMSE (Degree = 8) 14.1908525449
```

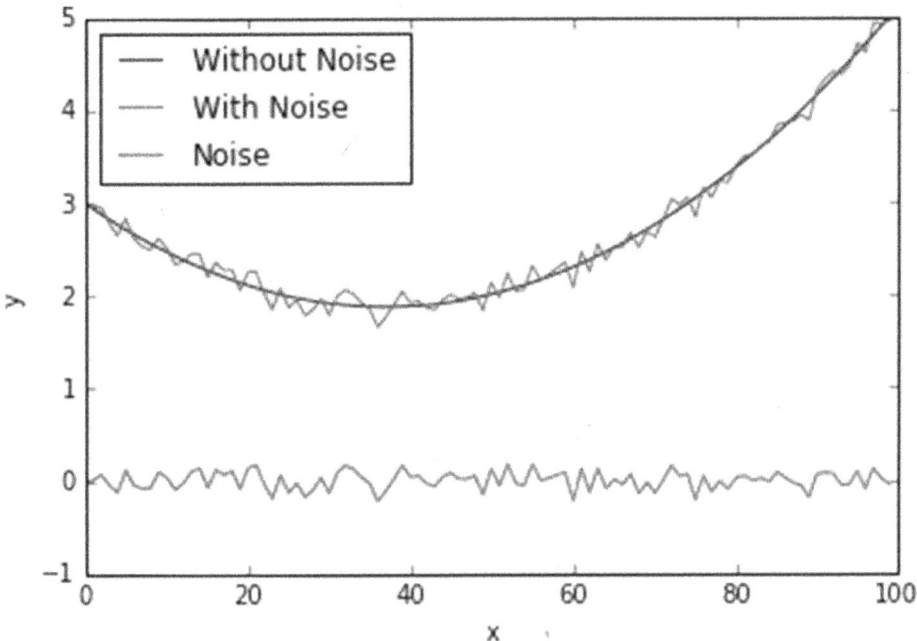

Figure 2-1. *Generate a toy problem dataset for regression*

In order to simulate seen and unseen data, we use the first 80 data points as seen data and the rest we treat as unseen data. That is, we build the model using only the first 80 data points and use the rest for evaluating the model.

Next, we use a very simple algorithm to generate a model, commonly referred to as Least Squares. Given a data set of the form $D = \{(x_1, y_1), (x_2, y_2), \ldots, (x_n, y_n)\}$ where $x \in \mathbb{R}^n$ and $y \in \mathbb{R}$, the least squares model takes the form $y = \beta x$ where β is a vector such that $\|X\beta - y\|_2^2$ is minimized. Here X is a matrix where each row is an x, thus $X \in \mathbb{R}^{m \times n}$ with m being the number of examples (in our case 80). The value of β can be derived using the closed form $\beta = (X^T X)^{-1} X^T y$. We are glossing over a lot of important details of the least squares method but those are secondary to the current discussion. The more pertinent detail is how we transform the input variable to a suitable form. In our first model, we will transform x to be a vector of values $[x^0, x^1, x^2]$. That is, if $x = 2$, it will be transformed to $[1, 2, 4]$. Post this transformation, we can generate a least squares model β using the formula described above. What is happening under the hood is that we are approximating the given data with a second order polynomial (degree = 2) equation, and the least squares algorithm is simply curve fitting or generating the coefficients for each of $[x^0, x^1, x^2]$.

CHAPTER 2 ■ MACHINE LEARNING FUNDAMENTALS

We can evaluate the model on the unseen data using the RMSE metric. We can also compute the RMSE metric on the training data. The actual and predicted values are plotted in Figure 2-2 and listing 2-1 shows the source code for generating the model.

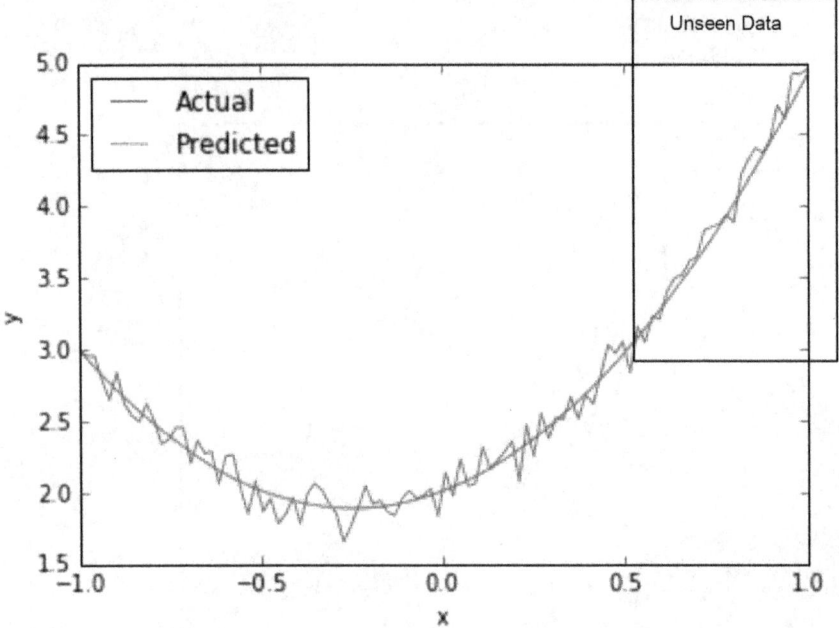

Figure 2-2. *Actual and predicted values for model with degree = 2*

Next, we generate another model with the least squares algorithm but we will transform *x* to $[x^0, x^1, x^2, x^3, x^4, x^5, x^6, x^7, x^8]$. That is, we are approximating the given data with a polynomial with degree = 8. The actual and predicted values are plotted in Figure 2-3 and listing 2-1 shows the source code for generating the model. As the last step we generate a model with degree = 1.

CHAPTER 2 ■ MACHINE LEARNING FUNDAMENTALS

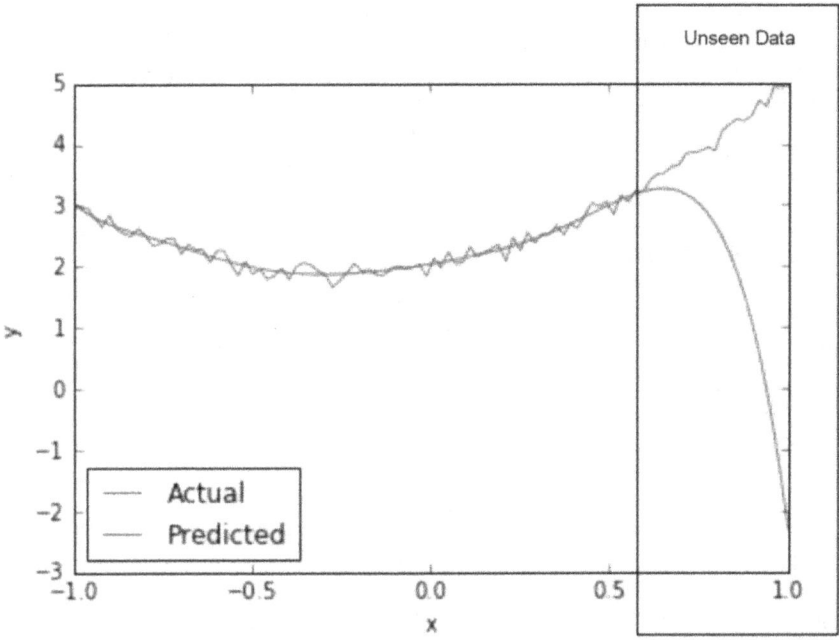

Figure 2-3. *Actual and predicted values for model with degree = 8*

The actual and predicted values are plotted in Figure 2-4 and listing 2-1 shows the source code for generating the model.

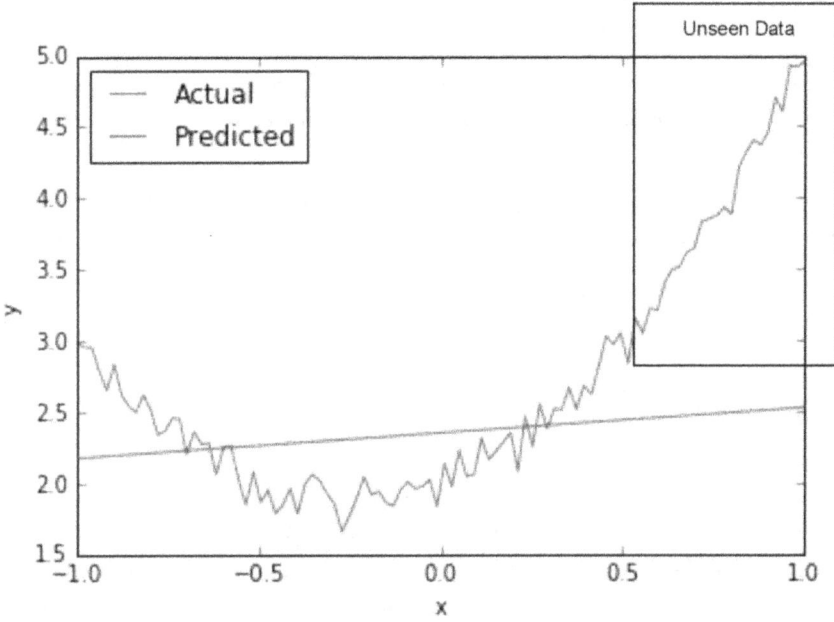

Figure 2-4. *Actual and predicted values for model with degree = 1*

13

We now have all the details in place to discuss the core concept of generalization. The key question to ask is which is the better model? The one with degree = 2 or the one with degree = 8 or the one with degree = 1?

Let us start by making a few observations about the three models. The model with degree = 1 performs poorly on both the seen as well as unseen data as compared to the other two models. The model with degree = 8 performs better on seen data as compared to the model with degree = 2. The model with degree = 2 performs better than the model with degree = 8 on unseen data. Table 2-1 visualizes this in table form for easy interpretation.

Table 2-1. Comparing the performance of the 3 different models

Degree	1	2	8
Seen Data	Worst	Worst	Better
Unseen Data	Worst	Better	Worst

Let us now understand the important concept of model capacity, which corresponds to the degree of the polynomial in this example. The data we generated was using a second order polynomial (degree = 2) with some noise. Then, we tried to approximate the data using three models of degree: 1, 2, and 8, respectively. The higher the degree, the more expressive is the model. That is, it can accommodate more variation. This ability to accommodate variation corresponds to the notion of capacity. That is, we say that the model with degree = 8 has a higher capacity that the model with degree = 2, which in turn has a higher capacity than the model with degree = 1. Isn't having higher capacity always a good thing? It turns out it is not, when we consider that all real world datasets contain some noise and a higher capacity model will end up just fitting the noise in addition to the signal in the data. This is why we observe that the model with degree = 2 does better on the unseen data as compared to the model with degree = 8. In this example, we knew how the data was generated (with a second order polynomial (degree = 2) with some noise); hence, this observation is quite trivial. However, in the real world, we don't know the underlying mechanism by which the data is generated. This leads us to the fundamental challenge in machine learning, which is, does the model truly generalize? And the only true test for that is the performance over unseen data.

In a sense the concept of capacity corresponds to the simplicity or parsimony of the model. A model with high capacity can approximate more complex data. This is how many free variables/coefficients the model has. In our example, the model with degree = 1 does not have capacity sufficient to approximate the data and this is commonly referred to as under fitting. Correspondingly, the model with degree = 8 has extra capacity and it over fits the data.

As a thought experiment, consider what would happen if we had a model with degree equal to 80. Given that we had 80 data points as training data, we would have an 80-degree polynomial that would perfectly approximate the data. This is the ultimate pathological case wherein there is no learning at all. The model has 80 coefficients and can simply memorize the data. This is referred to as rote learning, the logical extreme of overfitting. This is why the capacity of the model needs to be tuned with respect to the amount of training data we have. If the dataset is small, we are better off training models with lower capacity.

Regularization

Building on the idea of model capacity, generalization, over fitting, and under fitting, let us now cover the idea of regularization. The key idea here is to penalize complexity of the model. A regularized version of least squares takes the form $y = \beta x$, where β is a vector such that $\|X\beta - y\|_2^2 + \lambda \|\beta\|_2^2$ is minimized and λ is a user-defined parameter that controls the complexity. Here, by introducing the term $\lambda \|\beta\|_2^2$, we are penalizing complex models. To see why this is the case, consider fitting a least square model using a polynomial of degree 10, but the values in the vector β has 8 zeros; 2 are non-zeros. Against this, consider the case where

CHAPTER 2 ■ MACHINE LEARNING FUNDAMENTALS

all values in the vector β are non-zeros. For all practical purposes, the former model is a model with degree = 2 and has a lower value of $\lambda \|\beta\|_2^2$. The λ term allows us to balance accuracy over the training data with the complexity of the model. Lower values of λ imply a simpler model.

We can compute the value of β using the closed form $\beta = \left(X^T X - \lambda I\right)^{-1} X^T y$. We illustrate keeping the degree fixed at a value of 80 and varying the value of λ in listing 2-2.

Listing 2-2. Regularization

```
import pylab
import numpy
x = numpy.linspace(-1,1,100)
signal = 2 + x + 2 * x * x
noise = numpy.random.normal(0, 0.1, 100)
y = signal + noise
x_train = x[0:80]
y_train = y[0:80]

train_rmse = []
test_rmse = []
degree = 80
lambda_reg_values = numpy.linspace(0.01,0.99,100)

for lambda_reg in lambda_reg_values:
    X_train = numpy.column_stack([numpy.power(x_train,i) for i in xrange(0,degree)])
    model = numpy.dot(numpy.dot(numpy.linalg.inv(numpy.dot(X_train.transpose(),X_train) + lambda_reg * numpy.identity(degree)),X_train.transpose()),y_train)
    predicted = numpy.dot(model, [numpy.power(x,i) for i in xrange(0,degree)])
    train_rmse.append(numpy.sqrt(numpy.sum(numpy.dot(y[0:80] - predicted[0:80], y_train - predicted[0:80]))))
    test_rmse.append(numpy.sqrt(numpy.sum(numpy.dot(y[80:] - predicted[80:], y[80:] - predicted[80:]))))

pylab.plot(lambda_reg_values, train_rmse)
pylab.plot(lambda_reg_values, test_rmse)
pylab.xlabel(r"$\lambda$")
pylab.ylabel("RMSE")
pylab.legend(["Train", "Test"], loc = 2)
```

The training RMSE (seen data) and test RMSE (unseen data) is plotted in Figure 2-5.

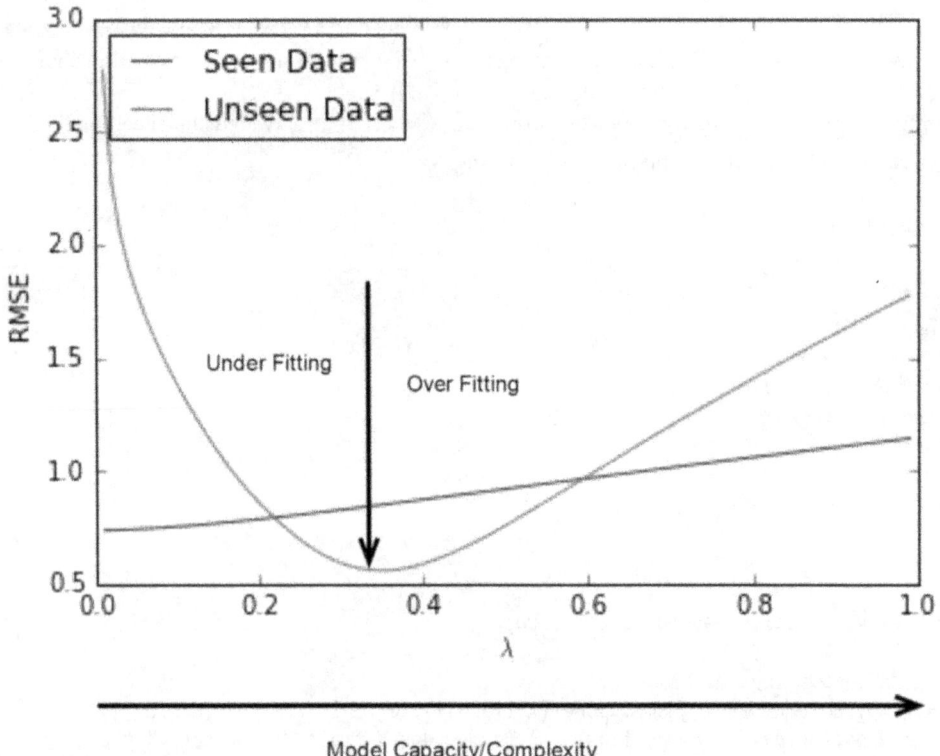

Figure 2-5. *Regularization*

Summary

In this chapter we covered the basics of Machine Learning. The key take-home points for this chapter are the concepts of generalizing over unseen examples, over-fitting and under-fitting the training data, the capacity of the model, and the notion of regularization. The reader is encouraged to try out the examples (in the source code listings). In the next chapter, we will build on these concepts and cover neural networks.

CHAPTER 3

Feed Forward Neural Networks

In this chapter we will cover some key concepts around Feed Forward neural networks. These concepts will serve as a foundation as we cover more technical topics in depth.

At an abstract level, a Neural Network can be thought of as a function $f_\theta : x \to y$, which takes an input $x \in \mathbb{R}^n$ and produces an output $y \in \mathbb{R}^m$, and whose behavior is parameterized by $\theta \in \mathbb{R}^p$. So for instance, f_θ could be simply $y = f_\theta(x) = \theta \cdot x$.

We will start by looking at the structure of a neural network, followed by how they are trained and used for making predictions.

Unit

A unit is the basic building of a neural network; refer to Figure 3-1. The following points should be noted:

1. A unit is a function that takes as input a vector $x \in \mathbb{R}^n$ and produces a scalar.

2. A unit is parameterized by a weight vector $w \in \mathbb{R}^n$ and a bias term denoted by b.

3. The output of the unit can be described as

$$f\left(\sum_{i=1}^{n} x_i \cdot w_i + b\right)$$

   where $f : \mathbb{R} \to \mathbb{R}$ is referred to as an activation function.

4. A variety of activation functions may be used, as we shall see later in the chapter; generally, it's a non-linear function.

CHAPTER 3 ■ FEED FORWARD NEURAL NETWORKS

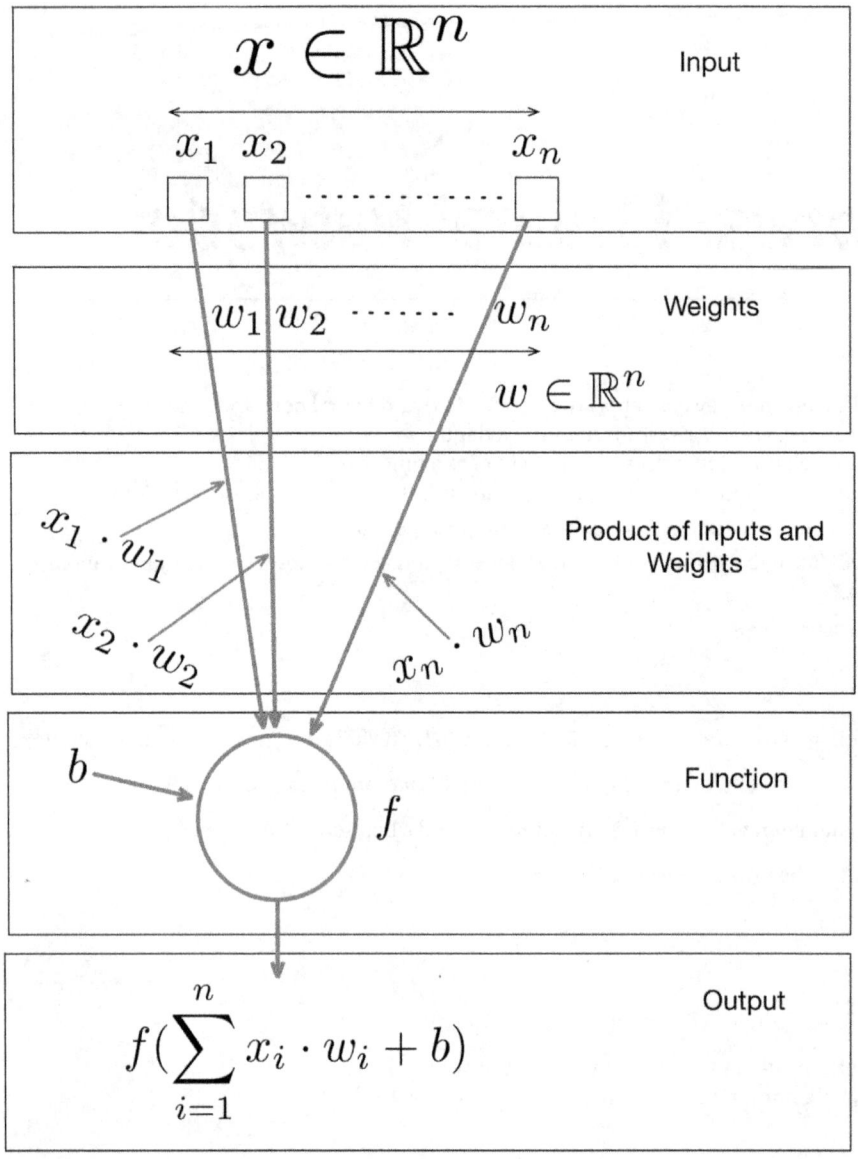

Figure 3-1. *A unit in a neural network*

CHAPTER 3 ■ FEED FORWARD NEURAL NETWORKS

Overall Structure of a Neural Network

Neural Networks are constructed using the unit as a basic building block (introduced earlier); refer to Figure 3-2.

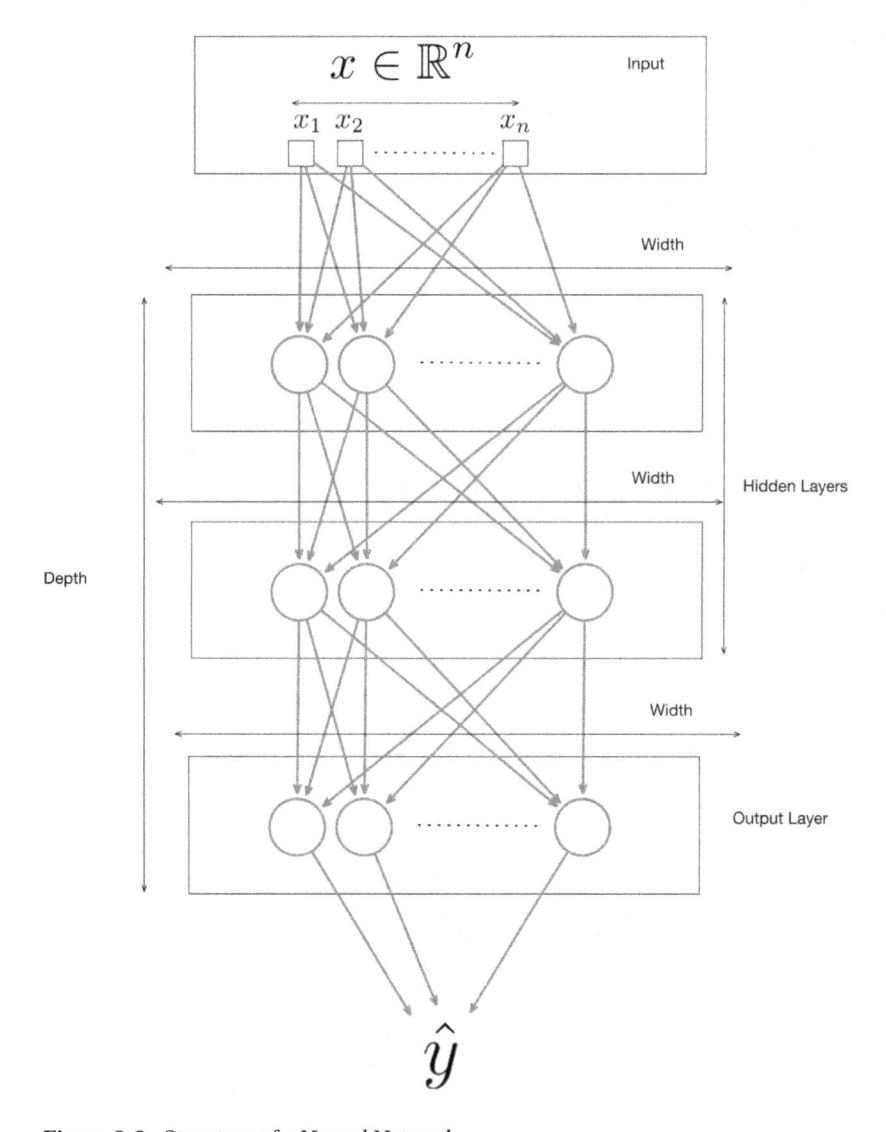

Figure 3-2. Structure of a Neural Network

The following points are to be noted:

1. Units are organized as layers, with every layer containing one or more units.
2. The last layer is referred to as the output layer.
3. All layers before the output layers are referred to as hidden layers.
4. The number of units in a layer is referred to as the width of the layer.

5. The width of each layer need not be the same, but the dimension should be aligned, as we shall see later in the chapter.

6. The number of layers is referred to as the depth of the network. This is where the notion of *deep* (as in deep learning) comes from.

7. Every layer takes as input the output produced by the previous layer, except for the first layer, which consumes the input.

8. The output of the last layer is the output of the network and is the prediction generated based on the input.

9. As we have seen earlier, a neural network can be seen as a function $f_\theta : x \to y$, which takes as input $x \in \mathbb{R}^n$ and produces as output $y \in \mathbb{R}^m$ and whose behavior is parameterized by $\theta \in \mathbb{R}^p$. We can now be more precise about θ; it's simply a collection of all the weights w for all the units in the network.

10. Designing a neural network involves, amongst other things, defining the overall structure of the network, including the number of layers and the width of these layers.

Expressing the Neural Network in Vector Form

Let us now take a look at the layers of a Neural Network and their dimensions in a bit more detail. Refer to Figure 3-3; the following points should be noted:

1. If we assume that the dimensionality of the input is $x \in \mathbb{R}^n$ and the first layer has p_1 units, then each of the units has $w \in \mathbb{R}^n$ weights associated with them. That is, the weights associated with the first layer are a matrix of the form $w_1 \in \mathbb{R}^{n \times p_1}$. While this is not shown in the diagram, each of the p_1 units also has a bias term associated with it.

2. The first layer produces an output $o_1 \in \mathbb{R}^{p_1}$ where $o_i = f\left(\sum_{k=1}^{n} x_k \cdot w_k + b_i\right)$. Note that the index k corresponds to each of the inputs/weights (going from $1 \ldots n$) and the index i corresponds to the units in the first layer (going from $1 .. p_1$).

3. Let us now look at the output of the first layer in a vectorised notation. By vectorised notation, we simply mean linear algebraic operations like vector matrix multiplications and computation of the activation function on a vector producing a vector (rather than scalar to scalar). The output of the first layer can be represented as $f(x \cdot w_1 + b_1)$. Here we are treating the input $x \in \mathbb{R}^n$ to be of dimensionality $1 \times n$, the weight matrix w_1 to be of dimensionality $n \times p_1$, and the bias term to be a vector of dimensionality $1 \times p_1$. Notice then that $x \cdot w_1 + b$ produces a vector of dimensionality $1 \times p_1$ and the function f simply transforms each element of the vector to produce $o_1 \in \mathbb{R}^{p_1}$.

4. A similar process follows for the second layer that goes from $o_1 \in \mathbb{R}^{p_1}$ to $o_2 \in \mathbb{R}^{p_2}$. This can be written in vectorised form as $f(o_1 \cdot w_2 + b_2)$. We can also write the entire computation up to layer 2 in vectorised form as $f(f(x \cdot w_1 + b_1) \cdot w_2 + b_2)$.

CHAPTER 3 ■ FEED FORWARD NEURAL NETWORKS

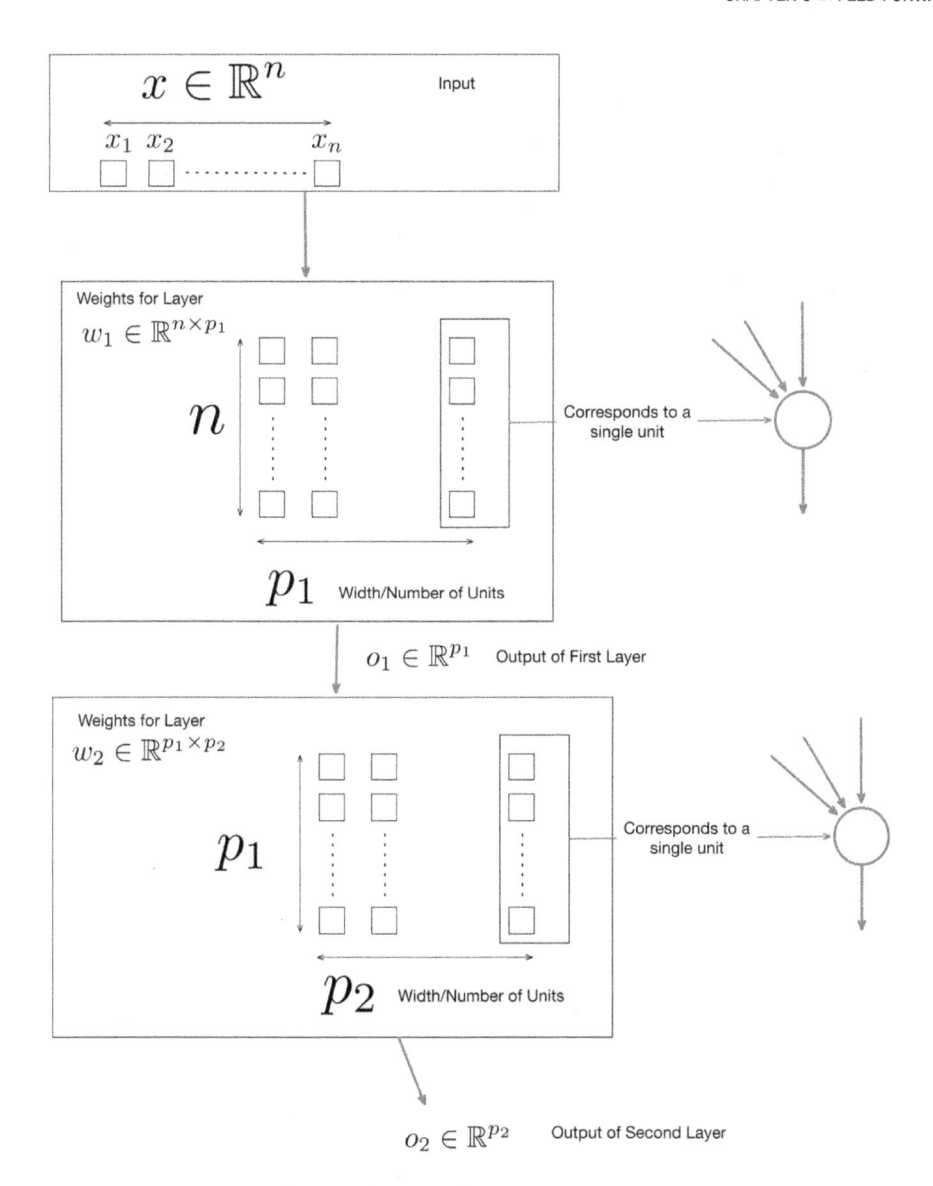

Figure 3-3. Expressing the Neural Network in Vector Form

Evaluating the output of the Neural Network

Now that we have looked at the structure of a Neural Network, let's look at how the output of the neural network can be evaluated against labeled data. Refer to Figure 3-4. The following points are to be noted:

1. We can assume that our data has the form $D = \{(x_1, y_1), (x_2, y_2), \ldots (x_n, y_n)\}$ where $x \in \mathbb{R}^n$ and $y \in \{0, 1\}$, which is the target of interest (currently this is binary, but it may be categorical or real valued depending on whether we are dealing with a multi-class or regression problem, respectively).

2. For a single data point we can compute the output of the Neural Network, which we denote as $\hat{y}$.

21

CHAPTER 3 ■ FEED FORWARD NEURAL NETWORKS

3. Now we need to compute how good the prediction of our Neural Network $\hat{y}$ is as compared to y. Here comes the notion of a loss function.

4. A loss function measures the disagreement between $\hat{y}$ and y which we denote by l. There are a number of loss functions appropriate for the task at hand: binary classification, multi-classification, or regression, which we shall cover later in the chapter (typically derived using Maximum Likelihood).

5. A loss function typically computes the disagreement between $\hat{y}$ and y over a number of data points rather than a single data point.

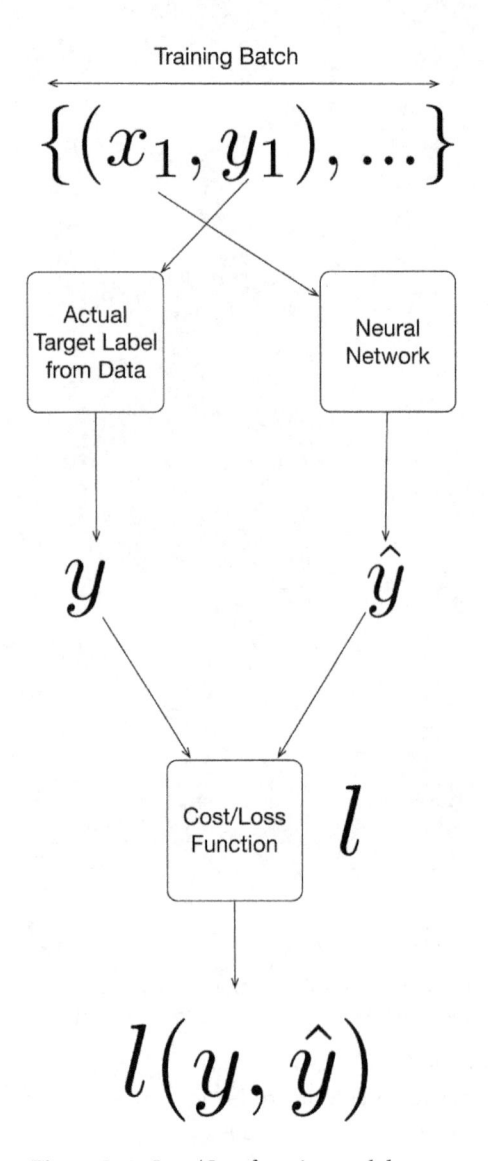

Figure 3-4. Loss/Cost function and the computation of cost/loss w.r.t, a neural network

Training the Neural Network

Let us now look at how the Neural Network is Trained. Refer to Figure 3-5. The following points are to be noted:

1. Assuming the same notation as earlier, we denote by θ the collection of all the weights and bias terms of all the layers of the network. Let us assume that θ has been initialized with random values. We denote by f_{NN} the overall function representing the Neural Network.

2. As we have seen earlier, we can take a single data point and compute the output of the Neural Network $\hat{y}$. We can also compute the disagreement with the actual output y using the loss function $l(\hat{y}, y)$ that is $l(f_{NN}(x, \theta), y)$.

3. Let us now compute the gradient of this loss function and denote it by $\nabla l(f_{NN}(x, \theta), y)$.

4. We can now update θ using steepest descent as $\theta_s = \theta_{s-1} - \alpha \cdot l(f_{NN}(x, \theta), y)$ where s denotes a single step (we can take many such steps over different data points in our training set over and over again until we have a reasonably good value for $l(f_{NN}(x, \theta), y)$.

Note For now, we will stay away from the computation of gradients of loss functions $\nabla l(f_{NN}(x, \theta), y)$. These can be generated using automatic differentiation (covered elsewhere in the book) quite easily (even for arbitrary complicated loss functions) and need not be derived manually. Also, the method of steepest descent and stochastic gradient descent is covered in a separate chapter.

CHAPTER 3 ■ FEED FORWARD NEURAL NETWORKS

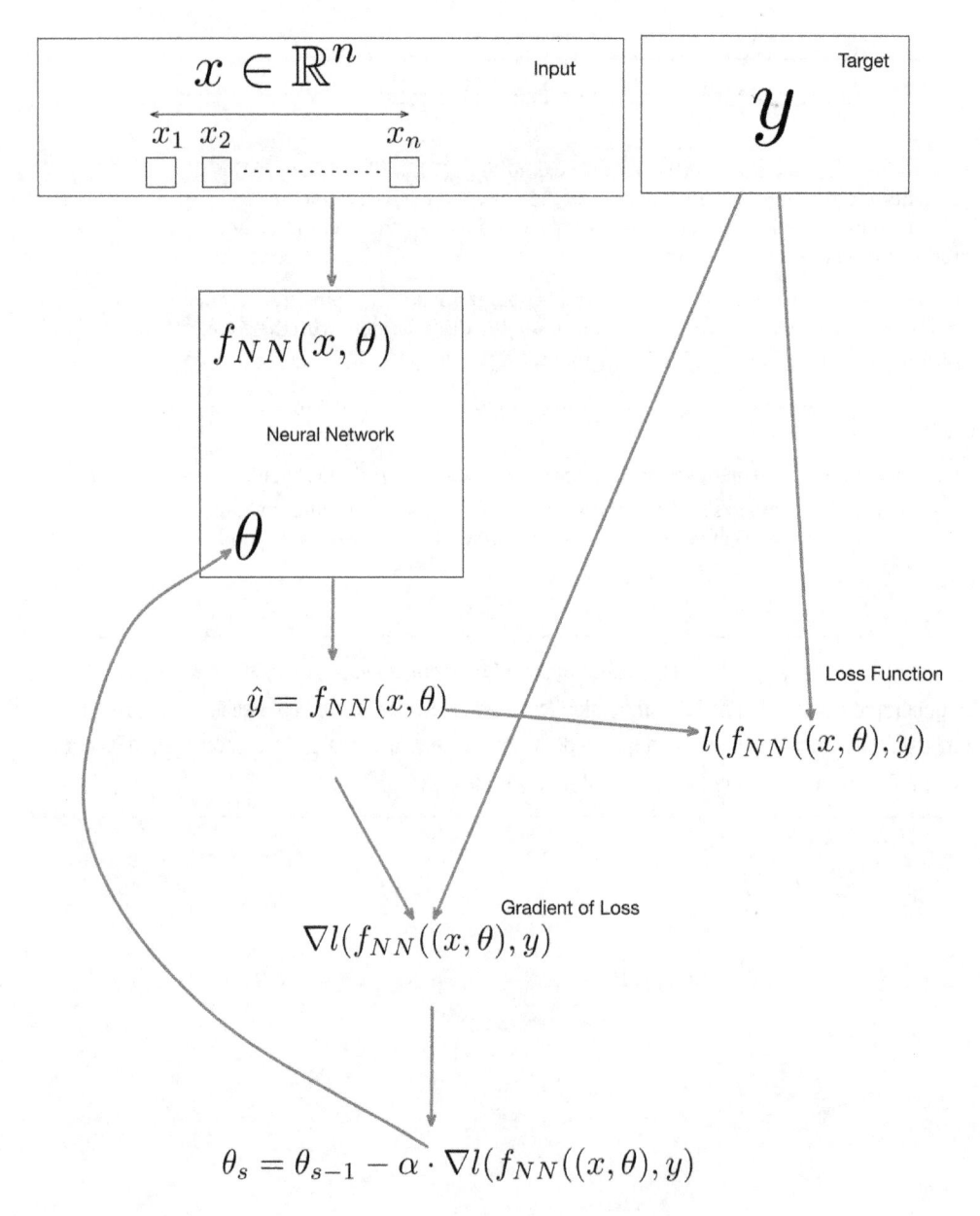

Figure 3-5. Training a Neural Network

Deriving Cost Functions using Maximum Likelihood

We will now look into how loss functions are derived using Maximum Likelihood. Specifically, we will see how commonly used loss functions in deep learning like binary cross entropy, cross entropy, and squared error can be derived using the Maximum Likelihood principle.

CHAPTER 3 ■ FEED FORWARD NEURAL NETWORKS

Binary Cross Entropy

Instead of starting with the general idea of Maximum Likelihood, let's directly jump to the binary classification problem. We have some data consisting of $D = \{(x_1, y_1), (x_2, y_2), \ldots (x_n, y_n)\}$ where $x \in \mathbb{R}^n$ and $y \in \{0, 1\}$, which is the target of interest (currently this is binary, but it may be categorical or real valued depending on whether we are dealing with a multi-class or regression problem, respectively).

Let us assume that we have somehow generated a model that predicts the probability of y given x. Let us denote this model by $f(x, \theta)$ where θ represents the parameters of the model. The idea behind Maximum Likelihood is to find a θ that maximizes $P(D|\theta)$. Assuming a Bernoulli distribution and given that each of the examples $\{(x_1, y_1), (x_2, y_2), \ldots (x_n, y_n)\}$ are independent, we have the following expression:

$$P(D|\theta) = \prod_{i=1}^{n} f(x_i, \theta)^{y_i} \cdot (1 - f(x_i, \theta))^{(1-y_i)}$$

We can take a logarithm operation on both sides to arrive at the following:

$$\log P(D|\theta) = \log \prod_{i=1}^{n} f(x_i, \theta)^{y_i} \cdot (1 - f(x_i, \theta))^{(1-y_i)}$$

which simplifies to the expression below:

$$\log P(D|\theta) = \sum_{i=1}^{n} y_i \log f(x_i, \theta) + (1 - y_i) \log(1 - f(x_i, \theta))$$

Instead of maximizing the RHS, we minimize its negative value as follows:

$$-\log P(D|\theta) = -\sum_{i=1}^{n} y_i \log f(x_i, \theta) + (1 - y_i) \log(1 - f(x_i, \theta))$$

This leads us to the binary cross entropy function as below:

$$-\sum_{i=1}^{n} y_i \log f(x_i, \theta) + (1 - y_i) \log(1 - f(x_i, \theta))$$

The idea of Maximum Likelihood thus allows us to derive the binary cross entropy function which can be used as a loss function in the context of binary classification.

Cross Entropy

Building on the idea of binary cross entropy, let us now consider deriving the cross entropy loss function to be used in the context of multi-classification. Let us assume in this case that $y \in \{0, 1, \ldots k\}$, which are the classes. We also denote $n_1, n_2 \cdots n_k$ to be the observed counts of each of the k classes. Observe that $\sum_{i=1}^{k} n_i = n$.

In this case, too, let us assume that we have somehow generated a model that predicts the probability of y given x. Let us denote this model by $f(x, \theta)$ where θ represents the parameters of the model. Let us again use the idea behind Maximum Likelihood, which is to find a θ that maximizes $P(D|\theta)$. Assuming a Multinomial distribution and given that each of the examples $\{(x_1, y_1), (x_2, y_2), \ldots (x_n, y_n)\}$ are independent, we have the following expression:

$$P(D|\theta) = \frac{n!}{n_1! \cdot n_2! \cdots n_k!} \prod_{i=1}^{n} f(x_i, \theta)^{y_i}$$

We can take a logarithm operation on both sides to arrive at the following:

$$\log P(D|\theta) = \log n! - \log n_1! \cdot n_2! \cdots n_k! + \log \prod_{i=1}^{n} f(x_i,\theta)^{y_i}$$

This can be simplified to the following:

$$\log P(D|\theta) = \log n! - \log n_1! \cdot n_2! \cdots n_k! + \sum_{i=1}^{n} y_i \log f(x_i,\theta)$$

The terms $\log n!$ and $\log n_1! \cdot n_2! \cdots n_k!$ are not parameterized by θ and can be safely ignored as we try to find a θ that maximizes $P(D|\theta)$. Thus we have the following:

$$\log P(D|\theta) = \sum_{i=1}^{n} y_i \log f(x_i,\theta)$$

As before, instead of maximizing the RHS we minimize its negative value as follows:

$$-\log P(D|\theta) = -\sum_{i=1}^{n} y_i \log f(x_i,\theta)$$

This leads us to the binary cross entropy function as below:

$$-\sum_{i=1}^{n} y_i \log f(x_i,\theta)$$

The idea of Maximum Likelihood thus allows us to derive the cross entropy function, which can be used as a loss function in the context of multi-classification.

Squared Error

Let us now look into deriving the squared error to be used in the context of regression using Maximum Likelihood. Let us assume in this case that $y \in \mathbb{R}$. Unlike the previous cases where we assumed that we had a model that predicted a probability, here we will assume that we have a model that predicts the value of y. To apply the Maximum Likelihood idea, we assume that the difference between the actual y and the predicted $\hat{y}$ has a Gaussian distribution with zero mean and a variance of σ^2. Then it can be shown that minimizing

$$\sum_{i=1}^{n}(y-\hat{y})^2$$

leads to the minimization of $-\log P(D|\theta)$.

Summary of Loss Functions

We now summarize three key points with respect to loss functions and the appropriateness of a particular loss function given the problem at hand.

1. The Binary Cross entropy given by the expression

    $$-\sum_{i=1}^{n} y_i \log f(x_i,\theta) + (1-y_i)\log(1-f(x_i,\theta))$$

    is the recommended loss function for binary classification. This loss function should typically be used when the Neural Network is designed to predict the probability of the outcome. In such cases, the output layer has a single unit with a suitable sigmoid as the activation function.

2. The Cross entropy function given by the expression

    $$-\sum_{i=1}^{n} y_i \log f(x_i,\theta)$$

    is the recommended loss function for multi-classification. This loss function should typically be used with the Neural Network and is designed to predict the probability of the outcomes of each of the classes. In such cases, the output layer has softmax units (one for each class).

3. The squared loss function given by $\sum_{i=1}^{n}(y-\hat{y})^2$ should be used for regression problems. The output layer in this case will have a single unit.

Types of Units/Activation Functions/Layers

We will now look at a number of Units/Activation Functions/Layers commonly used for Neural Networks. Let's start by enumerating a few properties of interest for activation functions.

1. In theory, when an activation function is non-linear, a two-layer Neural Network can approximate any function (given a sufficient number of units in the hidden layer). Thus, we do seek non-linear activation functions in general.

2. A function that is continuously differentiable allows for gradients to be computed and gradient-based methods to be used for finding the parameters that minimize our loss function over the data. If a function is not continuously differentiable, gradient-based methods cannot make progress.

3. A function whose range is finite (as against infinite) leads to a more stable performance w.r.t gradient-based methods.

4. Smooth functions are preferred (empirical evidence) and Monolithic functions for a single layer lead to convex error surfaces (this is typically not a consideration w.r.t deep learning).

5. Are symmetric around the origin and behave like identity functions near the origin ($f(x)=x$).

Linear Unit

The Linear unit is the simplest unit which transforms the input as $y = w.x + b$. As the name indicates, the unit does not have a non-linear behavior and is typically used to generate the mean of a conditional Gaussian distribution. Linear units make gradient-based learning a fairly straightforward task.

Sigmoid Unit

The Sigmoid unit transforms the input as follows:

$$y = \frac{1}{1+e^{-(wx+b)}}.$$

The underlying activation function (refer to Figure 3-6) is given by

$$f(x) = \frac{1}{1+e^{-x}}.$$

Sigmoid units can be used in the output layer in conjunction with binary cross entropy for binary classification problems. The output of this unit can model a Bernoulli distribution over the output y conditioned over x.

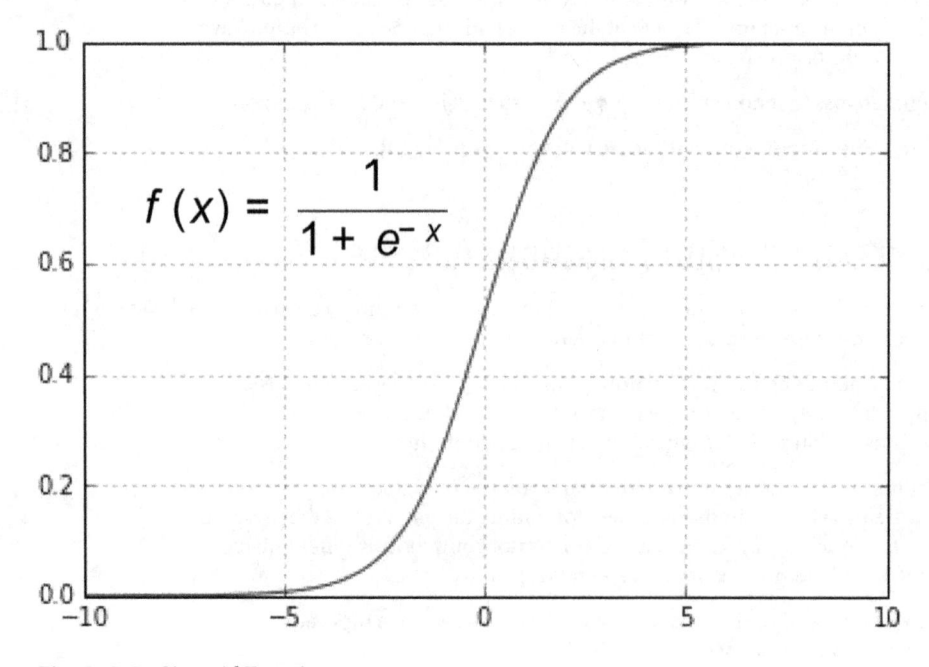

Figure 3-6. Sigmoid Function

Softmax Layer

The Softmax layer is typically used as an output layer for multi-classification tasks in conjunction with the Cross Entropy loss function. Refer to Figure 3-7. The Softmax layer normalizes outputs of the previous layer so that they sum up to one. Typically, the units of the previous layer model an un-normalized score of how likely the input is to belong to a particular class. The softmax layer is thus normalized so that the output represents the probability for every class.

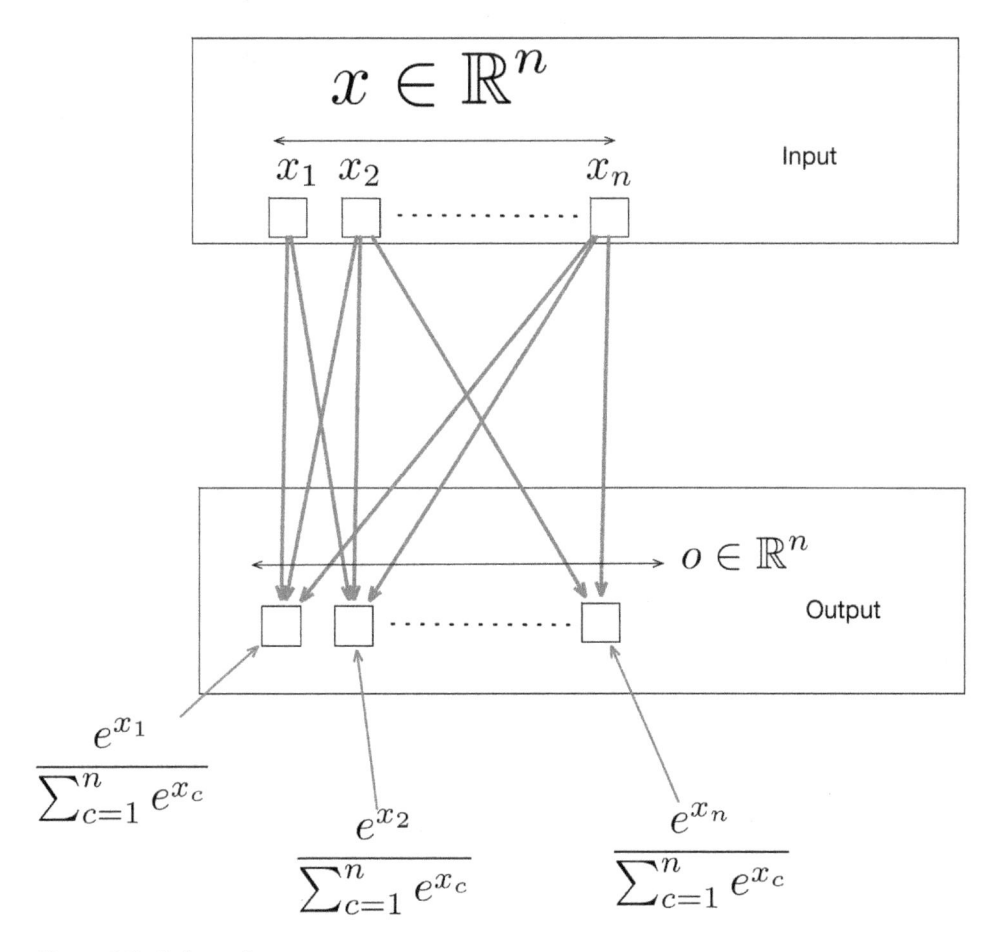

Figure 3-7. Softmax Layer

Rectified Linear Unit (ReLU)

Rectified Linear Unit used in conjunction with a linear transformation transforms the input as

$$f(x) = \max(0, wx + b).$$

CHAPTER 3 ■ FEED FORWARD NEURAL NETWORKS

The underlying activation function is $f(x) = \max(0, x)$; refer to Figure 3-8. The ReLU unit is more commonly used as a hidden unit in recent times. Results show that ReLU units lead to large and consistent gradients, which helps gradient-based learning.

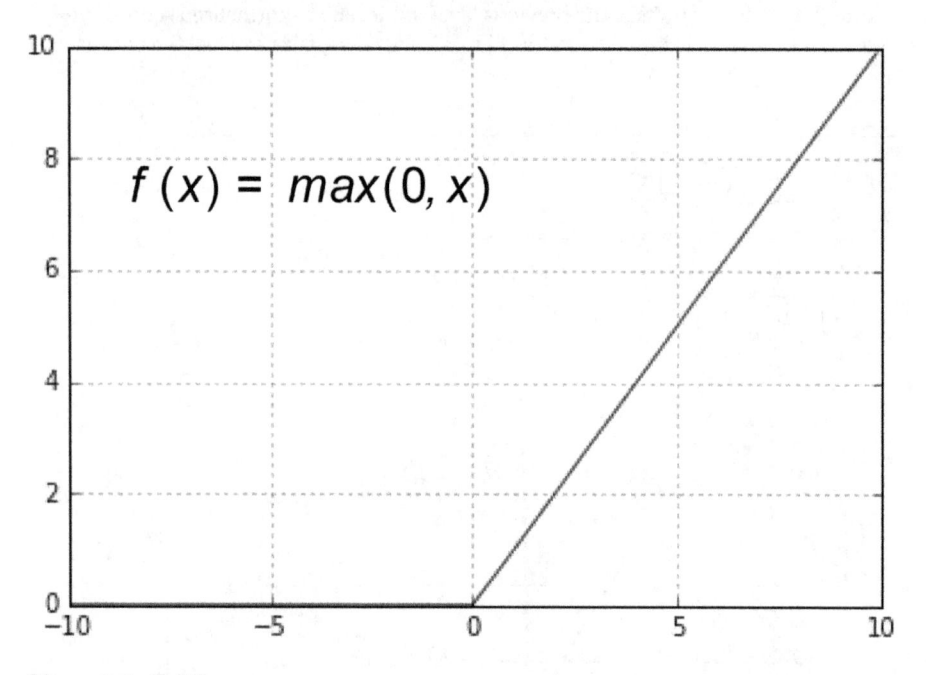

Figure 3-8. ReLU

Hyperbolic Tangent

The Hyperbolic Tangent unit transforms the input (used in conjunction with a linear transformation) as follows:

$$y = \tanh(wx + b).$$

The underlying activation function (refer to Figure 3-9) is given by

$$f(x) = \tanh(x).$$

The hyperbolic tangent unit is also commonly used as a hidden unit.

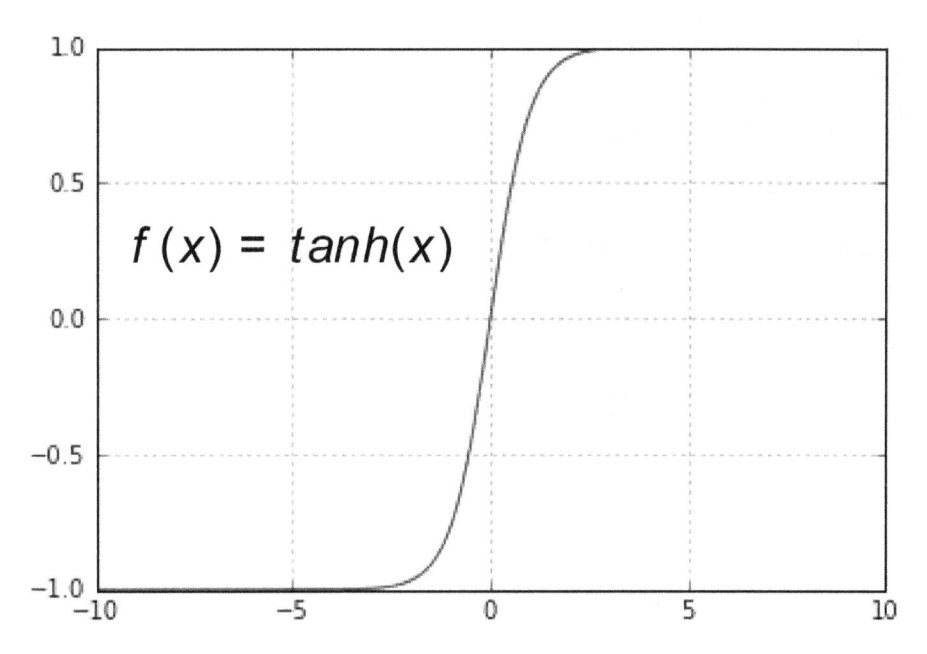

Figure 3-9. The tanh activation function

Listing 3-1. A 2-Layer Neural Network for Regression

```
import autograd.numpy as np
import autograd.numpy.random as npr
from autograd import grad
import sklearn.metrics
import pylab

# Generate Dataset
examples = 1000
features = 100
D = (npr.randn(examples, features), npr.randn(examples))

# Specify the network
layer1_units = 10
layer2_units = 1
w1 = npr.rand(features, layer1_units)
b1 = npr.rand(layer1_units)
w2 = npr.rand(layer1_units, layer2_units)
b2 = 0.0
theta = (w1, b1, w2, b2)

# Define the loss function
def squared_loss(y, y_hat):
    return np.dot((y - y_hat),(y - y_hat))

# Output Layer
def binary_cross_entropy(y, y_hat):
    return np.sum(-((y * np.log(y_hat)) + ((1-y) * np.log(1 - y_hat))))
```

31

CHAPTER 3 ■ FEED FORWARD NEURAL NETWORKS

```
# Wraper around the Neural Network
def neural_network(x, theta):
    w1, b1, w2, b2 = theta
    return np.tanh(np.dot((np.tanh(np.dot(x,w1) + b1)), w2) + b2)

# Wrapper around the objective function to be optimised
def objective(theta, idx):
    return squared_loss(D[1][idx], neural_network(D[0][idx], theta))

# Update
def update_theta(theta, delta, alpha):
    w1, b1, w2, b2 = theta
    w1_delta, b1_delta, w2_delta, b2_delta = delta
    w1_new = w1 - alpha * w1_delta
    b1_new = b1 - alpha * b1_delta
    w2_new = w2 - alpha * w2_delta
    b2_new = b2 - alpha * b2_delta
    new_theta = (w1_new,b1_new,w2_new,b2_new)
    return new_theta

# Compute Gradient
grad_objective = grad(objective)

# Train the Neural Network
epochs = 10
print "RMSE before training:", sklearn.metrics.mean_squared_error(D[1],neural_network(D[0],
theta))
rmse = []
for i in xrange(0, epochs):
    for j in xrange(0, examples):
        delta = grad_objective(theta, j)
        theta = update_theta(theta,delta, 0.01)

rmse.append(sklearn.metrics.mean_squared_error(D[1],neural_network(D[0], theta)))
print "RMSE after training:", sklearn.metrics.mean_squared_error(D[1],neural_network(D[0],
theta))

pylab.plot(rmse)
pylab.show()

#Output
#RMSE before training: 1.88214665439
#RMSE after training: 0.739508975012
```

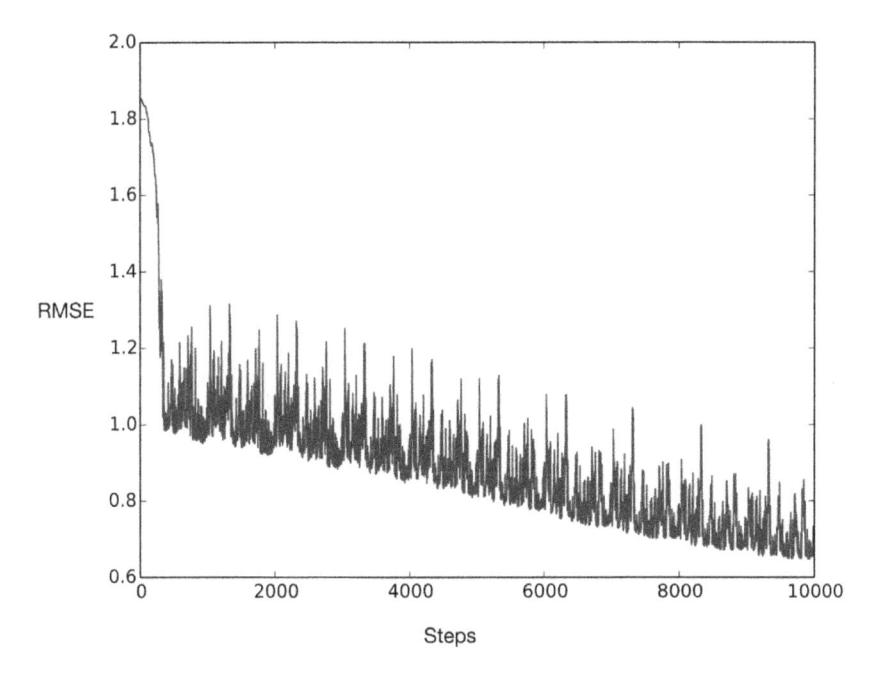

Figure 3-10. RMSE over training steps

Neural Network Hands-on with AutoGrad

We will now build a simple Neural Network from scratch (refer to Listing 3-1). The only external library we will be using is Autograd. Autograd is an automatic differentiation library that will allow us to compute gradients for arbitrary functions written with Numpy.

> **Note** Autograd is covered in more detail in the chapter on Automatic Differentiation.

Summary

In this chapter we covered feed forward neural networks, which will serve as the conceptual foundation for the rest of the chapters. The key concepts we covered were the overall structure of the neural network, the input, hidden and output layers, cost functions, and their basis on the principle of Maximum Likelihood. We encourage the reader to try out the example in the source code listing; although it is a toy example, it will help reinforce the concepts. The next chapter will provide a hands-on introduction to the reader on Theano, which will enable the reader to implement full-fledged neural networks.

CHAPTER 4

Introduction to Theano

In this chapter we introduce the reader to Theano, which is a Python library for defining mathematical functions (operating over vectors and matrices), and computing the gradients of these functions. Theano is the foundational layer on which many deep learning packages like Keras are based.

What is Theano

As we have seen before, building deep learning models fundamentally involves optimizing loss functions using stochastic gradient descent (SGD), requiring the computation of the gradient of loss function. As loss functions in deep learning are complicated, it is not convenient to manually derive such gradients. This is where Theano comes in handy. Theano allows the user to define mathematical expressions that encode loss functions and, once these are defined, Theano allows the user to compute the gradients of these expressions.

A typical workflow for using Theano is as follows:

1. Write symbolic expressions in Python that implement the loss function of the model to be built. This usually amounts to only a few lines of code because of the expressiveness of the Python language and a tight integration with Numpy that allows the user to quickly and elegantly define mathematical expressions involving vectors and matrices.

2. Use the symbolic/automatic differentiation capabilities in Theano to generate an expression that produces the gradient of the loss function.

3. Pass this gradient function as a parameter to a SGD optimization routine to optimize the loss function.

Theano allows a user to focus on the model rather than on the mechanics of deriving the gradient. The specific capabilities of Theano that make it a great toolbox for building deep learning models are as follows:

1. A very seamless integration with Numpy that allows the user to use Numpy objects (vectors and matrices) in the definition of loss functions

2. Theano can generate optimized code for both CPU as well as GPU under the hood without the user having to rewrite the code, which defines the loss function.

3. Optimised automatic/symbolic differentiation

4. Numerical stability for the generated code via automatic/symbolic differentiation

CHAPTER 4 ■ INTRODUCTION TO THEANO

Theano Hands-On

Let us now start getting our hands dirty with Theano. We will start with simple examples, which will serve as conceptual building blocks for more complicated examples. It is recommended that the reader go over the source code listing and corresponding computational graph for each example and give careful consideration to how the source code translates to the computational graph.

In our first example in Listing 4-1 (and the corresponding computational graph in Figure 4-1) we will define a simple function with scalars. The reader should note the following:

1. Scalars are defined before they can be used in a mathematical expression.

2. Every scalar is given a unique name.

3. Once defined, the scalar can be operated upon with operations like +, -, * and /.

4. The function construct in Theano allows one to relate inputs and outputs. So, in the example from Listing 4-1, we have defined a function with the name g, which takes a, b, c, d, and e as input and produces f as the output.

5. We can now compute the result of the function g given the input and check that it evaluates exactly as the non-Theano expression.

6. While this seems like a trivial example, the non-trivial bit is that now we will be able to easily compute the gradient of such a function g quite easily using Theano, as we will see soon.

Listing 4-1. Functions with Scalars

```
import theano.tensor as T
from theano import function

a = T.dscalar('a')
b = T.dscalar('b')
c = T.dscalar('c')
d = T.dscalar('d')
e = T.dscalar('e')

f = ((a - b + c) * d )/e

g = function([a, b, c, d, e], f)

print "Expected: ((1 - 2 + 3) * 4)/5.0 = ", ((1 - 2 + 3) * 4)/5.0
print "Via Theano: ((1 - 2 + 3) * 4)/5.0 = ", g(1, 2, 3, 4, 5)

# Expected: ((1 - 2 + 3) * 4)/5.0 =  1.6
# Via Theano: ((1 - 2 + 3) * 4)/5.0 =  1.6
```

CHAPTER 4 ■ INTRODUCTION TO THEANO

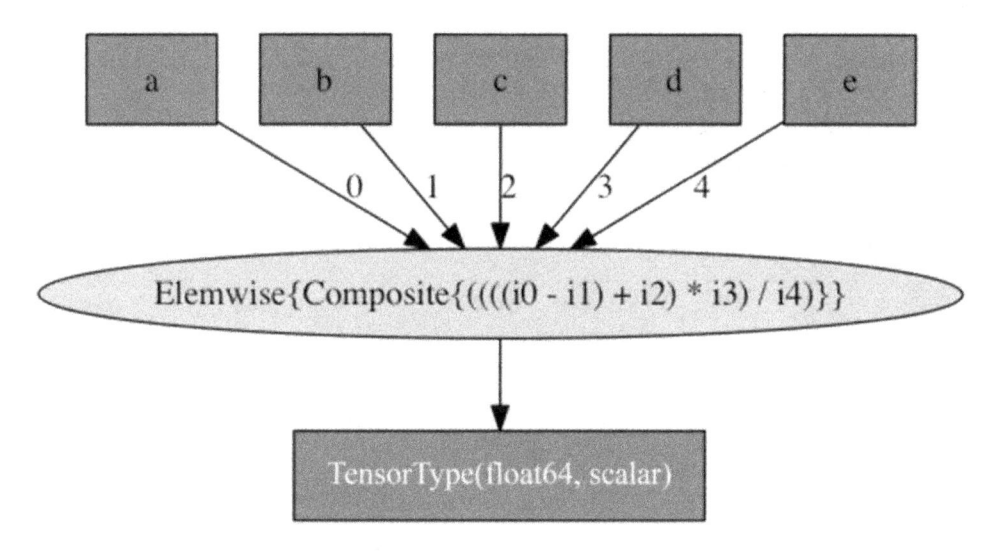

Figure 4-1. Functions with scalars

In our second example in Listing 4-2 (and the corresponding computational graph in Figure 4-2) we will define a simple function with vectors. The reader should note the following:

1. Vectors/Matrices are defined before they can be used in a mathematical expression.
2. Every Vector/Matrix is given a unique name.
3. The dimensions of the Vectors/Matrices are not specified.
4. Once Vectors/Matrices are defined, the user can define operations like matrix addition, subtraction, and multiplication. The user should take care that vector/matrix operations respect the intended dimensionality.
5. As before, the user can define a function based on the defined expressions. In this case we define a function f that takes a, b, c, and d as input and produces e as output.
6. The use can pass Numpy arrays to the function and compute the output. The user should take care that vector/matrix inputs respect the intended dimensionality.

Listing 4-2. Functions with Vectors

```
import numpy
import theano.tensor as T
from theano import function

a = T.dmatrix('a')
b = T.dmatrix('b')
c = T.dmatrix('c')
d = T.dmatrix('d')
```

37

CHAPTER 4 ■ INTRODUCTION TO THEANO

```
e = (a + b - c) * d

f = function([a,b,c,d], e)

a_data = numpy.array([[1,1],[1,1]])
b_data = numpy.array([[2,2],[2,2]])
c_data = numpy.array([[5,5],[5,5]])
d_data = numpy.array([[3,3],[3,3]])

print "Expected:", (a_data + b_data - c_data) * d_data
print "Via Theano:", f(a_data,b_data,c_data,d_data)

# Expected: [[-6 -6]
#  [-6 -6]]
# Via Theano: [[-6. -6.]
#  [-6. -6.]]
```

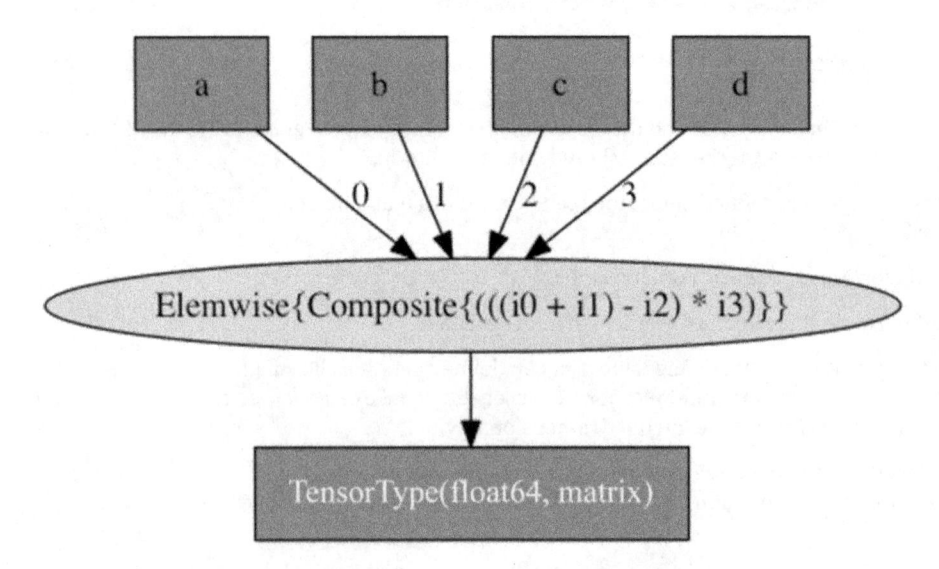

Figure 4-2. Functions with Vectors

In our next example in Listing 4-3 (and the corresponding computational graph in Figure 4-3) we will define a function with both scalars and vectors. The reader should note the following:

1. Scalars and vectors/matrices can be used together in expressions.
2. The user needs to take care that vector/matrices respect the dimensionality both while defining the expressions as well as passing inputs to the expressions.

Listing 4-3. Functions with Scalars and Vectors

```
import numpy
import theano.tensor as T
from theano import function
```

CHAPTER 4 ■ INTRODUCTION TO THEANO

```
a = T.dmatrix('a')
b = T.dmatrix('b')
c = T.dmatrix('c')
d = T.dmatrix('d')

p = T.dscalar('p')
q = T.dscalar('q')
r = T.dscalar('r')
s = T.dscalar('s')
u = T.dscalar('u')

e = (((a * p) + (b - q) - (c + r )) * d/s) * u

f = function([a,b,c,d,p,q,r,s,u], e)

a_data = numpy.array([[1,1],[1,1]])
b_data = numpy.array([[2,2],[2,2]])
c_data = numpy.array([[5,5],[5,5]])
d_data = numpy.array([[3,3],[3,3]])

print "Expected:", (((a_data * 1.0) + (b_data - 2.0) - (c_data + 3.0 )) * d_data/4.0) * 5.0
print "Via Theano:", f(a_data,b_data,c_data,d_data,1,2,3,4,5)

# Expected: [[-26.25 -26.25]
#  [-26.25 -26.25]]
# Via Theano: [[-26.25 -26.25]
#  [-26.25 -26.25]]
```

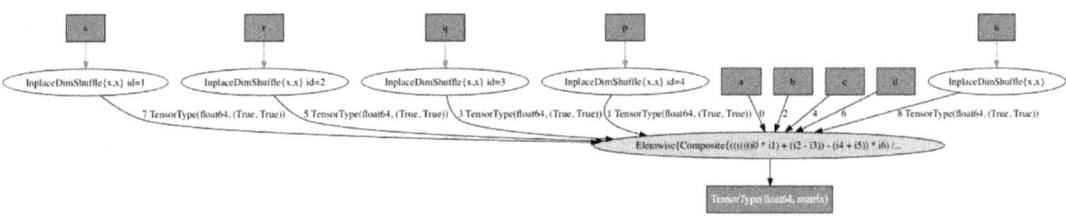

Figure 4-3. Functions with Scalars and Vectors

In our next example in Listing 4-4 (and the corresponding computational graph in Figure 4-4) we will define a few activation functions with Theano. The nnet package in Theano defines a number of common activation functions.

Listing 4-4. Activiation Functions

```
import theano.tensor as T
from theano import function

# sigmoid
a = T.dmatrix('a')
f_a = T.nnet.sigmoid(a)
f_sigmoid = function([a],[f_a])
print "sigmoid:", f_sigmoid([[-1,0,1]])
```

39

```
# tanh
b = T.dmatrix('b')
f_b = T.tanh(b)
f_tanh = function([b],[f_b])
print "tanh:", f_tanh([[-1,0,1]])

# fast sigmoid
c = T.dmatrix('c')
f_c = T.nnet.ultra_fast_sigmoid(c)
f_fast_sigmoid = function([c],[f_c])
print "fast sigmoid:", f_fast_sigmoid([[-1,0,1]])

# softplus
d = T.dmatrix('d')
f_d = T.nnet.softplus(d)
f_softplus = function([d],[f_d])
print "soft plus:",f_softplus([[-1,0,1]])

# relu
e = T.dmatrix('e')
f_e = T.nnet.relu(e)
f_relu = function([e],[f_e])
print "relu:",f_relu([[-1,0,1]])

# softmax
f = T.dmatrix('f')
f_f = T.nnet.softmax(f)
f_softmax = function([f],[f_f])
print "soft max:",f_softmax([[-1,0,1]])
```

CHAPTER 4 ■ INTRODUCTION TO THEANO

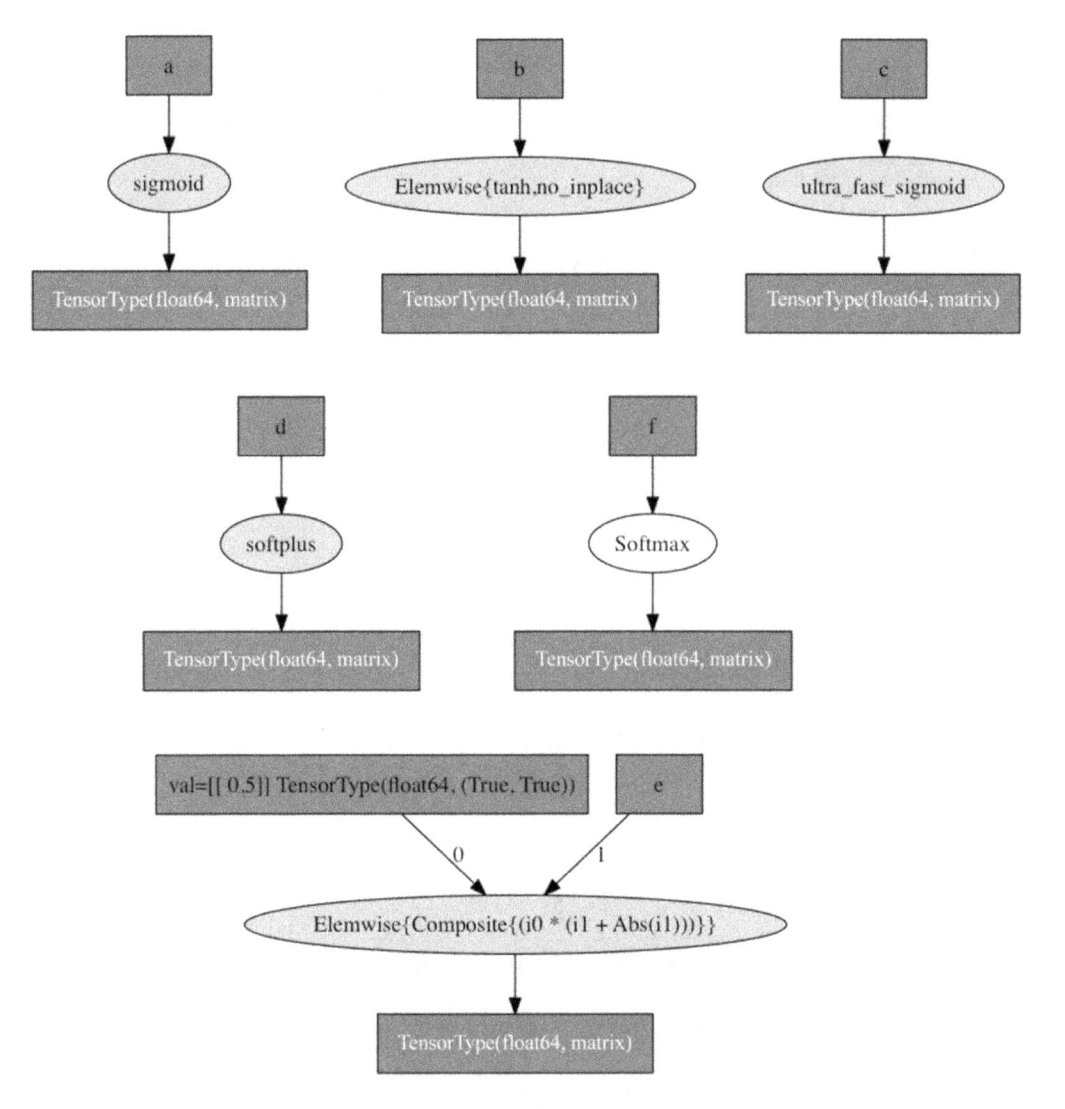

Figure 4-4. Activation Functions

In our next example in Listing 4-5 (and the corresponding computational graph in Figure 4-5) we will define a function with internal state. The reader should note the following:

1. All models (deep learning or otherwise) will involve defining functions with internal state, which will typically be weights that need to be learned or fitted.

2. A shared variable is defined using the shared construct in Theano.

3. A shared variable can be initialized with Numpy constructs.

4. Once the shared variable is defined and initialized, it can be used in the definition of expressions and functions in a manner similar to scalars and vectors/matrices, as we have seen earlier.

5. A user can get the value of the shared variable using the get_value method.

41

CHAPTER 4 ■ INTRODUCTION TO THEANO

6. A user can set the value for the shared variable using the set_value method.

7. A function defined using the shared variable computes its output based on the current value of the shared variable. That is, as soon as the shared variable updates, a function defined using the shared variable will produce a different value for the same input.

8. A shared variable allows a user to define a function with internal state, which can be updated arbitrarily without needing to redefine the function defined using the shared variable.

Listing 4-5. Shared Variables

```
import theano.tensor as T
from theano import function
from theano import shared

import numpy

x = T.dmatrix('x')
y = shared(numpy.array([[4, 5, 6]]))
z = x + y
f = function(inputs = [x], outputs = [z])

print "Original Shared Value:", y.get_value()
print "Original Function Evaluation:", f([[1, 2, 3]])

y.set_value(numpy.array([[5, 6, 7]]))

print "Original Shared Value:", y.get_value()
print "Original Function Evaluation:", f([[1, 2, 3]])

# Couldn't import dot_parser, loading of dot files will not be possible.
# Original Shared Value: [[4 5 6]]
# Original Function Evaluation: [array([[ 5.,  7.,  9.]])]
# Original Shared Value: [[5 6 7]]
# Original Function Evaluation: [array([[ 6.,  8., 10.]])]
```

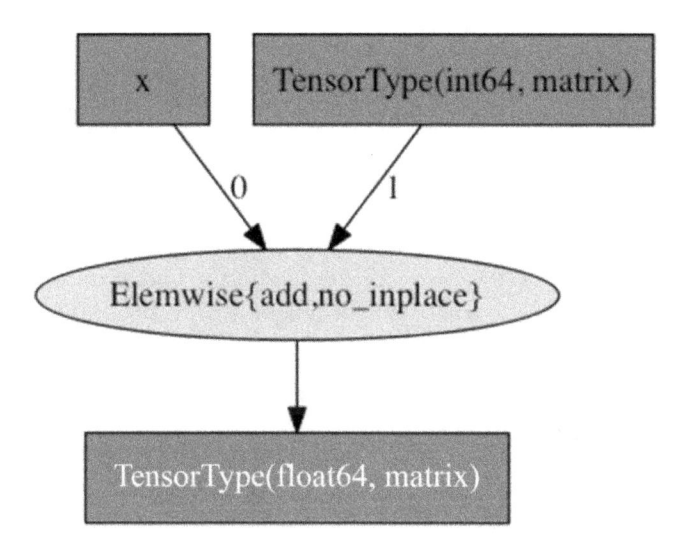

Figure 4-5. Shared Variables

In our next example in Listing 4-6 (and the corresponding computational graph in Figure 4-6) we will define a function and generate a function that computes its gradient. The reader should note the following:

1. A function needs to be defined using expressions before the gradient of the function can be generated.

2. The grad construct in Theano allows the user to generate the gradient of a function (as an expression). Users can then define a function over the expression, which gives them the gradient function.

3. Gradients can be computed for any set of expressions/functions as in the earlier examples. So, for instance, we could generate gradients for functions with a shared state. As the shared state updates, so do the function and the gradient function.

Listing 4-6. Gradients

```
import theano.tensor as T
from theano import function
from theano import shared

import numpy

x = T.dmatrix('x')
y = shared(numpy.array([[4, 5, 6]]))
z = T.sum(((x * x) + y) * x)

f = function(inputs = [x], outputs = [z])

g = T.grad(z,[x])
g_f = function([x], g)
```

CHAPTER 4 ■ INTRODUCTION TO THEANO

```
print "Original:", f([[1, 2, 3]])
print "Original Gradient:", g_f([[1, 2, 3]])

y.set_value(numpy.array([[1, 1, 1]]))
print "Updated:", f([[1, 2, 3]])
print "Updated Gradient", g_f([[1, 2, 3]])

# Original: [array(68.0)]
# Original Gradient: [array([[  7.,  17.,  33.]])]
# Updated: [array(42.0)]
# Updated Gradient [array([[  4.,  13.,  28.]])]
```

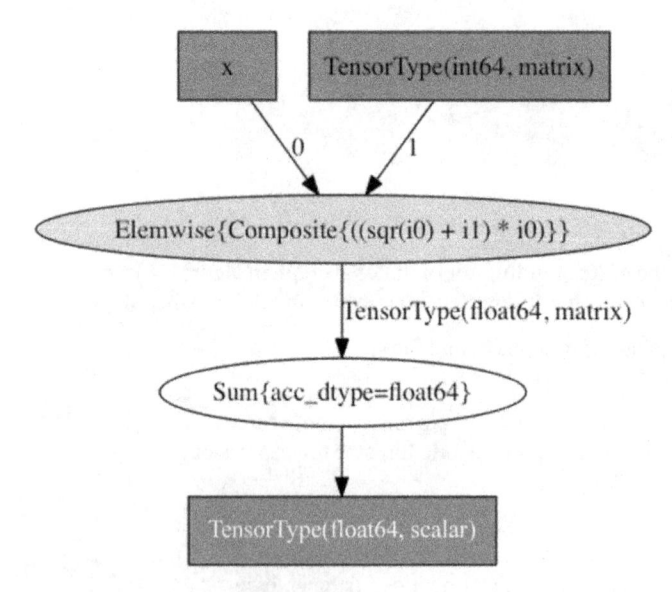

Figure 4-6. Computing Gradients

In our next example in Listing 4-7 (and the corresponding computational graph in Figure 4-7 (a) and Figure 4-7 (b)) we will define a few loss functions using Theano. The nnet package in Theano implements many standard loss functions.

Listing 4-7. Loss Functions

```
import theano.tensor as T
from theano import function

# binary cross entropy
a1 = T.dmatrix('a1')
a2 = T.dmatrix('a2')
f_a = T.nnet.binary_crossentropy(a1, a2).mean()
f_sigmoid = function([a1, a2],[f_a])
print "Binary Cross Entropy [[0.01,0.01,0.01]],[[0.99,0.99,0.01]]:",
f_sigmoid([[0.01,0.01,0.01]],[[0.99,0.99,0.01]])
```

```
# categorical cross entropy
b1 = T.dmatrix('b1')
b2 = T.dmatrix('b2')
f_b = T.nnet.categorical_crossentropy(b1, b2)
f_sigmoid = function([b1, b2],[f_b])
print "Categorical Cross Entropy [[0.01,0.01,0.01]],[[0.99,0.99,0.01]]:",
f_sigmoid([[0.01,0.01,0.01]],[[0.99,0.99,0.01]])

# squared error
def squared_error(x,y):
    return (x - y) ** 2

c1 = T.dmatrix('b1')
c2 = T.dmatrix('b2')
f_c = squared_error(c1, c2)
f_squared_error = function([c1, c2],[f_c])
print "Squared Error [[0.01,0.01,0.01]],[[0.99,0.99,0.01]]:",
f_sigmoid([[0.01,0.01,0.01]],[[0.99,0.99,0.01]])

# Binary Cross Entropy [[0.01,0.01,0.01]],[[0.99,0.99,0.01]]: [array(3.058146503109446)]
# Categorical Cross Entropy [[0.01,0.01,0.01]],[[0.99,0.99,0.01]]: [array([ 9.16428867])]
# Squared Error [[0.01,0.01,0.01]],[[0.99,0.99,0.01]]: [array([ 9.16428867])]
```

Figure 4-7 (a). *Loss Functions – Binary Cross Entropy*

CHAPTER 4 ■ INTRODUCTION TO THEANO

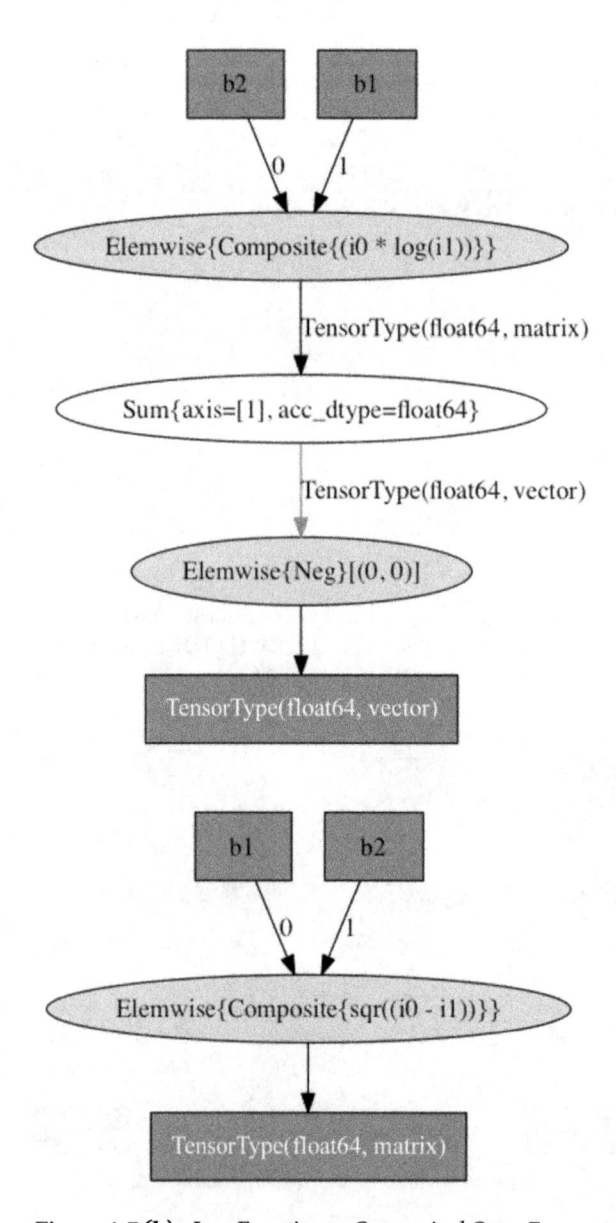

Figure 4-7 (b). *Loss Functions – Categorical Cross Entropy and Squared Error*

In our next example in Listing 4-8 (and corresponding computational graph in Figure 4-8) we will define L1 and L2 regularization using Theano.

Listing 4-8. Regularization

```
import theano.tensor as T
from theano import function

# L1 Regularization
def l1(x):
    return T.sum(abs(x))

# L2 Regularization
def l2(x):
    return T.sum(x**2)

a = T.dmatrix('a')
f_a = l1(a)
f_l1 = function([a], f_a)
print "L1 Regularization:", f_l1([[0,1,3]])

b = T.dmatrix('b')
f_b = l2(b)
f_l2 = function([b], f_b)
print "L2 Regularization:", f_l2([[0,1,3]])

# L1 Regularization: 4.0
# L2 Regularization: 10.0
```

```
a
 │
 ▼
Elemwise{abs_,no_inplace}
 │ TensorType(float64, matrix)
 ▼
Sum{acc_dtype=float64}
 │
 ▼
TensorType(float64, scalar)


b
 │
 ▼
Elemwise{sqr,no_inplace}
 │ TensorType(float64, matrix)
 ▼
Sum{acc_dtype=float64}
 │
 ▼
TensorType(float64, scalar)
```

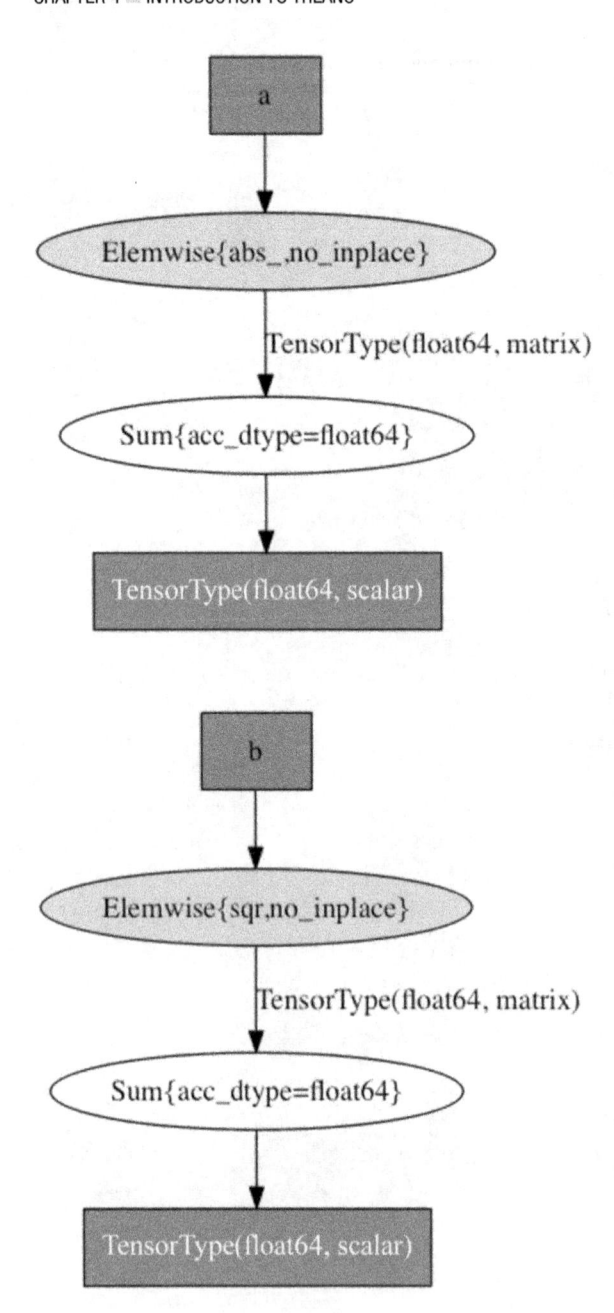

Figure 4-8. Regularization

In our next example in Listing 4-9 (and corresponding computational graph in Figure 4-9) we will define a function with a random variable. The reader should note the following:

1. There are cases/situations where we want to define functions having a random variable (for instance introducing minor corruptions in inputs).

2. Such a random element in the function is different from having an internal state, like in the case of shared variables.

CHAPTER 4 ■ INTRODUCTION TO THEANO

3. Basically, the desired outcome in such cases/situations is that the user wants to define a function with a random variable with a particular distribution.

4. Theano provides a construct called RandomStreams, which allows the user to define functions with a random variable. RandomStreams is initialized with a seed.

5. The user defines a variable using RandomStreams and specifies a distribution by calling the appropriate function (in our case, normal).

6. Once defined, the random variable can be used in the definition of expression or functions in a manner similar to scalars and vectors/matrices.

7. Every invocation of the function defined with a random variable will internally draw a sample point from the set distribution (in our case, normal).

Listing 4-9. Random Streams

```
import theano.tensor as T
from theano import function
from theano.tensor.shared_randomstreams import RandomStreams
import numpy

random = RandomStreams(seed=42)

a = random.normal((1,3))
b = T.dmatrix('a')

f1 = a * b

g1 = function([b], f1)

print "Invocation 1:", g1(numpy.ones((1,3)))
print "Invocation 2:", g1(numpy.ones((1,3)))
print "Invocation 3:", g1(numpy.ones((1,3)))

# Invocation 1: [[ 1.25614218 -0.53793023 -0.10434045]]
# Invocation 2: [[ 0.66992188 -0.70813926  0.99601177]]
# Invocation 3: [[ 0.0724739  -0.66508406  0.93707751]]
```

CHAPTER 4 ■ INTRODUCTION TO THEANO

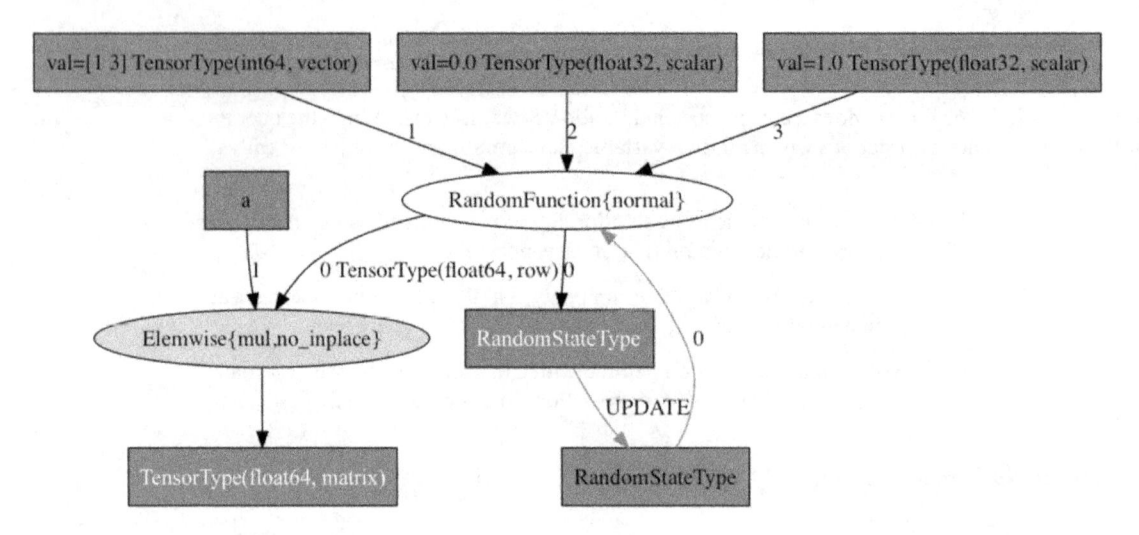

Figure 4-9. Random Streams

In our next example in Listing 4-10 (and corresponding computational graph in Figure 4-10) we will build a model for Logistic regression. The reader should note the following:

1. The example generates some artificial/toy data, fits a logistic regression model and computes the accuracy before and after training. This is a toy dataset for the purposes of illustration; the model is not generalizing/learning, as the data is generated randomly.

2. We define a function to compute L2 regularization as covered in listing 4-8 earlier.

3. We generate input data, which consists of 1000 vectors of dimensionality 100. Basically, 1000 examples with 100 features.

4. We generate random target/output labels as zeros and ones.

5. We define the expressions for logistic regression involving the data (denoted by x), the outputs (denoted by y), the bias term (denoted by b), and the weight vector (denoted by w). The weight vector and the bias term are shared variables.

6. We compute the prediction, the error, and the loss using binary cross entropy as introduced in listing 4-7 earlier.

7. Having defined these expressions, we can now use the grad construct in Theano (introduced in listing (4-6)) to compute the gradient.

8. We define a train function based on the gradient function. The train function defines the inputs, outputs, and how the internal state (shared variables) are to be updated.

9. The train function is invoked for 1000 steps; in each step the gradient is computed internally and the shared variables are updated.

10. Accuracy is computed before and after the training steps using sklearn.metrics

Listing 4-10. Logistic Regression

```
import numpy
import theano
import theano.tensor as T
import sklearn.metrics

def l2(x):
    return T.sum(x**2)

examples = 1000
features = 100

D = (numpy.random.randn(examples, features), numpy.random.randint(size=examples,
low=0, high=2))
training_steps = 1000

x = T.dmatrix("x")
y = T.dvector("y")
w = theano.shared(numpy.random.randn(features), name="w")
b = theano.shared(0., name="b")

p = 1 / (1 + T.exp(-T.dot(x, w) - b))
error = T.nnet.binary_crossentropy(p,y)
loss = error.mean() + 0.01 * l2(w)
prediction = p > 0.5
gw, gb = T.grad(loss, [w, b])

train = theano.function(inputs=[x,y],outputs=[p, error], updates=((w, w - 0.1 * gw),
(b, b - 0.1 * gb)))
predict = theano.function(inputs=[x], outputs=prediction)

print "Accuracy before Training:",sklearn.metrics.accuracy_score(D[1], predict(D[0]))

for i in range(training_steps):
    prediction, error = train(D[0], D[1])

print "Accuracy before Training:", sklearn.metrics.accuracy_score(D[1], predict(D[0]))

# Accuracy before Training: 0.481
# Accuracy before Training: 0.629
```

CHAPTER 4 ■ INTRODUCTION TO THEANO

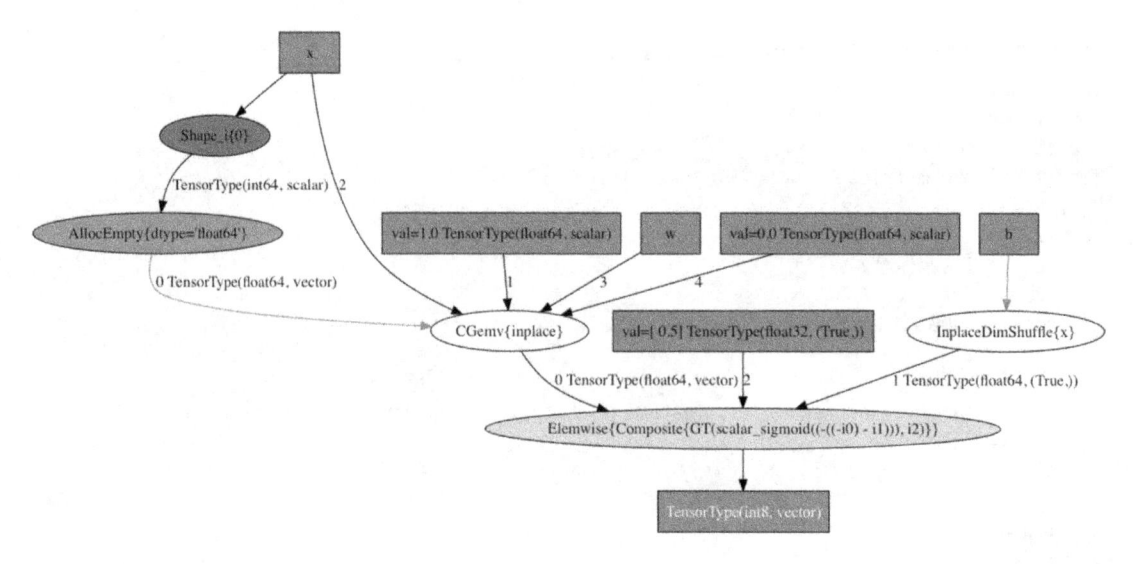

Figure 4-10. Logistic Regression

In our next example in Listing 4-11 (and corresponding computational graph in Figure 4-11) we will build a model for Linear regression. The reader should note the following:

1. The example generates some artificial/toy data, fits a linear regression model and computes the accuracy before and after training. This is a toy dataset for the purposes of illustration, the model is not generalizing/learning as the data is generated randomly.

2. We define a function to compute L2 regularization as covered in listing 4-8 earlier.

3. We define a function for squared error as covered in listing 4-7.

4. We generate input data, which consists of 1000 vectors of dimensionality 100. Basically, 1000 examples with 100 features.

5. We generate random target/output labels values between 0 and 1.

6. We define the expressions for linear regression involving the data (denoted by x), the outputs (denoted by y), the bias term (denoted by b) and the weight vector (denoted by w). The weight vector and the bias term are shared variables.

7. We compute the prediction, the error and the loss using squared error as introduced in listing 4-7 earlier.

8. Having defined these expressions, we can now use the grad construct in Theano introduced in listing (4-6) to compute the gradient.

9. We define a train function based on the gradient function. The train function defines the inputs, outputs and how the internal state (shared variables) are to be updated.

10. The train function is invoked for a 1000 steps, in each step the gradient is computed internally and the shared variables are updated.

11. Root mean squared error (RMSE) is computed before and after the training steps using sklearn.metrics

Listing 4-11. Linear Regression

```
import numpy
import theano
import theano.tensor as T
import sklearn.metrics

def l2(x):
    return T.sum(x**2)

def squared_error(x,y):
    return (x - y) ** 2

examples = 1000
features = 100

D = (numpy.random.randn(examples, features), numpy.random.randn(examples))
training_steps = 1000

x = T.dmatrix("x")
y = T.dvector("y")
w = theano.shared(numpy.random.randn(features), name="w")
b = theano.shared(0., name="b")

p = T.dot(x, w) + b
error = squared_error(p,y)
loss = error.mean() + 0.01 * l2(w)
gw, gb = T.grad(loss, [w, b])

train = theano.function(inputs=[x,y],outputs=[p, error], updates=((w, w - 0.1 * gw),
(b, b - 0.1 * gb)))
predict = theano.function(inputs=[x], outputs=p)

print "RMSE before training:", sklearn.metrics.mean_squared_error(D[1],predict(D[0]))

for i in range(training_steps):
    prediction, error = train(D[0], D[1])

print "RMSE after training:", sklearn.metrics.mean_squared_error(D[1],predict(D[0]))

# RMSE before training: 90.4707491496
# RMSE after training: 0.915701676631
```

CHAPTER 4 ■ INTRODUCTION TO THEANO

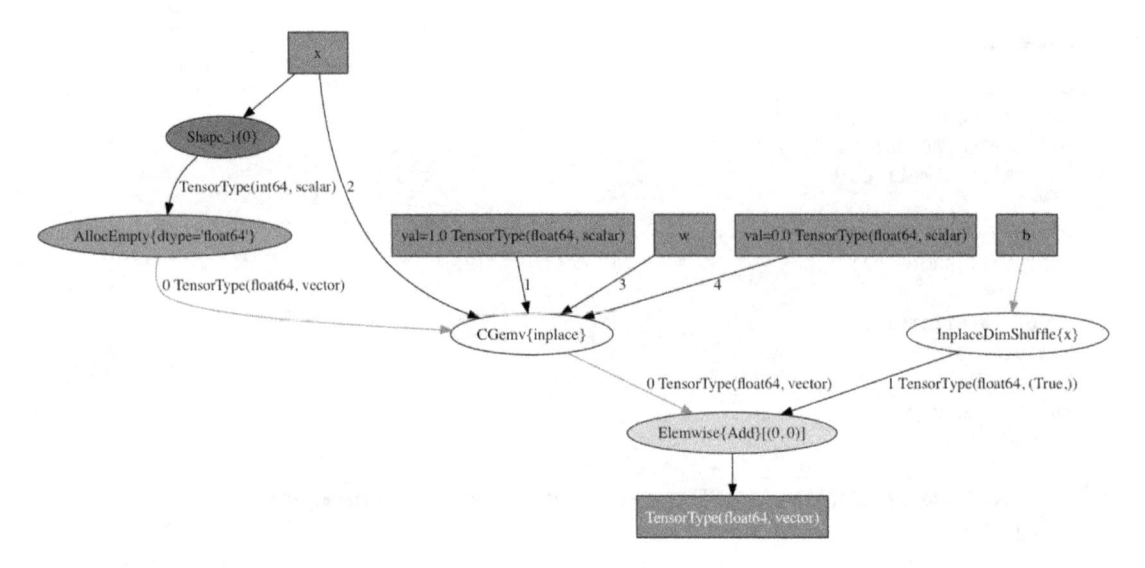

Figure 4-11. Linear Regression

In our next example in Listing 4-12 (and corresponding computational graph in Figure 4-12) we will build a neural network model with 2 layers. The reader should note the following:

1. The example generates some artificial/toy data, fits a logistic regression model and computes the accuracy before and after training. This is a toy dataset for the purposes of illustration; the model is not generalizing/learning, as the data is generated randomly.

2. We define a function to compute L2 regularization as covered in listing 4-8 earlier.

3. We generate input data, which consists of 1000 vectors of dimensionality 100. Basically, 1000 examples with 100 features.

4. We generate random target/output labels as zeros and ones.

5. We define the expressions for the 2-layer neural network involving the data (denoted by x), the outputs (denoted by y), the bias term of the first layer (denoted by b1), the weight vector of the first layer (denoted by w1), the bias term of the second layer (denoted by b2), and, the weight vector of the second layer (denoted by w2). The weight vectors and the bias terms are shared variables.

6. We use the tanh activation function as covered in listing 4-4 to encode the neural network.

7. We compute the prediction, the error, and the loss using binary cross entropy as introduced in listing 4-7 earlier.

8. Having defined these expressions, we can now use the grad construct in Theano (introduced in listing (4-6)) to compute the gradient.

9. We define a train function based on the gradient function. The train function defines the inputs, outputs, and how the internal state (shared variables) are to be updated.

CHAPTER 4 ■ INTRODUCTION TO THEANO

10. The train function is invoked for 1000 steps; in each step the gradient is computed internally and the shared variables are updated.

11. Accuracy is computed before and after the training steps using sklearn.metrics

Listing 4-12. Neural Network

```
import numpy
import theano
import theano.tensor as T
import sklearn.metrics

def l2(x):
    return T.sum(x**2)

examples = 1000
features = 100
hidden = 10

D = (numpy.random.randn(examples, features), numpy.random.randint(size=examples,
low=0, high=2))
training_steps = 1000

x = T.dmatrix("x")
y = T.dvector("y")

w1 = theano.shared(numpy.random.randn(features, hidden), name="w1")
b1 = theano.shared(numpy.zeros(hidden), name="b1")

w2 = theano.shared(numpy.random.randn(hidden), name="w2")
b2 = theano.shared(0., name="b2")

p1 = T.tanh(T.dot(x, w1) + b1)
p2 = T.tanh(T.dot(p1, w2) + b2)

prediction = p2 > 0.5

error = T.nnet.binary_crossentropy(p2,y)

loss = error.mean() + 0.01 * (l2(w1) + l2(w2))
gw1, gb1, gw2, gb2 = T.grad(loss, [w1, b1, w2, b2])

train = theano.function(inputs=[x,y],outputs=[p2, error], updates=((w1, w1 - 0.1 * gw1),
(b1, b1 - 0.1 * gb1), (w2, w2 - 0.1 * gw2), (b2, b2 - 0.1 * gb2)))
predict = theano.function(inputs=[x], outputs=[prediction])

print "Accuracy before Training:", sklearn.metrics.accuracy_score(D[1], numpy.
array(predict(D[0])).ravel())

for i in range(training_steps):
    prediction, error = train(D[0], D[1])
```

55

CHAPTER 4 ■ INTRODUCTION TO THEANO

```
print "Accuracy after Training:", sklearn.metrics.accuracy_score(D[1],
numpy.array(predict(D[0])).ravel())

# Accuracy before Training: 0.51
# Accuracy after Training: 0.716
```

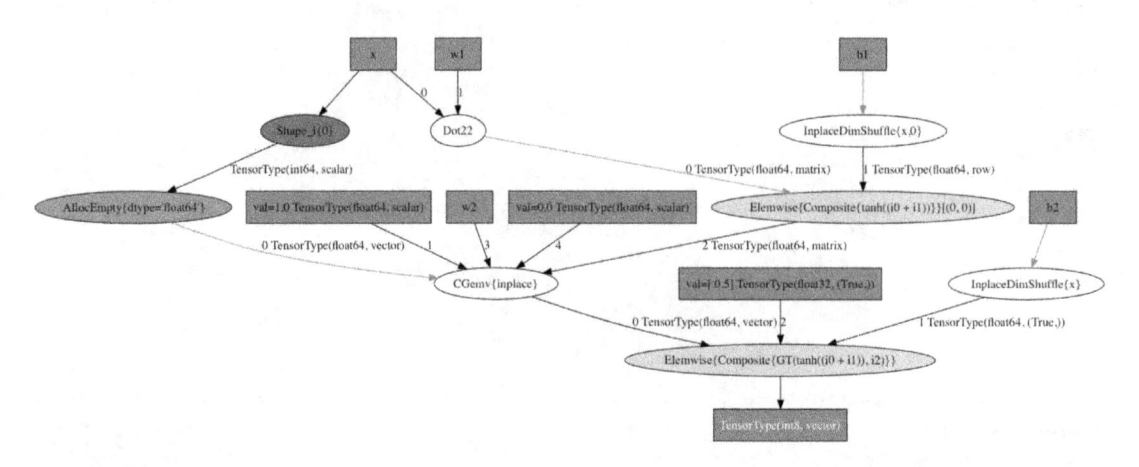

Figure 4-12. Neural Network

In our next example in Listing 4-13 (and corresponding computational graphs in Figures 4-13 (a), 4-13 (b) and 4-13 (c)) we will define a function using the if-else and switch construct. The reader should note the following:

1. Certain functions need an if-else (or switch) clause for their evaluation. For such cases Theano provides an if-else and switch constructs.

2. Expressions and functions can be defined using the if-else and switch constructs and gradients can be generated as with other expressions/constructs.

3. In the example we demonstrate the computation of the hinge lose using the if-else and switch construct and verify that it matches to the one defined with max.

Listing 4-13. Switch/If-Else

```
import numpy
import theano
import theano.tensor as T
from theano.ifelse import ifelse

def hinge_a(x,y):
    return T.max([0 * x, 1-x*y])

def hinge_b(x,y):
    return ifelse(T.lt(1-x*y,0), 0 * x, 1-x*y)

def hinge_c(x,y):
    return T.switch(T.lt(1-x*y,0), 0 * x, 1-x*y)
```

```
x = T.dscalar('x')
y = T.dscalar('y')

z1 = hinge_a(x, y)
z2 = hinge_b(x, y)
z3 = hinge_b(x, y)

f1 = theano.function([x,y], z1)
f2 = theano.function([x,y], z2)
f3 = theano.function([x,y], z3)

print "f(-2, 1) =",f1(-2, 1), f2(-2, 1), f3(-2, 1)
print "f(-1,1 ) =",f1(-1, 1), f2(-1, 1), f3(-1, 1)
print "f(0,1) =",f1(0, 1), f2(0, 1), f3(0, 1)
print "f(1, 1) =",f1(1, 1), f2(1, 1), f3(1, 1)
print "f(2, 1) =",f1(2, 1), f2(2, 1), f3(2, 1)

# f(-2, 1) = 3.0 3.0 3.0
# f(-1,1 ) = 2.0 2.0 2.0
# f(0,1) = 1.0 1.0 1.0
# f(1, 1) = 0.0 0.0 0.0
# f(2, 1) = 0.0 0.0 0.0
```

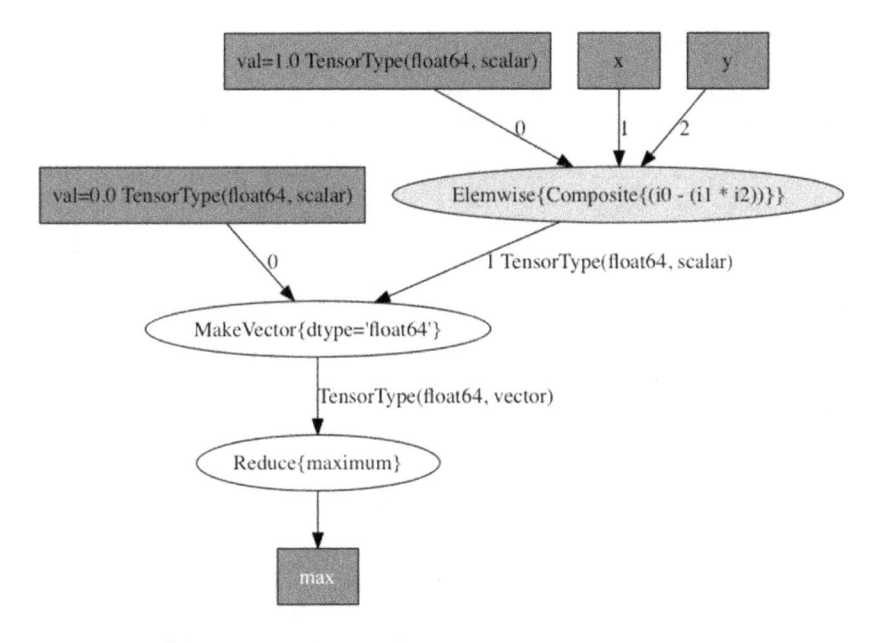

Figure 4-13 (a). *Hinge implemented using Max*

Figure 4-13 (a) illustrates the implementation of the hinge loss using the max operation that is $l(y) = \max(0, 1 - x \cdot y)$ where x is the correct/actual output and y is the output produced by the model. The computational graph closely corresponds to the formula/equation for hinge loss.

CHAPTER 4 ■ INTRODUCTION TO THEANO

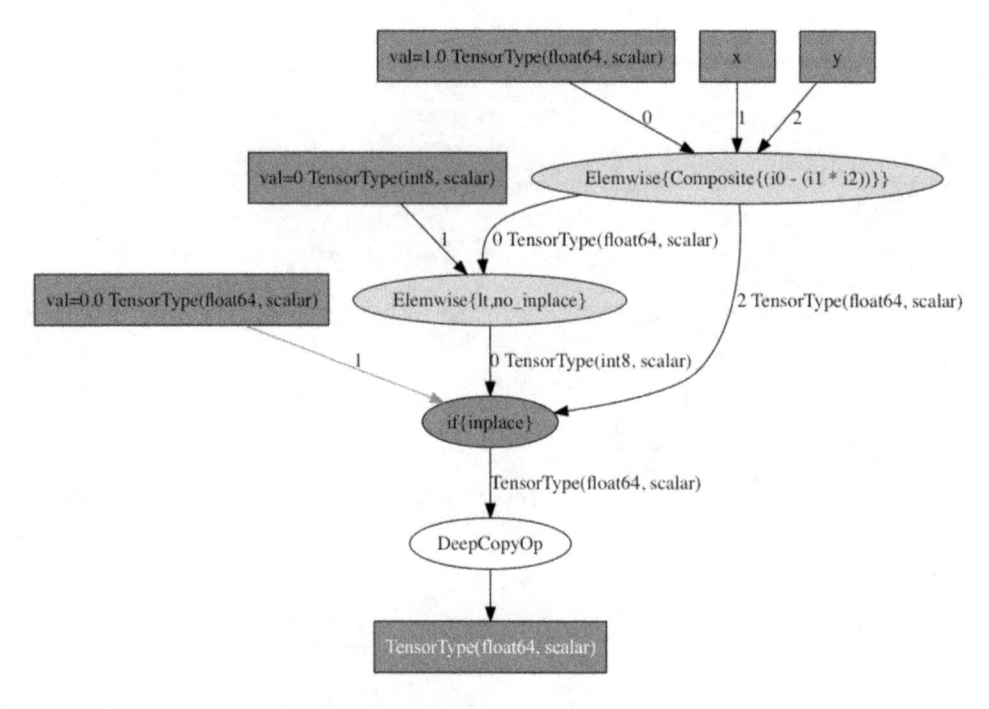

Figure 4-13 (b). Hinge implemented using ifelse

Figure 4-13 (b) illustrates the implementation of the hinge loss using the if-else construct. Note how the computational graph implements the condition and the intended out for each of the condition.

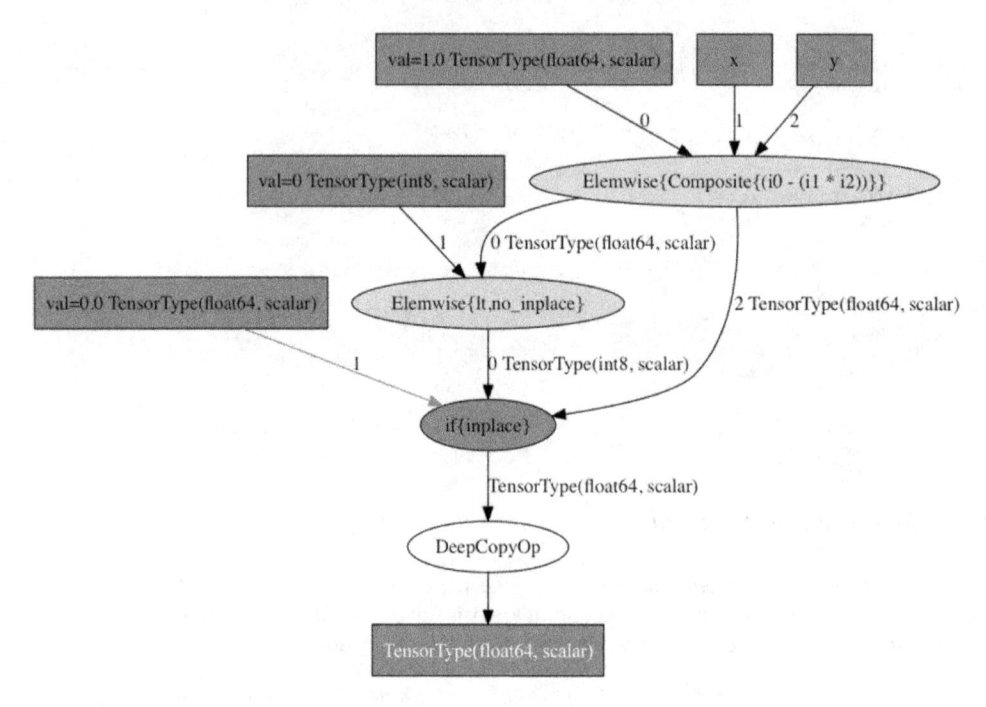

Figure 4-13 (c). Hinge implemented using switch

58

CHAPTER 4 ■ INTRODUCTION TO THEANO

In our next example in listing 4-14 (and the corresponding computational graph in Figure 4-14) we illustrate the scan construct that allows the user to define functions involving iterative computation. The reader should note the following.

1. Computation of certain functions requires iterative constructs for which Theano provides the scan construct.

2. In our example we compute the power operation with the scan construct and match the output with using the standard operator for power.

3. Expressions and functions can be defined using the scan construct and gradients can be generated as with other expressions/constructs.

Listing 4-14. Scan

```
import theano
import theano.tensor as T
import theano.printing
k = T.iscalar("k")
a = T.dscalar("a")
result, updates = theano.scan(fn=lambda prior_result, a: prior_result * a, outputs_info=a,
non_sequences=a, n_steps=k-1)
final_result = result[-1]
a_pow_k = theano.function(inputs=[a,k], outputs=final_result, updates=updates)
print a_pow_k(2,5), 2 ** 5
print a_pow_k(2,5), 2 ** 5
# 32.0 32
```

59

CHAPTER 4 ■ INTRODUCTION TO THEANO

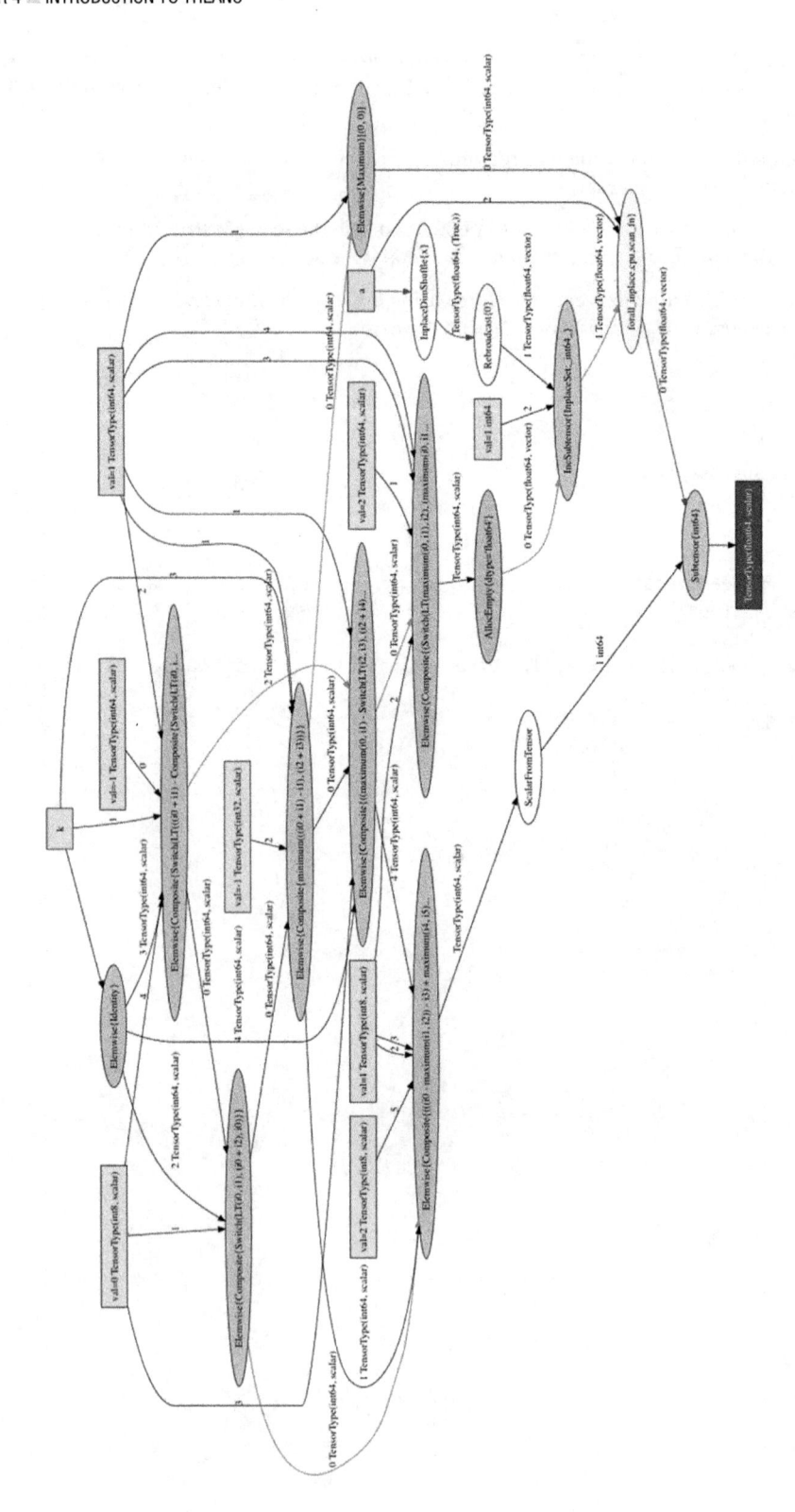

Figure 4-14. Scan Operation

Summary

In this chapter we covered the basics of Theano which is a low level library for building and training neural networks. Theano allows users to build computational graphs and compute gradients and is the ideal tool when it comes to building new architectures/networks as it gives the user a very fine grained control over the computational graph. A number of libraries like Keras (covered in Chapter 7) and Lasagne are built over Theano and provide higher level abstractions so that users need not build networks using computational graphs themselves. Such higher level libraries make the user much more productive, but the user does not have precise control over the network/architecture. In general, higher level libraries are recommended when the higher library provides a close enough implementation of the network/ architecture the user wants to build. In case, this is not available, it is recommended that the user build the network using Theano which will give him complete control. Basically using such high level libraries versus Theano is a tradeoff between productivity and control, much similar to programming in Python vs. programming in C.

CHAPTER 5

Convolutional Neural Networks

Convolution Neural Networks (CNNs) in essence are neural networks that employ the convolution operation (instead of a fully connected layer) as one of its layers. CNNs are an incredibly successful technology that has been applied to problems wherein the input data on which predictions are to be made has a known grid like topology like a time series (which is a 1-D grid) or an image (which is a 2-D grid).

Convolution Operation

Let us start developing intuition for the convolution operation in one dimension. Given an input $I(t)$ and a kernel $K(a)$ the convolution operation is given by

$$s(t) = \sum_a I(a) \cdot K(t-a)$$

An equivalent form of this operation given commutativity of the convolution operation is as follows:

$$s(t) = \sum_a I(t-a) \cdot K(a)$$

Furthermore, the negative sign (flipping) can be replaced to get cross-correlation given as follows:

$$s(t) = \sum_a I(t+a) \cdot K(a)$$

CHAPTER 5 CONVOLUTIONAL NEURAL NETWORKS

In deep learning literature and software implementations, convolution and cross-correlation are used interchangeably. The essence of the operation is that the Kernel is a much shorter set of data points as compared to the input, and the output of the convolution operation is higher when the input is similar to the kernel. Figures 5-1 and 5-2 illustrate this key idea. We take an arbitrary input and an arbitrary kernel, perform the convolution operation, and the highest value is achieved when the kernel is similar to a particular portion of the input.

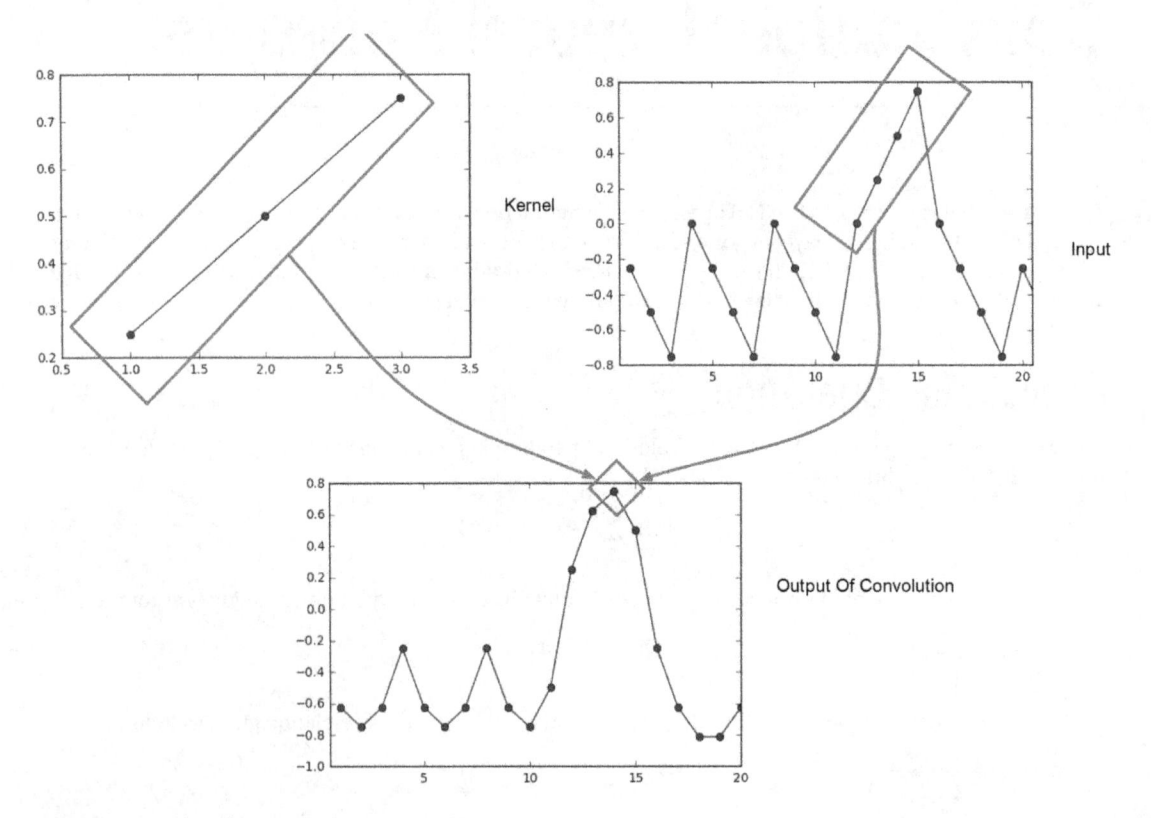

Figure 5-1. Convolution operation – Intuition

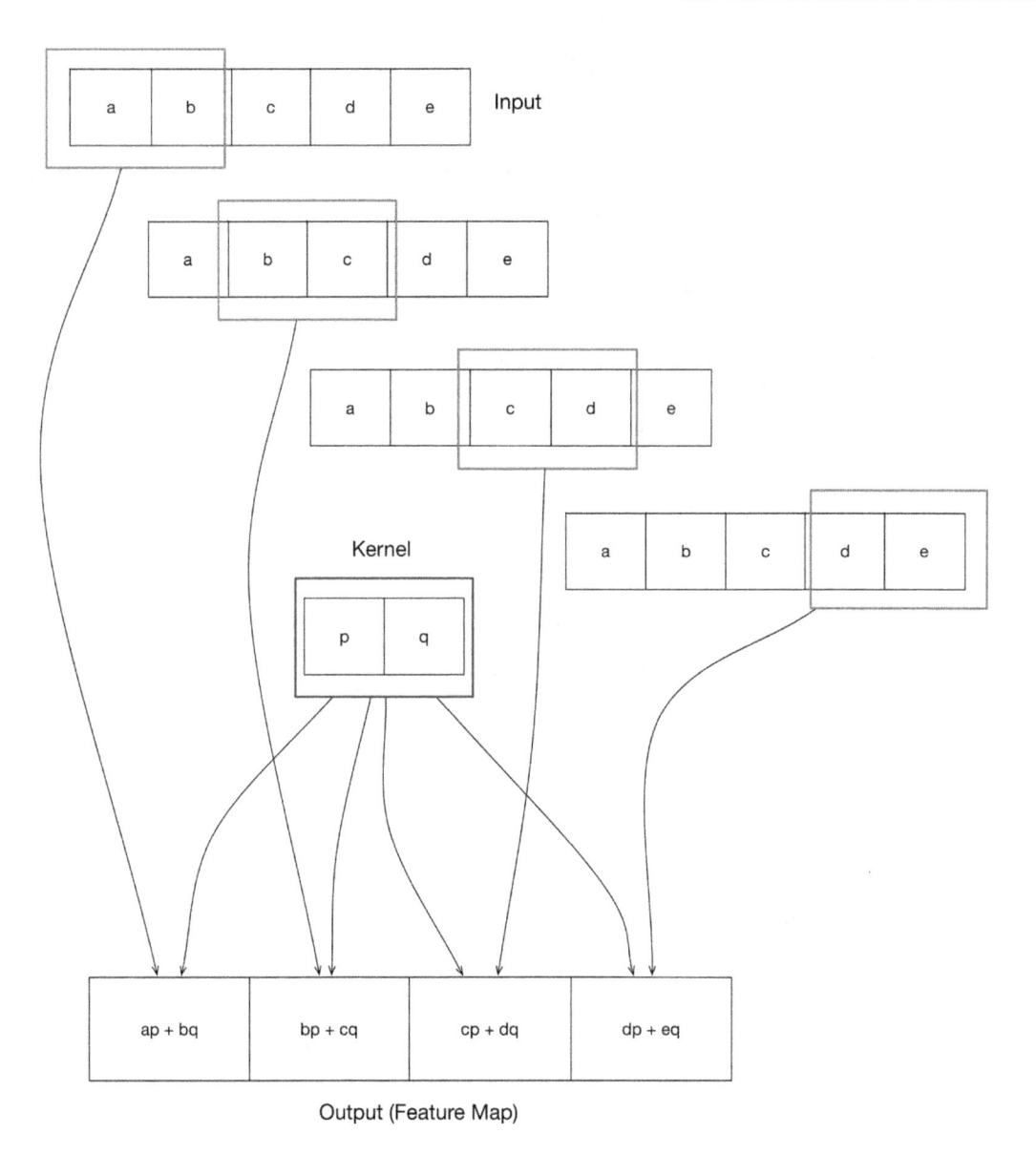

Figure 5-2. Convolution operation – One Dimension

CHAPTER 5 CONVOLUTIONAL NEURAL NETWORKS

Let us strengthen our intuition about convolution by observing Figures 5-1 and 5-2 and noting the following points:

1. The input is an arbitrary large set of data points.
2. The Kernel is a set of data points smaller in number to the input.
3. The convolution operation in a sense slides the kernel over the input and computes how similar the kernel is with the portion of the input.
4. The convolution operation produces the highest value where the Kernel is most similar with a portion of the input.

The convolution operation can be extended to two dimensions. Given an input $I(m, n)$ and a kernel $K(a, b)$ the convolution operation is given by

$$s(t) = \sum_a \sum_b I(a,b) \cdot K(m-a, n-b)$$

An equivalent form of this operation given commutativity of the convolution operation is as follows:

$$s(t) = \sum_a \sum_b I(m-a, n-b) \cdot K(a, b)$$

Furthermore, the negative sign (flipping) can be replaced to get cross-correlation given as follows:

$$s(t) = \sum_a \sum_b I(m+a, n+b) \cdot K(a, b)$$

Figure 5-3 illustrates the convolution operation in two dimensions. Note that this is simply extending the idea of convolution to two dimensions.

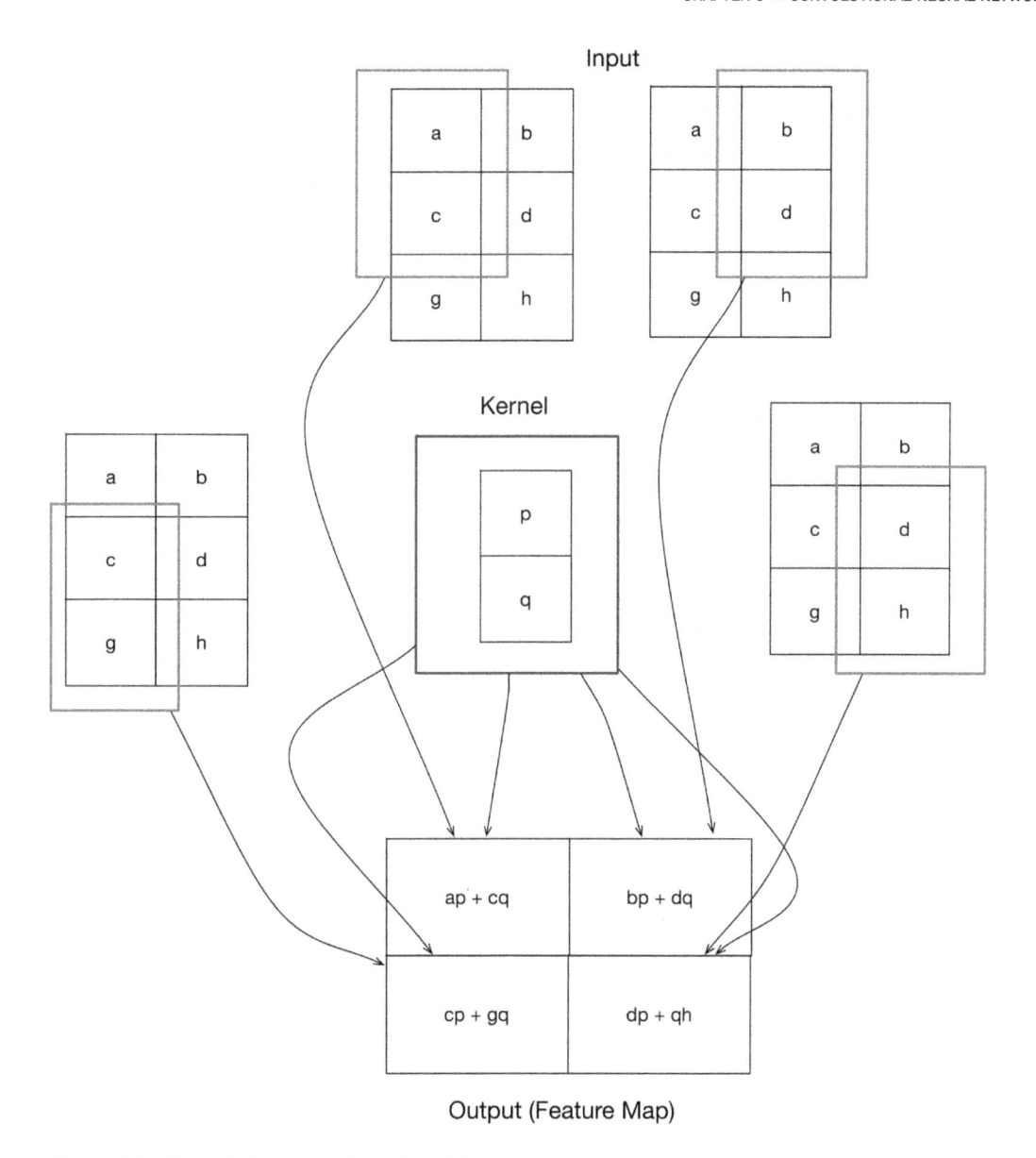

Figure 5-3. Convolution operation – Two Dimensions

Having introduced the convolution operation, we can now dive deeper into the key constituent parts of a CNN, were a convolution layer is used instead of a fully connected layer which involves a matrix multiplication. So, a fully connected layer can be described as $y = f(x \cdot w)$ where x is the input vector, y is the output vector, w is a set of weights, and f is the activation function. Correspondingly, a convolution layer can be described as $y = f(s(x \cdot w))$ where s denotes the convolution operation between the input and the weights.

CHAPTER 5 ■ CONVOLUTIONAL NEURAL NETWORKS

Let us now contrast the fully connected layer with the convolution layer. Figure 5-4 illustrates a fully connected layer and Figure 5-5 illustrates a convolution layer, schematically. Figure 5-6 illustrates parameter sharing in a convolution layer and the lack of it in a fully connected layer. The following points should be noted:

1. For the same number of inputs and outputs, the fully connected layer has a lot more connections, and correspondingly weights than a convolution layer.

2. The interactions amongst inputs to produce outputs are fewer in convolution layers as compared to many interactions in the case of a fully connected layer. This is referred to as sparse interactions.

3. Parameters/weights are shared across the convolution layer, given that the kernel is much smaller than the input and the kernel slides across the input. Thus, there are a lot fewer unique parameters/weights in a convolution layer.

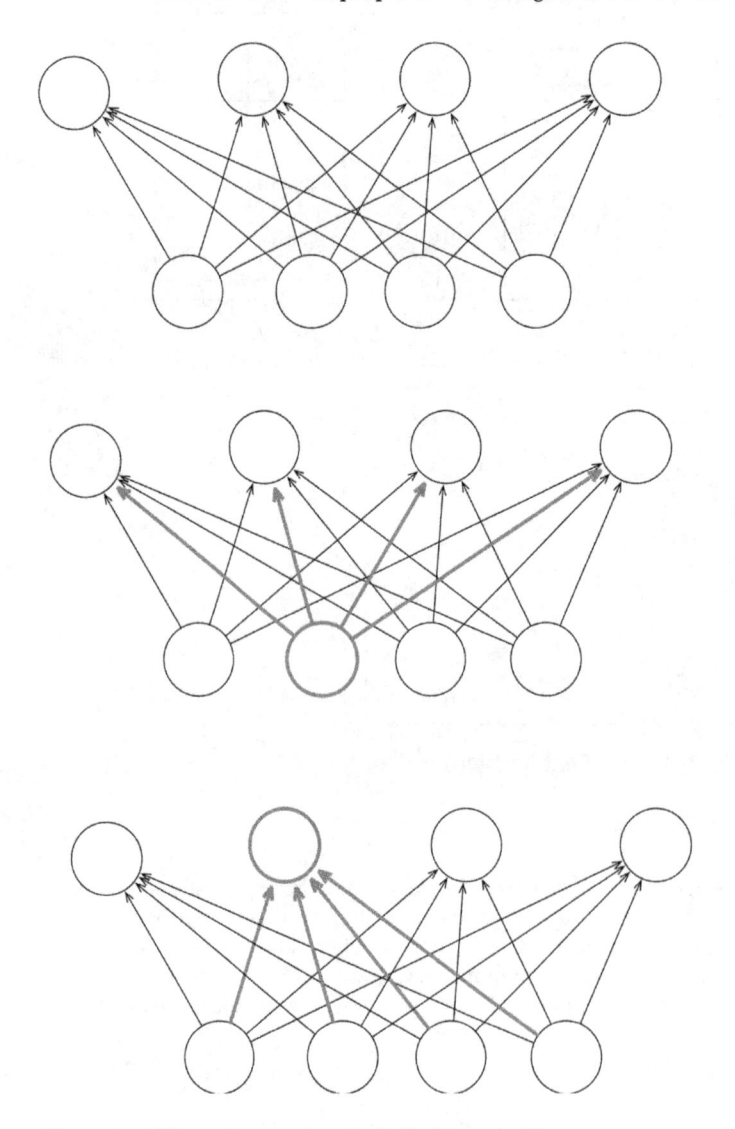

Figure 5-4. Dense Interactions in Fully Connected Layers

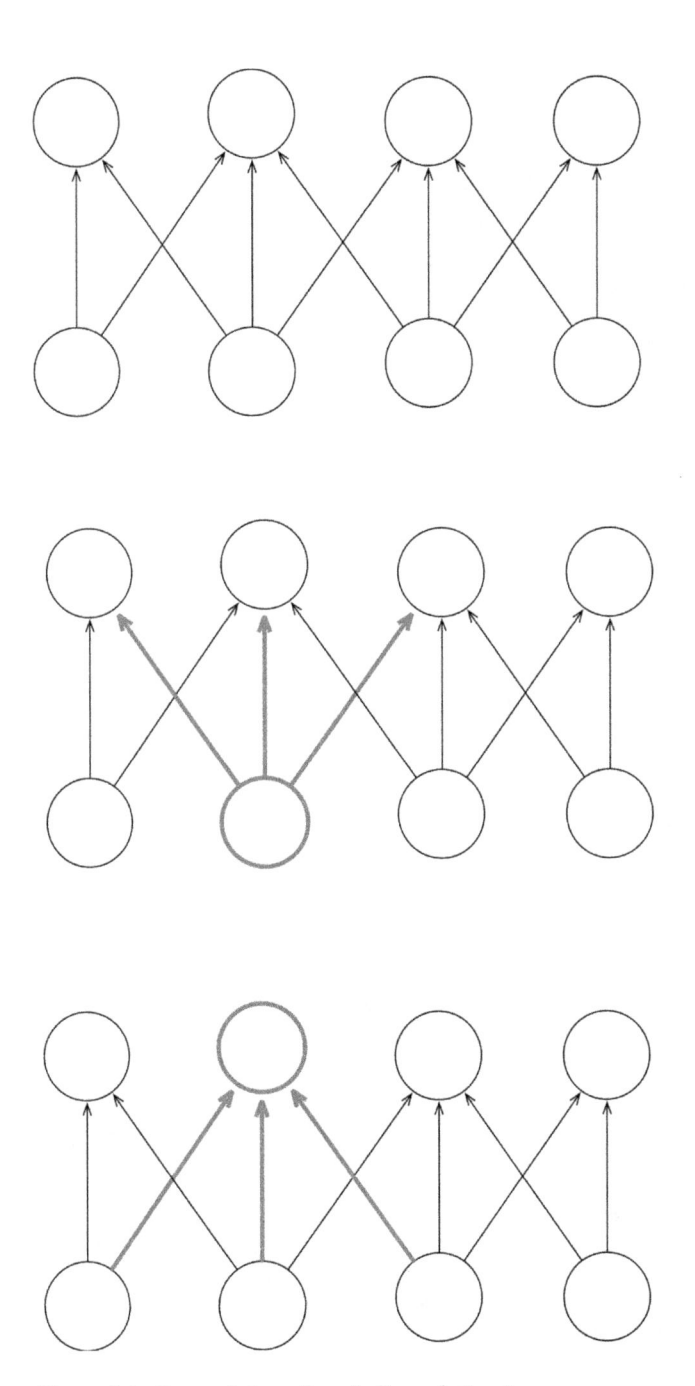

Figure 5-5. *Sparse Interactions in Convolution Layer*

CHAPTER 5 ■ CONVOLUTIONAL NEURAL NETWORKS

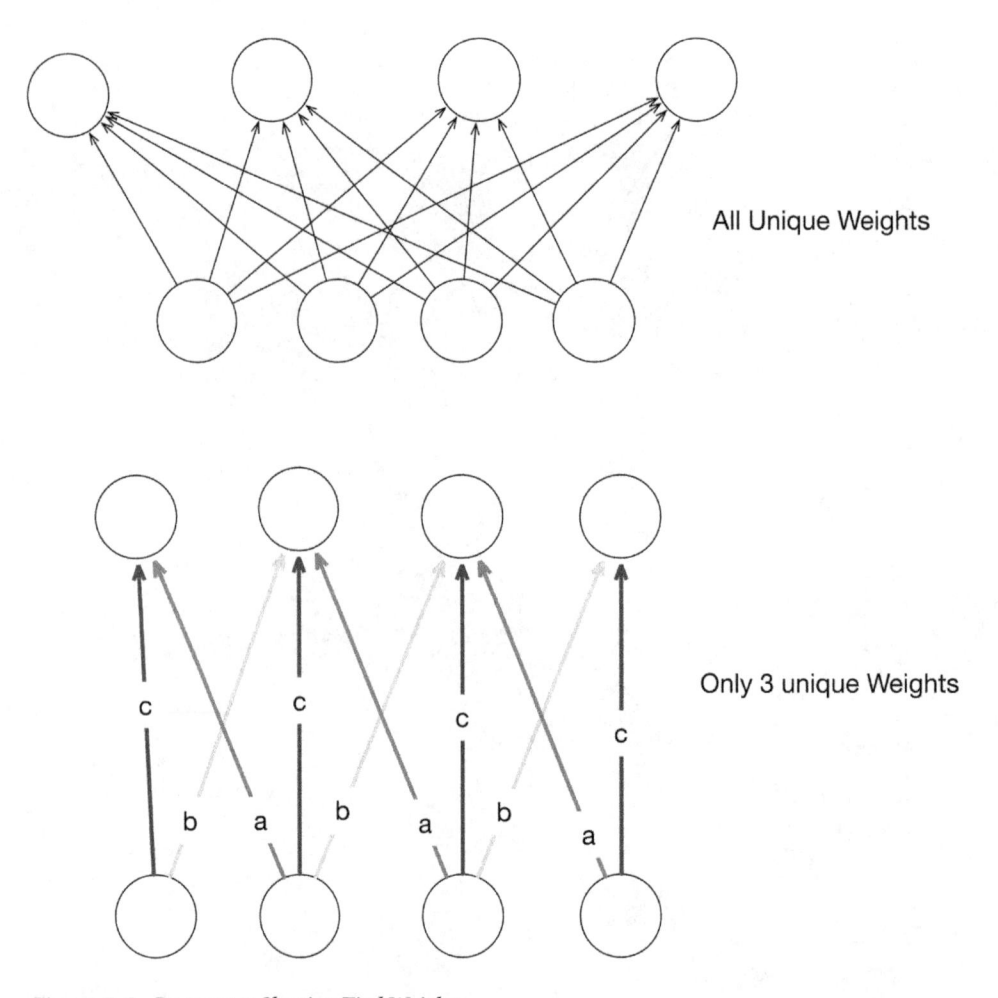

All Unique Weights

Only 3 unique Weights

Figure 5-6. Parameter Sharing Tied Weights

Pooling Operation

Let us now look at the pooling operation which is almost always used in CNNs in conjunction with convolution. The intuition behind the pooling operation is that the exact location of the feature is not a concern if in fact it has been discovered. It simply provides translation invariance. So, for instance, assume that the task at hand is to learn to detect faces in photographs. Let us also assume that the faces in the photograph are tilted (as they generally are) and suppose that we have a convolution layer that detects the eyes. We would like to abstract the location of the eyes in the photograph from their orientation. The pooling operation achieves this and is an important constituent of CNNs.

Figure 5-7 illustrates the pooling operation for a two-dimensional input. The following points are to be noted:

1. Pooling operates over a portion of the input and applies a function f over this input to produce the output.

2. The function f is commonly the *max* operation (leading to max pooling), but other variants such as average or L_2 norm can be used as an alternative.

CHAPTER 5 ■ CONVOLUTIONAL NEURAL NETWORKS

3. For a two-dimensional input, this is a rectangular portion.
4. The output produced as a result of pooling is much smaller in dimensionality as compared to the input.

Input

a	b	c	d
e	f	g	h
i	j	k	l
m	n	o	p

Output

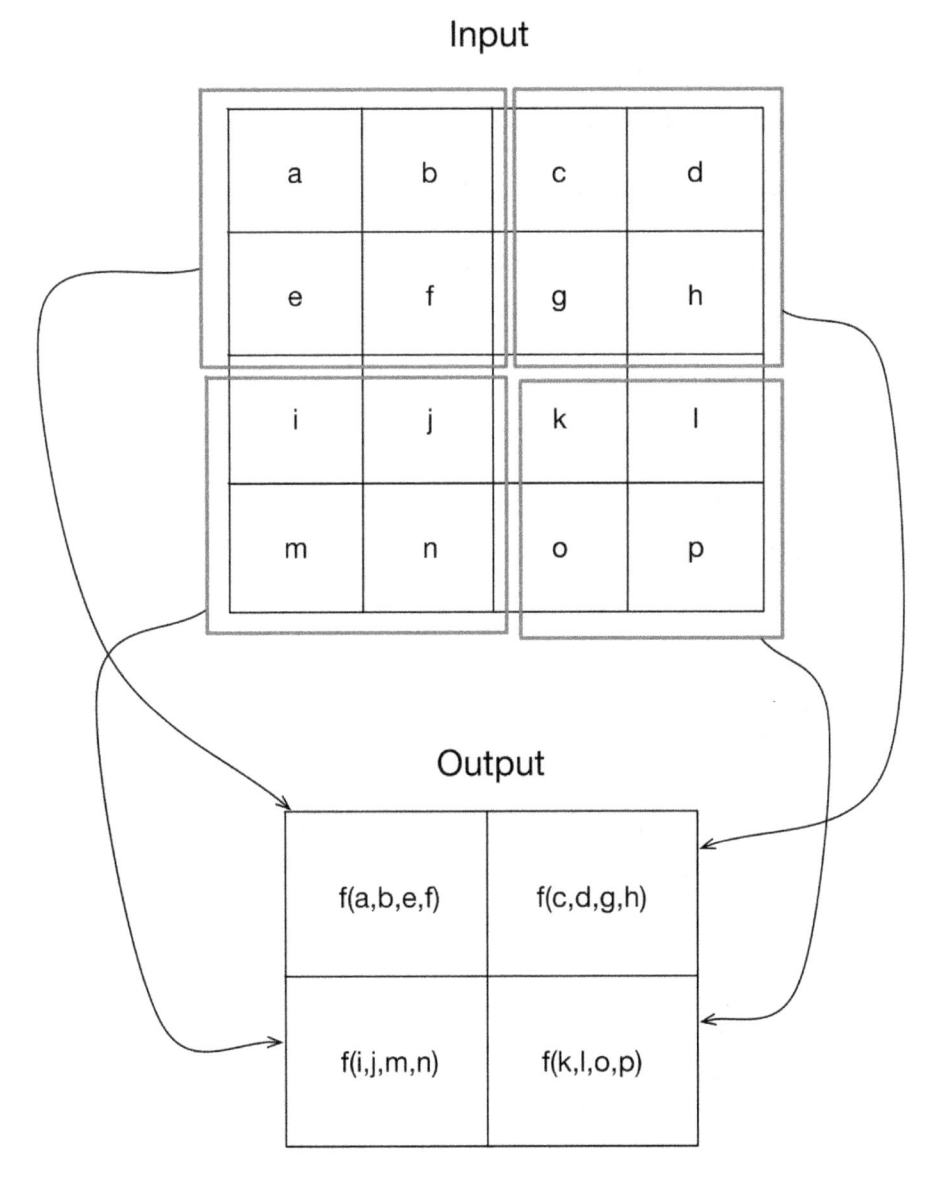

f(a,b,e,f)	f(c,d,g,h)
f(i,j,m,n)	f(k,l,o,p)

Figure 5-7. Pooling or Subsampling

Convolution-Detector-Pooling Building Block

Let us now look at the Convolution-Detector-Pooling block, which can be thought of as a building block of the CNN.

Let us now look at how all the operations we have covered earlier work in conjunction. Refer to Figure 5-8 and Figure 5-9. The following points are to be noted:

1. The detector stage is simply a non-linear activation function.

2. The convolution, detector, and pooling operations are applied in sequence to transform the input to the output. The output is referred to as a feature map.

3. The output typically is passed on to other layers (convolution or fully connected).

4. Multiple Convolution-Detector-Pooling blocks can be applied in parallel, consuming the same input and producing multiple outputs or feature maps.

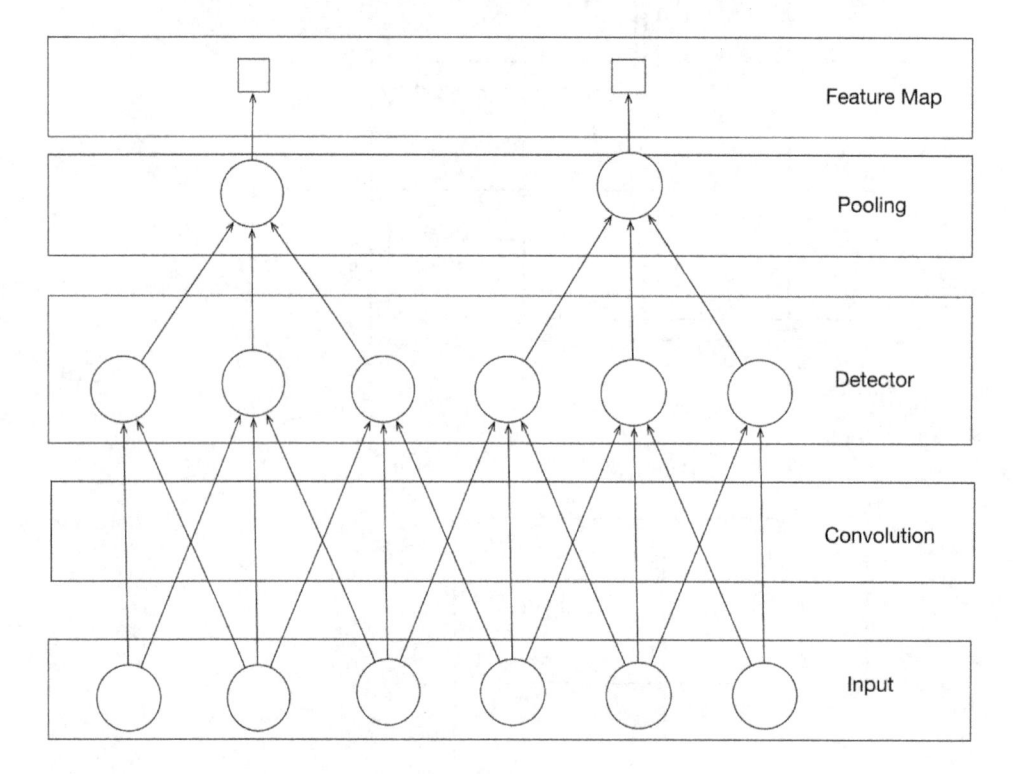

Figure 5-8. Convolution followed by detector stage and pooling

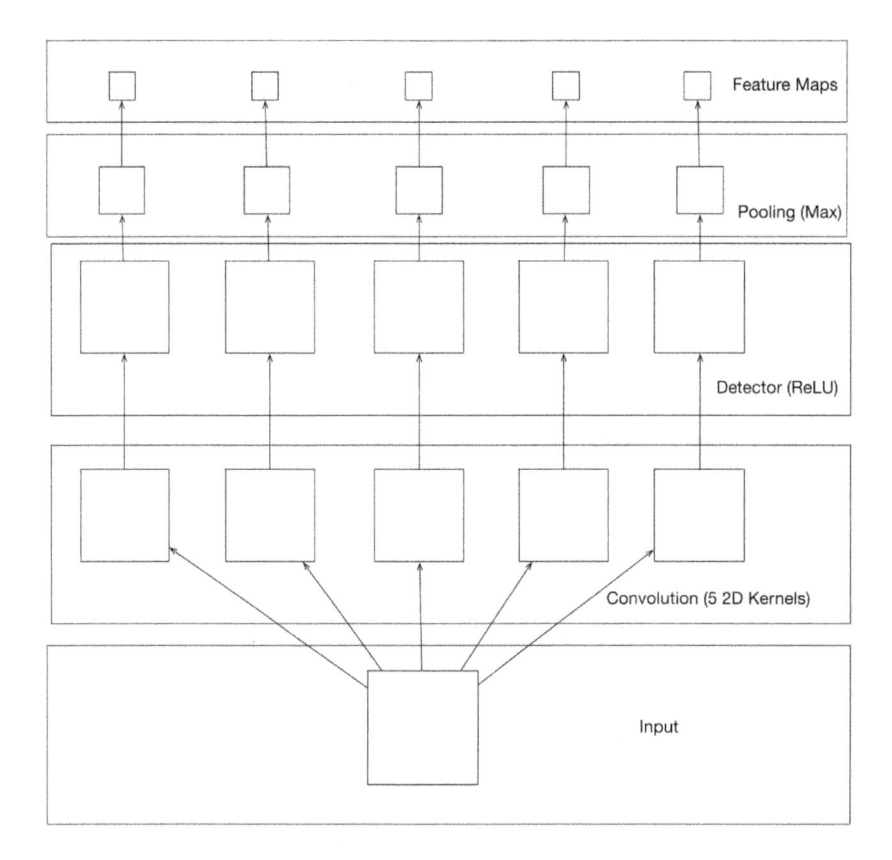

Figure 5-9. *Multiple Filters/Kernels giving Multiple Feature Maps*

CHAPTER 5 CONVOLUTIONAL NEURAL NETWORKS

In the case of image inputs, which consist of 3 channels, a separate convolution operation is applied to each channel and then outputs post the convolution are added up. This is illustrated in Figure 5-10.

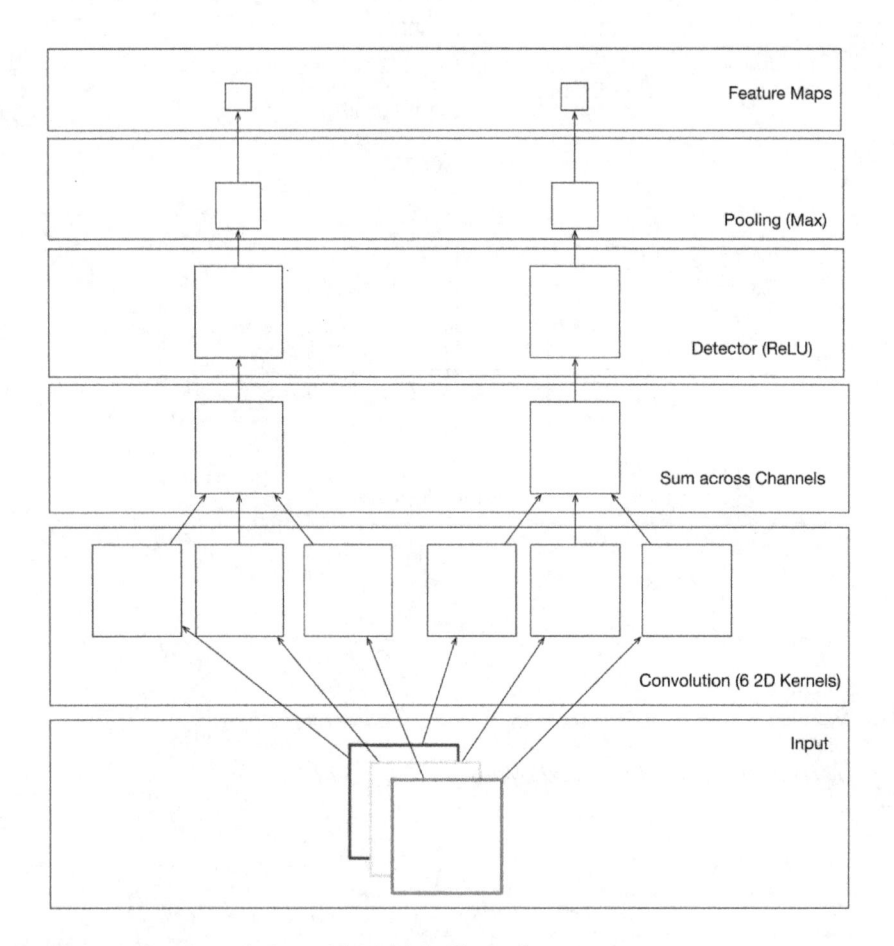

Figure 5-10. Convolution with Multiple Channels

CHAPTER 5 ■ CONVOLUTIONAL NEURAL NETWORKS

Having covered all the constituent elements of CNNs, we can now look at an exemplar CNN in its entirety as illustrated in Figure 5-11. The CNN consists of two stages of convolution-detector-pooling blocks with multiple filters/kernels at each stage producing multiple feature maps. Post these two stages we have a fully connected layer which produces the output. In general, a CNN may have multiple stages of convolution-detector-pooling blocks (employing multiple filters) typically followed by a fully connected layer.

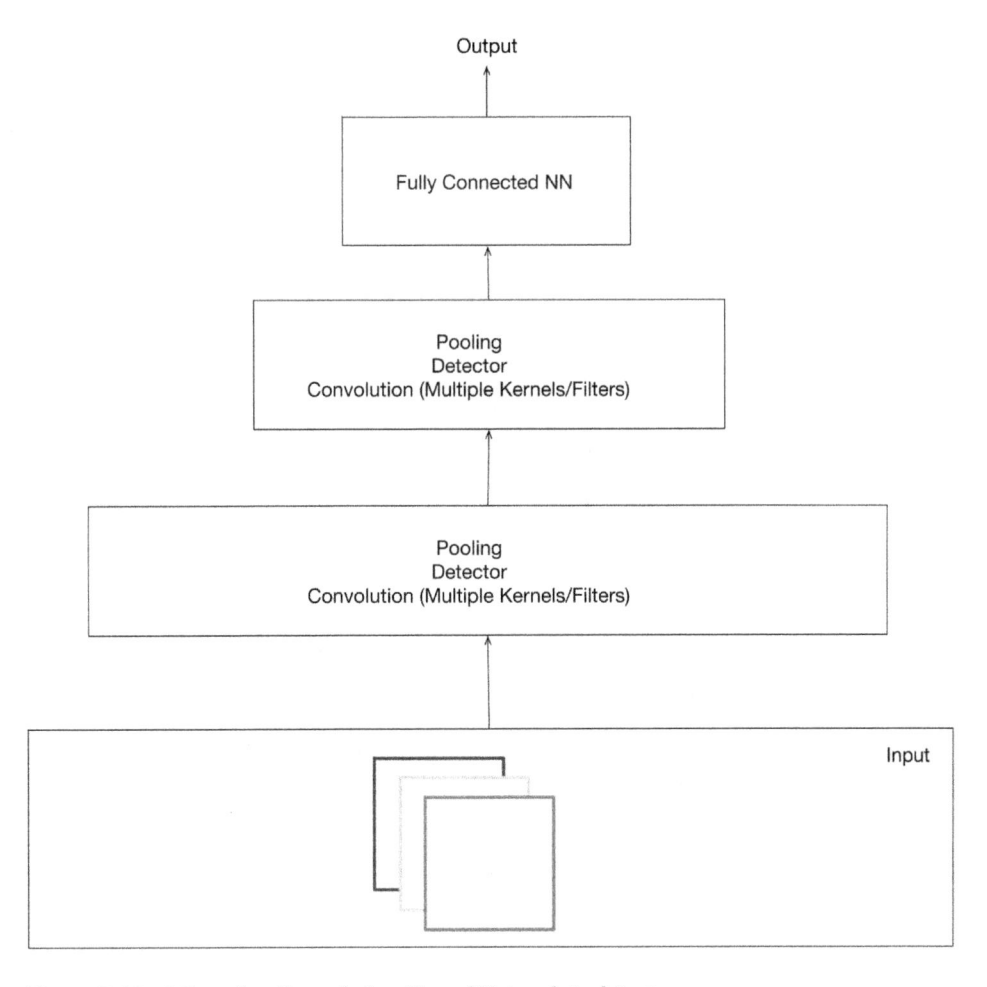

Figure 5-11. A Complete Convolution Neural Network Architecture

CHAPTER 5 CONVOLUTIONAL NEURAL NETWORKS

Convolution Variants

We will now cover some variations of convolution, illustrated in Figure 5-12. Strided convolution is a variant of the standard convolution where the kernel slides over the input by moving at a predefined stride. An alternative way of looking at this is that the standard convolution operated at a stride size equal to one. Another variation is tiled convolution where there are actually multiple kernels that are convoluted with the input alternately.

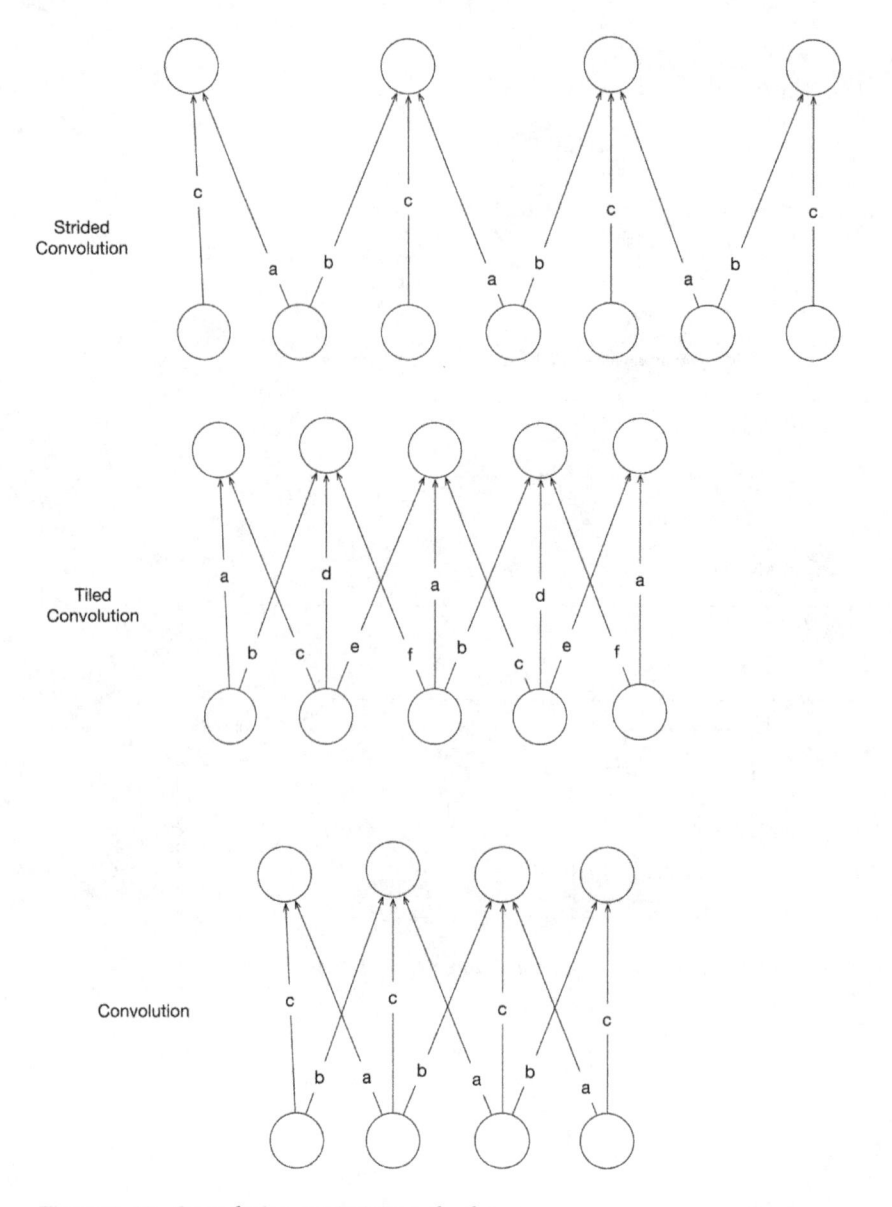

Figure 5-12. *Convolution, variation on the theme*

Another variation on the theme is locally connected layers which basically employ sparsity of interactions but do not employ parameter/weight sharing. This is illustrated in Figure 5-13.

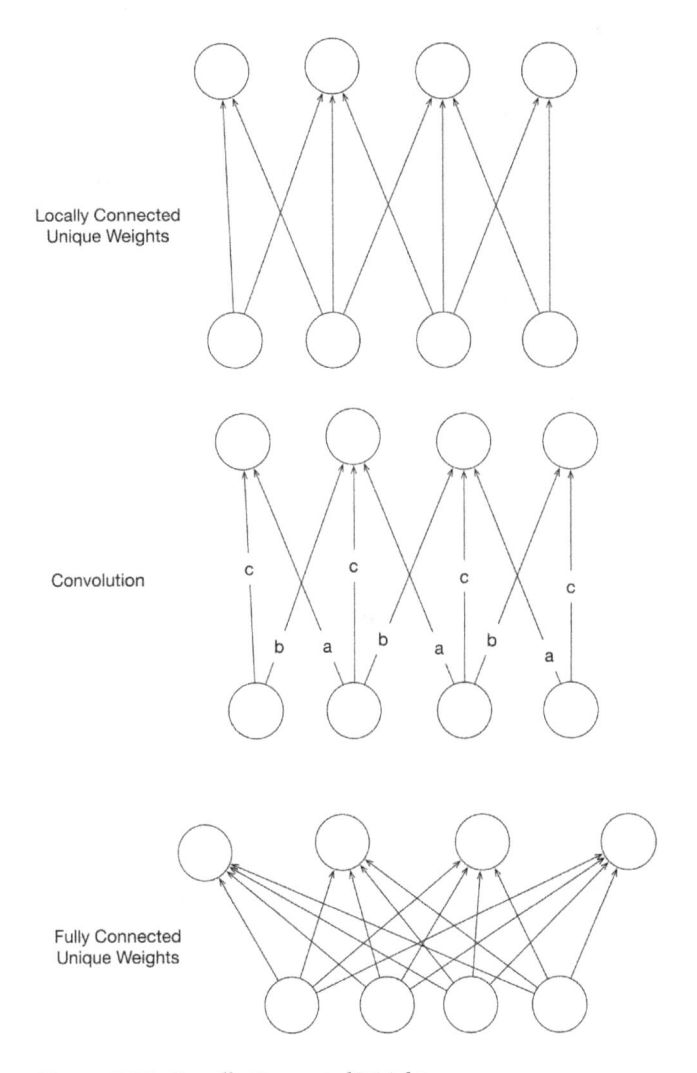

Figure 5-13. *Locally Connected Weights*

Intuition behind CNNs

So far in this chapter we have covered the key constituent concepts behind the CNN, namely the convolution operation, the pooling operation, and how they are used in conjunction. Let us now take a step back to internalize the intuition behind CNNs using these building blocks.

The first idea to consider is the capacity of CNNs (refer to Chapter 2 on the capacity of a machine learning model). CNNs, which replace at least one of the fully connected layers of a neural network by the convolution operation, have less capacity than a fully connected network. That is, there exist data sets that a fully connected network will be able to model that a CNN will not be. So, the first point to note is that CNNs achieve more by limiting the capacity, hence making the training efficient.

The second idea to consider is that learning the filters driving the convolution operation is, in a sense, representation learning. For instance, the learned filters might learn to detect edges, shapes, etc. The important point to consider here is that we are not manually describing the features to be extracted from the input data, but are describing an architecture that learns to engineer the features/representations.

The third idea to consider is the location invariance introduced by the pooling operation. The pooling operation separates the location of the feature from the fact that it is detected. A filter detecting straight lines might detect this filter in any portion of the image, but the pooling operation picks the fact that the feature is detected (max pooling).

The fourth idea is that of hierarchy. A CNN may have multiple convolution and pooling layers stacked up followed by a fully connected network. This allows the CNN to build a hierarchy of concepts wherein more abstract concepts are based on simpler concepts (refer to Chapter 1).

The fifth and last idea is the presence of a fully connected layer at the end of a series of convolution and pooling layers. The idea is that the series of convolution and pooling layers generates the features and a standard neural network learns the final classification/regression function. It is important to distinguish this aspect of the CNN from traditional machine learning. In traditional machine learning, an expert would hand engineer features and feed them to a neural network. In the case of CNNs, these features/representations are being learned from data.

Summary

In this chapter we covered the basics of CNNs. The key takeaway points are the convolution operation, the pooling operation, how they are used in conjunction, and how features are not hand engineered but learned. CNNs are the most successful application of deep learning and embody the idea of learning features/representations rather than hand engineering them.

CHAPTER 6

Recurrent Neural Networks

Recurrent Neural Networks (RNNs) in essence are neural networks that employ recurrence, which is basically using information from a previous forward pass over the neural network. Essentially, all RNN's can be described as a recurrence relationship. RNNs are suited and have been incredibly successful when applied to problems wherein the input data on which the predictions are to be made is in the form of a sequence (series of entities where order is important).

RNN Basics

Let us start by describing the moving parts of a RNN. First, we introduce some notation.

1. We will assume that input consists of a sequence of entities $x^{(1)}, x^{(2)}, ..., x^{(\tau)}$.

2. Corresponding to this input we either need to produce a sequence $y^{(1)}, y^{(2)}, ..., y^{(\tau)}$ or just one output for the entire input sequence y

3. To distinguish between what the RNN produces and what it is ideally expected to produce we will denote by $\hat{y}^{(1)}, \hat{y}^{(2)}, ..., \hat{y}^{(\tau)}$ or $\hat{y}$ the output the RNN produces. Note that this is distinct from what the RNN should ideally produce, which is denoted by $y^{(1)}, y^{(2)}, ..., y^{(\tau)}$ or y.

RNNs either produce an output for every entity in the input sequence or produce a single output for the entire sequence. Let us consider the case where an RNN produces one output for every entity in the input. The RNN can be described using the following equations:

$$h^{(t)} = \tanh\left(Ux^{(t)} + Wh^{(t-1)} + b\right)$$

$$\hat{y}^{(t)} = softmax\left(Vh^{(t)} + c\right)$$

The following points about the RNN equations should be noted:

1. The RNN computation involves first computing the hidden state for an entity in the sequence. This is denoted by $h^{(t)}$.

2. The computation of $h^{(t)}$ uses the corresponding input at entity $x^{(t)}$ and the previous hidden state $h^{(t-1)}$.

3. The output $\hat{y}^{(t)}$ is computed using the hidden state $h^{(t)}$.

4. There are weights associated with the input and the previous hidden state while computing the current hidden state. This is denoted by U and W respectively. There is also a bias term denoted by b.

CHAPTER 6 ■ RECURRENT NEURAL NETWORKS

5. There are weights associated with the hidden state while computing the output; this is denoted by V. There is also a bias term, which is denoted by c.
6. The tanh activation function (introduced in earlier chapters) is used in the computation of the hidden state.
7. The softmax activation function is used in the computation of the output.
8. The RNN as described by the equations can process an arbitrarily large input sequence.
9. The parameters of the RNN, namely, U, W, V, b, c, etc. are shared across the computation of the hidden layer and output value (for each of the entities in the sequence).

Figure 6-1 illustrates an RNN. Note how the illustration depicts the recurrence relation with the self-loop at the hidden state.

L

$y^{(t)}$

$L_t(y^{(t)}, \hat{y}^{(t)})$

$\hat{y}^{(t)} = softmax(Vh^{(t)} + c)$

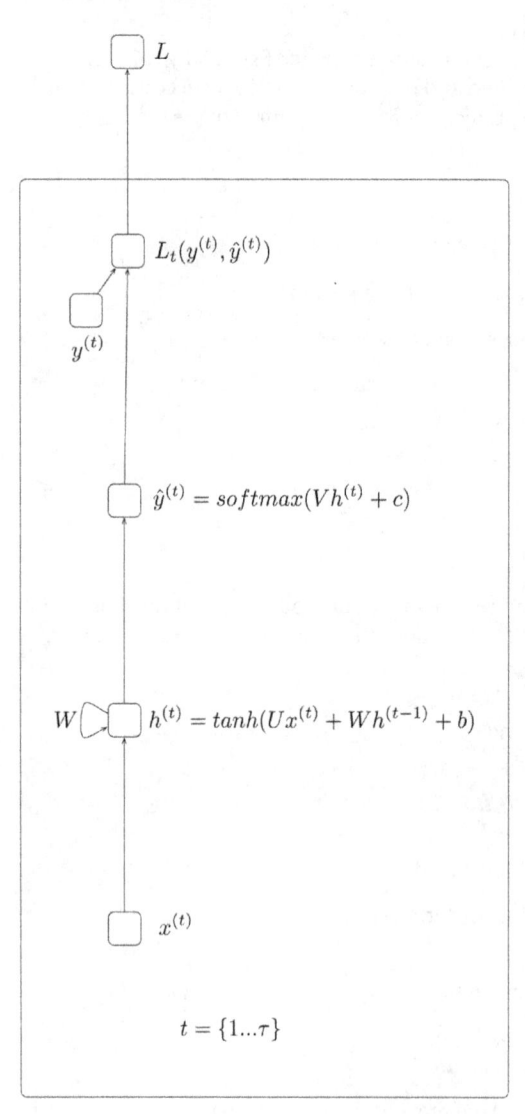

W $h^{(t)} = tanh(Ux^{(t)} + Wh^{(t-1)} + b)$

$x^{(t)}$

$t = \{1...\tau\}$

Figure 6-1. *RNN (Recurrence using the previous hidden state)*

CHAPTER 6 ■ RECURRENT NEURAL NETWORKS

The figure also depicts a loss function associated with each output associated with each input. We will refer back to it when we cover how RNNs are trained.

Presently, it's essential to internalize how an RNN is different from all the feedforward neural networks (including convolution networks) we have seen earlier. The key difference is the hidden state, which represents a summary of the entities seen in the past (for the same sequence).

Ignoring for the time being how RNNs are trained, it should be clear to the reader how a trained RNN could be used. For a given sequence of inputs, an RNN would produce an output for each entity in the input.

Let us now consider a variation in the RNN wherein instead of the recurrence using the hidden state, we have recurrence using the output produced in the previous state (refer to Figure 6-2).

L

$L_t(y^{(t)}, \hat{y}^{(t)})$

$y^{(t)}$

$\hat{y}^{(t)} = softmax(Vh^{(t)} + c)$

W

$h^{(t)} = tanh(Ux^{(t)} + W\hat{y}^{(t-1)} + b)$

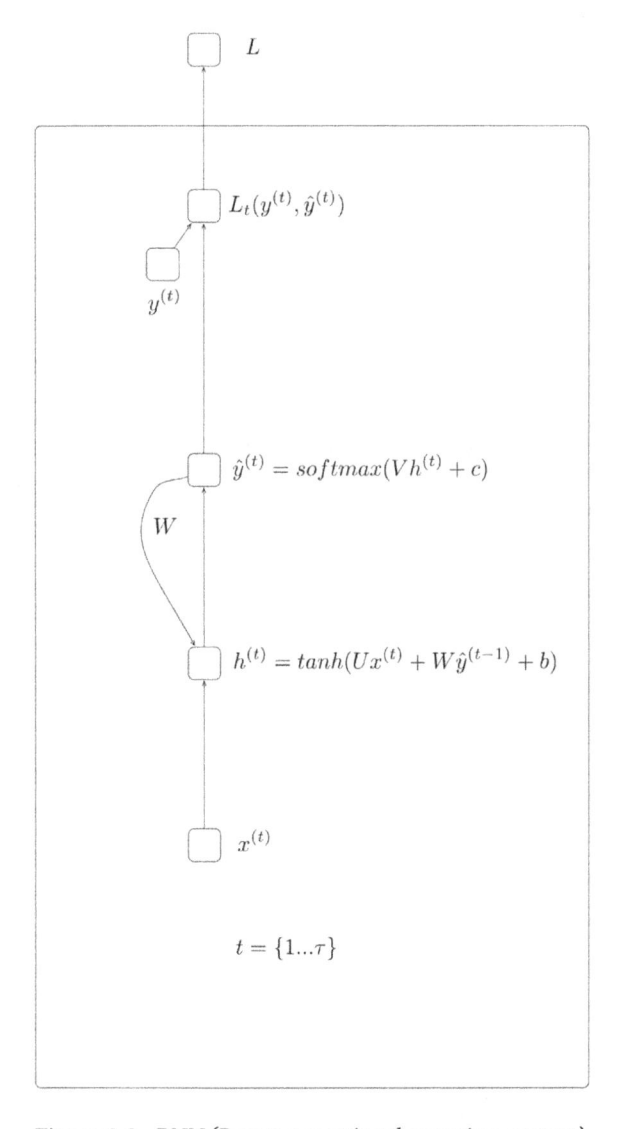

$x^{(t)}$

$t = \{1...\tau\}$

Figure 6-2. *RNN (Recurrence using the previous output)*

CHAPTER 6 RECURRENT NEURAL NETWORKS

The equations describing such an RNN are as follows:

$$h^{(t)} = \tanh(Ux^{(t)} + W\hat{y}^{(t-1)} + b)$$

$$\hat{y}^{(t)} = softmax\left(Vh^{(t)} + c\right)$$

The following points are to be noted:

1. The RNN computation involves first computing the hidden state for an entity in the sequence. This is denoted by $h^{(t)}$.

2. The computation of $h^{(t)}$ uses the corresponding input at entity $x^{(t)}$ and the previous output $\hat{y}^{(t-1)}$.

3. The output $\hat{y}^{(t)}$ is computed using the hidden state $h^{(t)}$.

4. There are weights associated with the input and the previous output while computing the current hidden state. This is denoted by U and W respectively. There is also a bias term denoted by c.

5. There are weights associated with the hidden state while computing the output; this is denoted by V. There is also a bias term, which is denoted by c.

6. The tanh activation function (introduced in earlier chapters) is used in the computation of the hidden state.

The softmax activation function is used in the computation of the output.

Let us now consider a variation in the RNN where only a single output is produced for the entire sequence (refer to Figure 6-3). Such an RNN is described using the following equations:

$$h^{(t)} = \tanh(Ux^{(t)} + W\hat{y}^{(t-1)} + b)$$

$$\hat{y} = softmax\left(Vh^{(\tau)} + c\right)$$

$$L(y, \hat{y})$$

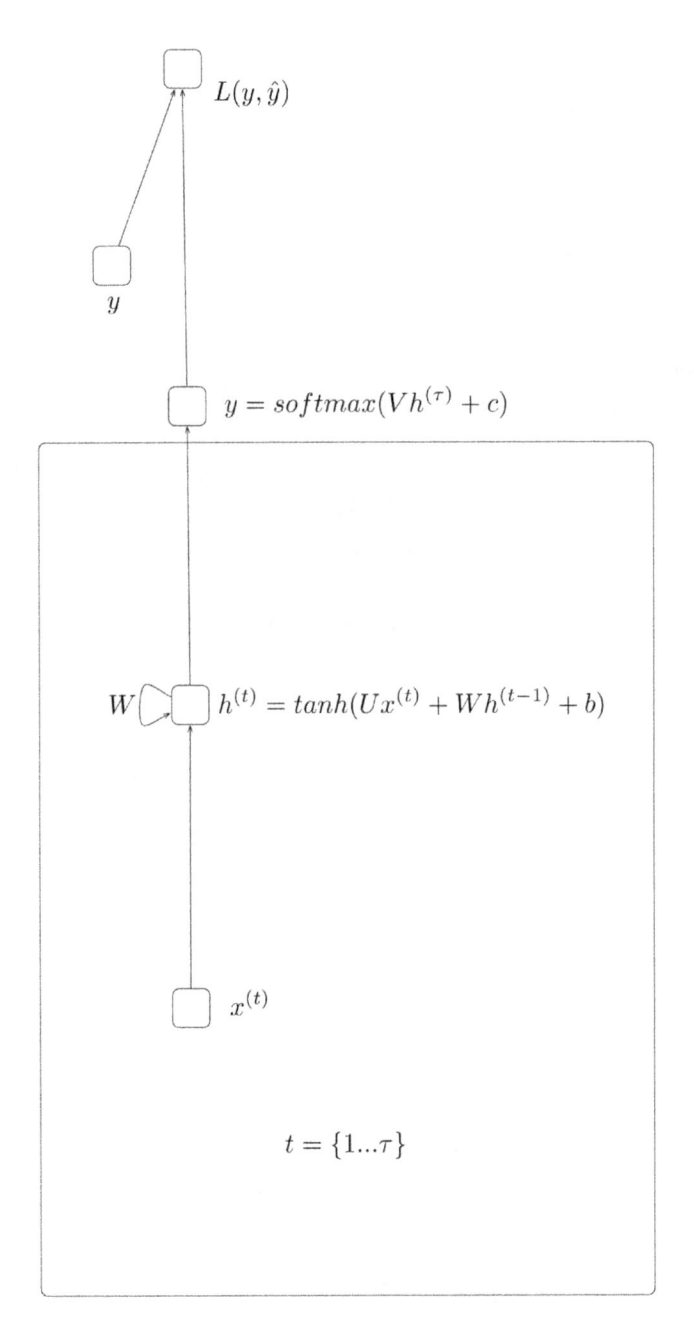

$$y$$

$$y = softmax(Vh^{(\tau)} + c)$$

$$W \quad h^{(t)} = tanh(Ux^{(t)} + Wh^{(t-1)} + b)$$

$$x^{(t)}$$

$$t = \{1...\tau\}$$

Figure 6-3. *RNN (Producing a single output for the entire input sequence)*

CHAPTER 6 ■ RECURRENT NEURAL NETWORKS

The following points are to be noted:

1. The RNN computation involves computing the hidden state for an entity in the sequence. This is denoted by $h^{(t)}$.

2. The computation of $h^{(t)}$ uses the corresponding input at entity $x^{(t)}$ and the previous hidden state $h^{(t-1)}$.

3. The computation of $h^{(t)}$ is done for each entity in the input sequence $x^{(1)}, x^{(2)}, ..., x^{(\tau)}$.

4. The output $\hat{y}$ is computed only using the last hidden state $h^{(\tau)}$.

5. There are weights associated with the input and the previous hidden state while computing the current hidden state. This is denoted by U and W respectively. There is also a bias term denoted by b.

6. There are weights associated with the hidden state while computing the output; this is denoted by V. There is also a bias term, which is denoted by c.

7. The tanh activation function (introduced in earlier chapters) is used in the computation of the hidden state.

8. The softmax activation function is used in the computation of the output.

Training RNNs

Let us now look at how RNNS are trained. To do this, we first need to look at how the RNN looks when we unroll the recurrence relation which is at the heart of the RNN.

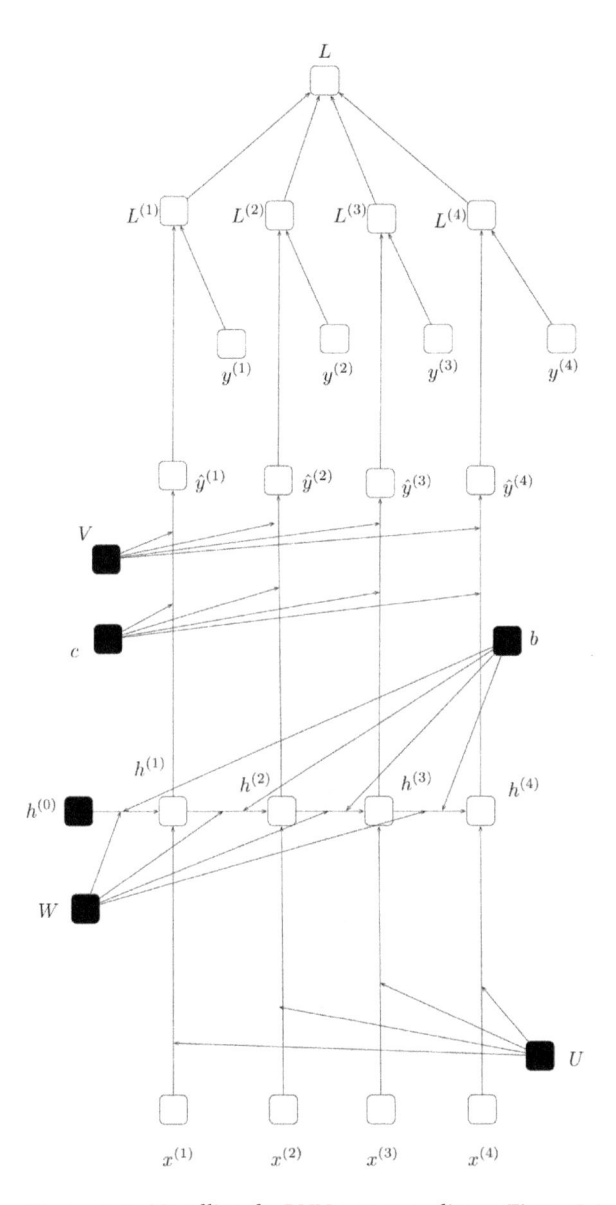

Figure 6-4. *Unrolling the RNN corresponding to Figure 6-1*

Unrolling the recurrence relation corresponding to RNN is simply writing out the equations by recursively substituting the value on which recurrence relation is defined. In the case of the RNN in Figure 6-1, this is $h^{(t)}$. That is, the value of $h^{(t)}$ is defined in terms of $h^{(t-1)}$, which in turn is defined in terms of $h^{(t-2)}$ and so on till $h^{(0)}$.

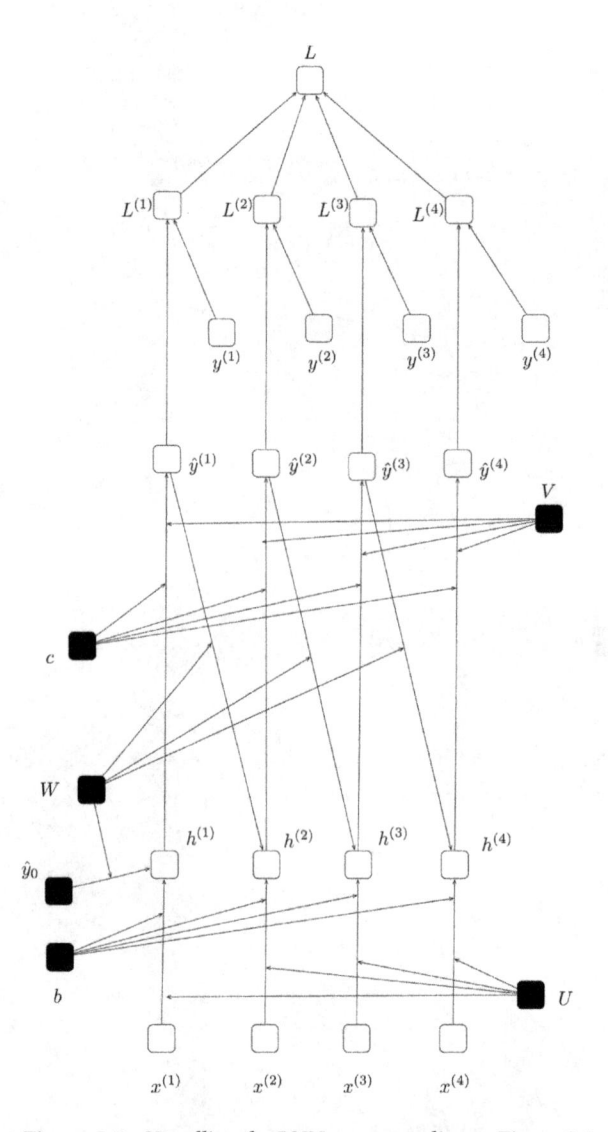

Figure 6-5. *Unrolling the RNN corresponding to Figure 6-2*

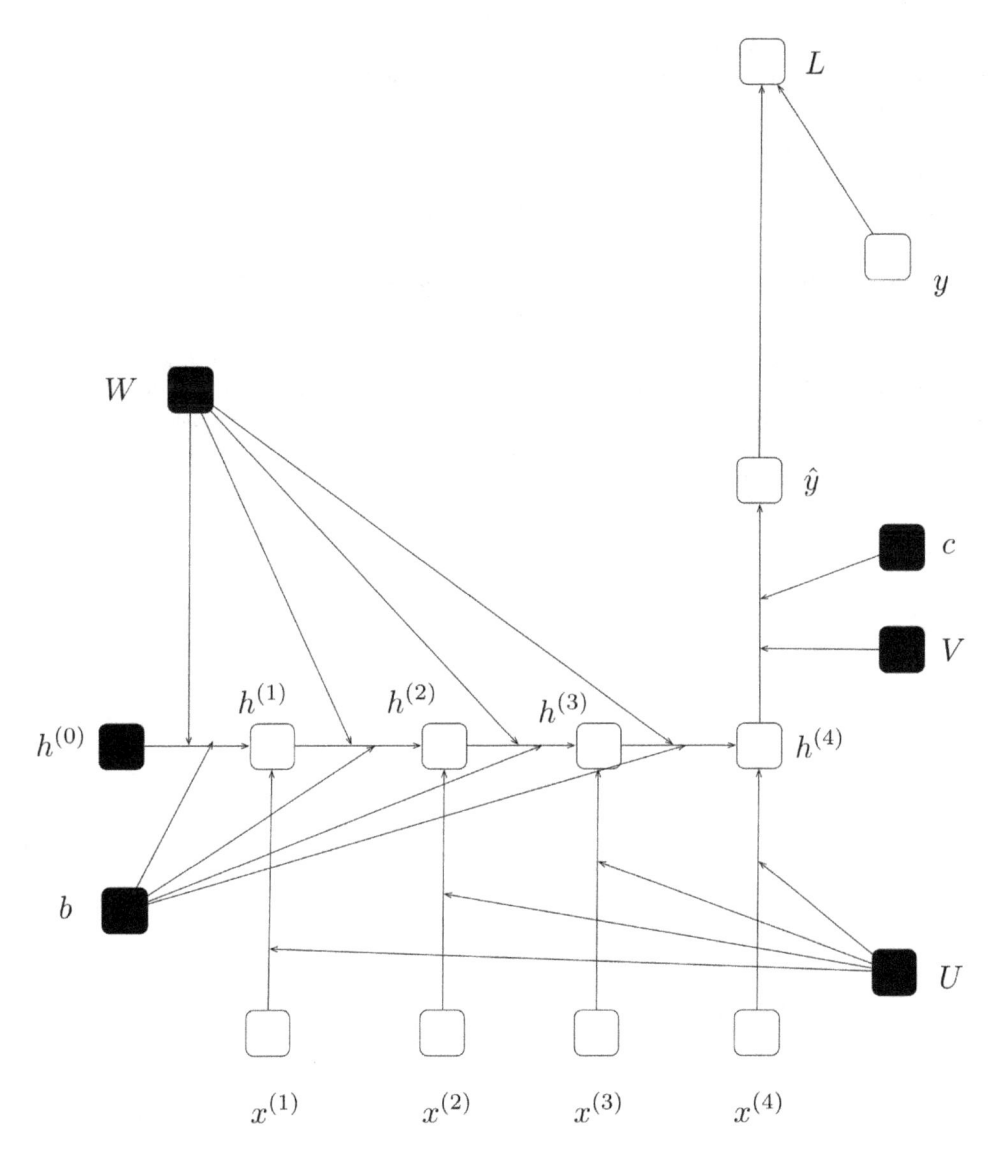

Figure 6-6. Unrolling the RNN corresponding to Figure 6-3

We will assume that $h^{(0)}$ is either predefined by the user, set to zero, or learned as another parameter/weight (learned like W, V, or b). Unrolling simply means writing out the equations describing the RNN in terms of $h^{(0)}$. Of course, in order to do so, we need to fix the length of the sequence, which is denoted by τ. Figure 6-4 illustrates the unrolled RNN corresponding to the RNN in Figure 6-1 assuming an input sequence of size 4. Similarly, Figure 6-5 and 6-6 illustrate the unrolled RNNs corresponding to the RNNs in Figure 6-2 and 6-3 respectively. The following points are to be noted:

1. The unrolling process operates on the assumption that the length of the input sequence is known beforehand and based on that the recurrence is unrolled.

2. Once unrolled, we essentially have a non-recurrent neural network.

CHAPTER 6 ■ RECURRENT NEURAL NETWORKS

3. The parameters to be learned, namely, U, W, V, b, c, etc. (denoted in dark in the diagram) are shared across the computation of the hidden layer and output value. We have seen such parameter sharing earlier in the context of CNNs.

4. Given an input and output of a given size, say τ (assumed to be 4 in Figures 6-4, 6-5, 6-6), we can unroll an RNN and compute gradients for the parameters to be learned with respect to a loss function (as we have seen in earlier chapters).

5. Thus, training an RNN is simply unrolling the RNN for a given size of input (and, correspondingly, the expected output) and training the unrolled RNN via computing the gradients and using stochastic gradient descent.

As mentioned earlier in the chapter, RNNs can deal with arbitrarily long inputs and correspondingly, they need to be trained on arbitrarily long inputs. Figure 6-7 illustrates how an RNN is unrolled for different sizes of inputs. Note that once the RNN is unrolled, the process of training the RNN is identical to training a regular neural network which we have covered in earlier chapters. In Figure 6-7 the RNN described in Figure 6-1 is unrolled for input sizes of 1,2,3 and 4.

CHAPTER 6 ■ RECURRENT NEURAL NETWORKS

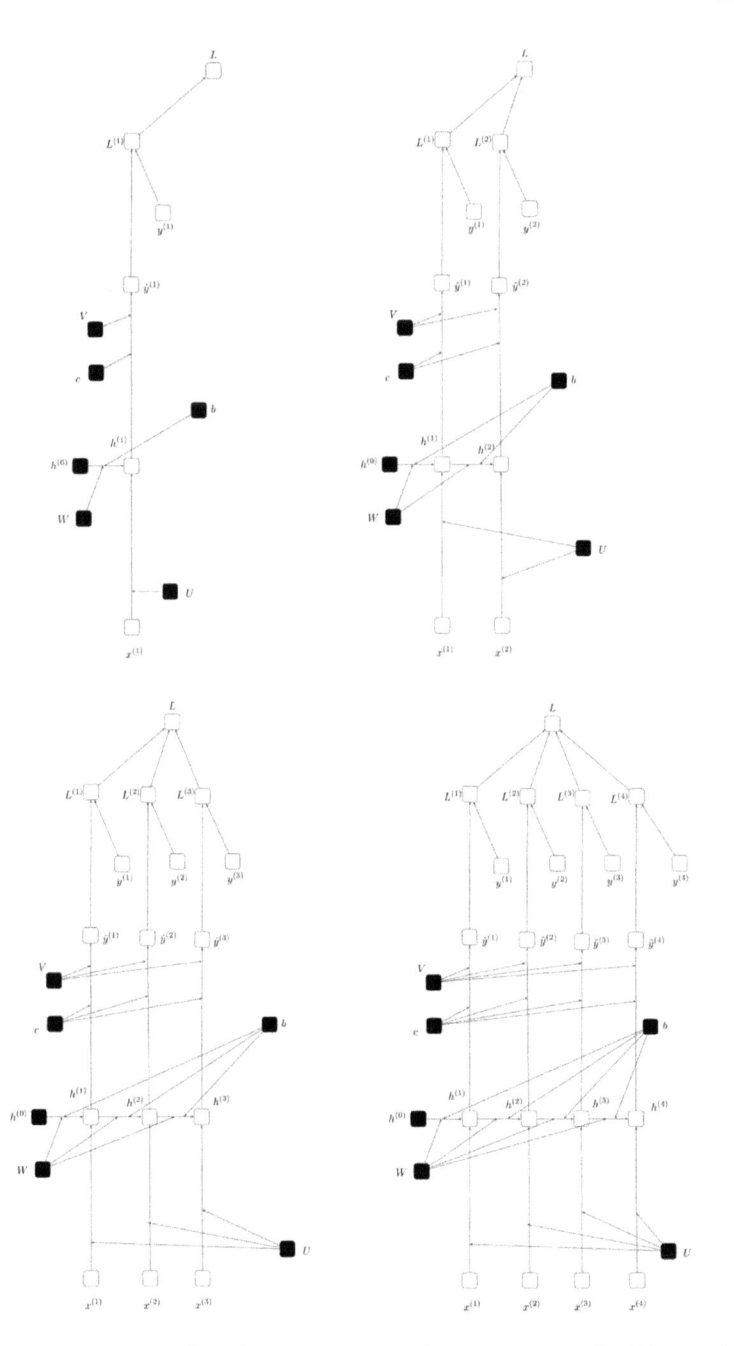

Figure 6-7. *Unrolling the RNN corresponding to Figure 6-1 for different sizes of inputs*

CHAPTER 6 ■ RECURRENT NEURAL NETWORKS

Given that the data set to be trained on consists of sequences of varying sizes, the input sequences are grouped so that the sequences of the same size fall in one group. Then for a group, we can unroll the RNN for the sequence length and train. Training for a different group will require the RNN to be unrolled for a different sequence length. Thus, it is possible to train the RNN on inputs of varying sizes by unrolling and training with the unrolling done based on the sequence length.

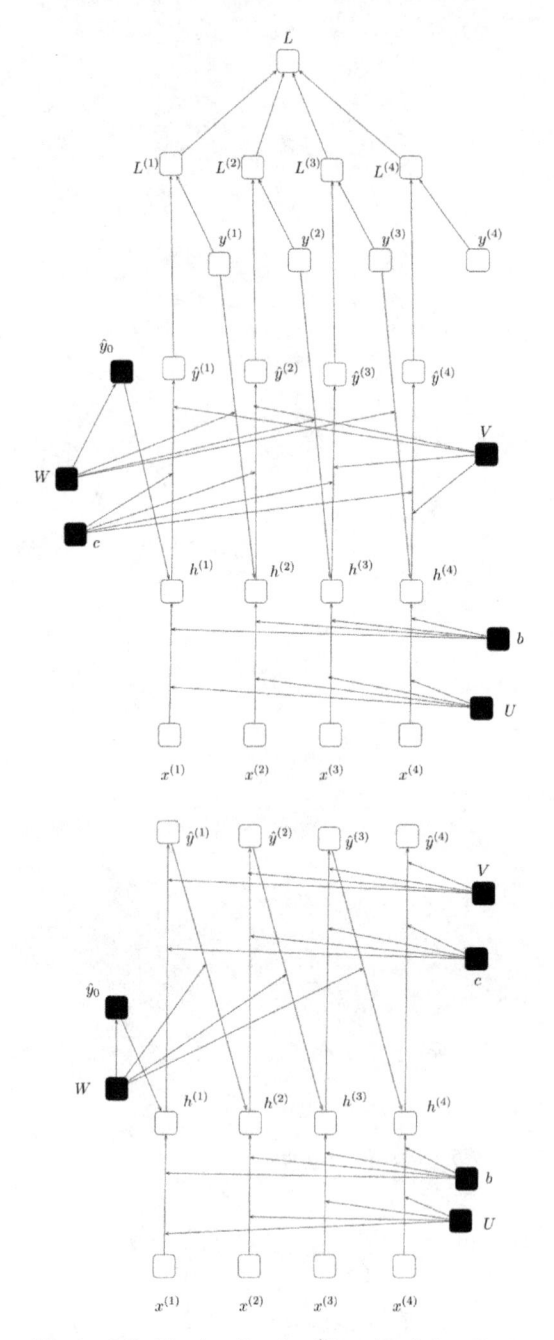

Figure 6-8. Teacher Forcing (Top – Training, Bottom – Prediction)

It must be noted that training the unrolled RNN (illustrated in Figure 6-1) is essentially a sequential process, as the hidden states are dependent on each other. In the case of RNNs wherein the recurrence is over the output instead of the hidden state (Figure 6-2), it is possible to use a technique called teacher forcing as illustrated in Figure 6-8. The key idea here is to use $y^{(t-1)}$ instead of $\hat{y}^{(t-1)}$ in the computation of $h^{(t)}$ while training. While making predictions (when the model is deployed for usage), however, $\hat{y}^{(t-1)}$ is used.

Bidirectional RNNs

Let us now take a look at another variation on RNNs, namely, the bidirectional RNN. The key intuition behind a bidirectional RNN is to use the entities that lie further in the sequence to make a prediction for the current entity. For all the RNNs we have considered so far, we have been using the previous entities (captured by the hidden state) and the current entity in the sequence to make the prediction. However, we have not been using information concerning the entities that lie further in the sequence to make predictions. A bidirectional RNN leverages this information and can give improved predictive accuracy in many cases.

A bidirectional RNN can be described using the following equations:

$$h_f^{(t)} = \tanh\left(U_f x^{(t)} + W_f h^{(t+1)} + b_f\right)$$

$$h_b^{(t)} = \tanh\left(U_b x^{(t)} + W_b h^{(t-1)} + b_b\right)$$

$$\hat{y}^{(t)} = softmax\left(V_b h_b^{(t)} + V_f h_f^{(t)} + c\right)$$

The following points are to be noted:

1. The RNN computation involves first computing the forward hidden state and backward hidden state for an entity in the sequence. This is denoted by $h_f^{(t)}$ and $h_b^{(t)}$ respectively.

2. The computation of $h_f^{(t)}$ uses the corresponding input at entity $x^{(t)}$ and the previous hidden state $h_f^{(t-1)}$.

3. The computation of $h_b^{(t)}$ uses the corresponding input at entity $x^{(t)}$ and the previous hidden state $h_b^{(t-1)}$.

4. The output $\hat{y}^{(t)}$ is computed using the hidden state $h_f^{(t)}$ and $h_b^{(t)}$

5. There are weights associated with the input and the previous hidden state while computing the current hidden state. This is denoted by U_f, W_f, U_b, and W_b respectively. There is also a bias term denoted by b_f and b_b.

6. There are weights associated with the hidden state while computing the output; this is denoted by V_b and V_f. There is also a bias term, which is denoted by c.

7. The tanh activation function (introduced in earlier chapters) is used in the computation of the hidden state.

8. The softmax activation function is used in the computation of the output.

9. The RNN as described by the equations can process an arbitrarily large input sequence.

10. The parameters of the RNN, namely, U_f, U_b, W_f, W_b, V_b, V_f, b_f, b_b, c, etc. are shared across the computation of the hidden layer and output value (for each of the entities in the sequence).

CHAPTER 6 ■ RECURRENT NEURAL NETWORKS

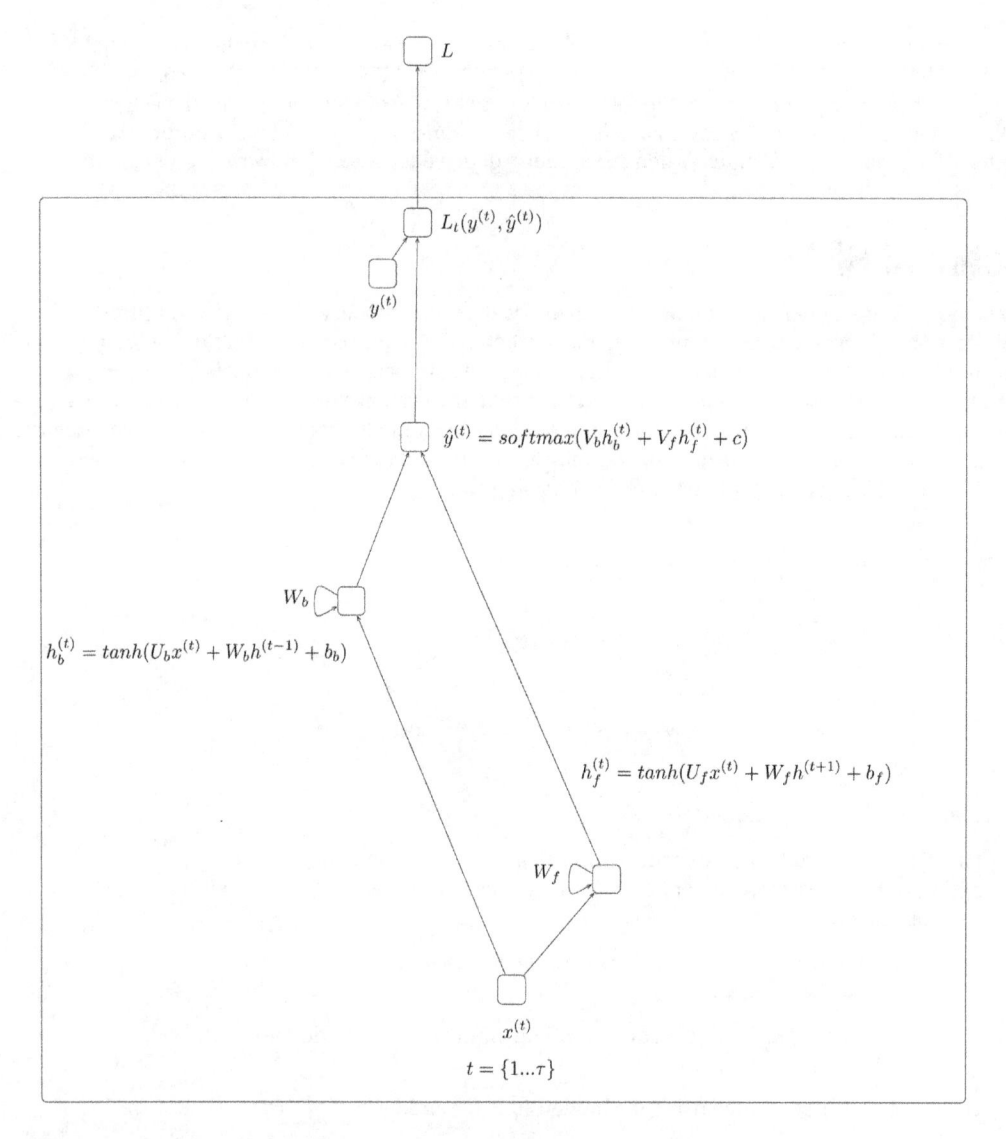

Figure 6-9. *Bidirectional RNN*

Gradient Explosion and Vanishing

Training RNNs suffers from the challenges of vanishing and explosion of gradients. Vanishing gradients means that, when computing the gradients on the unrolled RNNs, the value of the gradients can drop to a very small value (close to zero). Similarly, the gradients can increase to a very high value which is referred to as the exploding gradient problem. In both cases, training the RNN is a challenge.

Let us relook at the equations describing the RNN.

$$h^{(t)} = \tanh\left(Ux^{(t)} + Wh^{(t-1)} + b\right)$$

$$\hat{y}^{(t)} = softmax\left(Vh^{(t)} + c\right)$$

Let us derive the expression for the $\dfrac{\partial L}{\partial W}$ by applying the chain rule. This is illustrated in Figure 6-10.

$$\frac{\partial L}{\partial W} = \sum_{1 \leq t \leq \tau} \frac{\partial L^{(t)}}{\partial h^{(t)}} \left[\sum_{1 \leq k \leq t} \left[\prod_{k \leq j \leq t-1} \frac{\partial h^{(j+1)}}{\partial h^{(j)}} \right] \frac{\partial h^{(k)}}{\partial W} \right]$$

Let us now focus on the part of the expression $\prod_{k \leq j \leq t-1} \dfrac{\partial h^{(j+1)}}{\partial h^{(j)}}$ which involves a repeated matrix multiplication of W which contributes to both the vanishing and exploding gradient problems. Intuitively, this is similar to multiplying a real valued number over and over again, which might lead to the product shrinking to zero or exploding to infinity.

Gradient Clipping

One simple technique to deal with exploding gradients is to rescale the norm of gradient whenever it goes over a user-defined threshold. Specifically, if the gradient denoted by $\hat{g} = \dfrac{\partial L}{\partial W}$ and if $|\hat{g}| > c$ then we set $\hat{g} = \dfrac{c}{|\hat{g}|} \hat{g}$. This technique is both simple and computationally efficient but does introduce an extra hyperparameter.

CHAPTER 6 ■ RECURRENT NEURAL NETWORKS

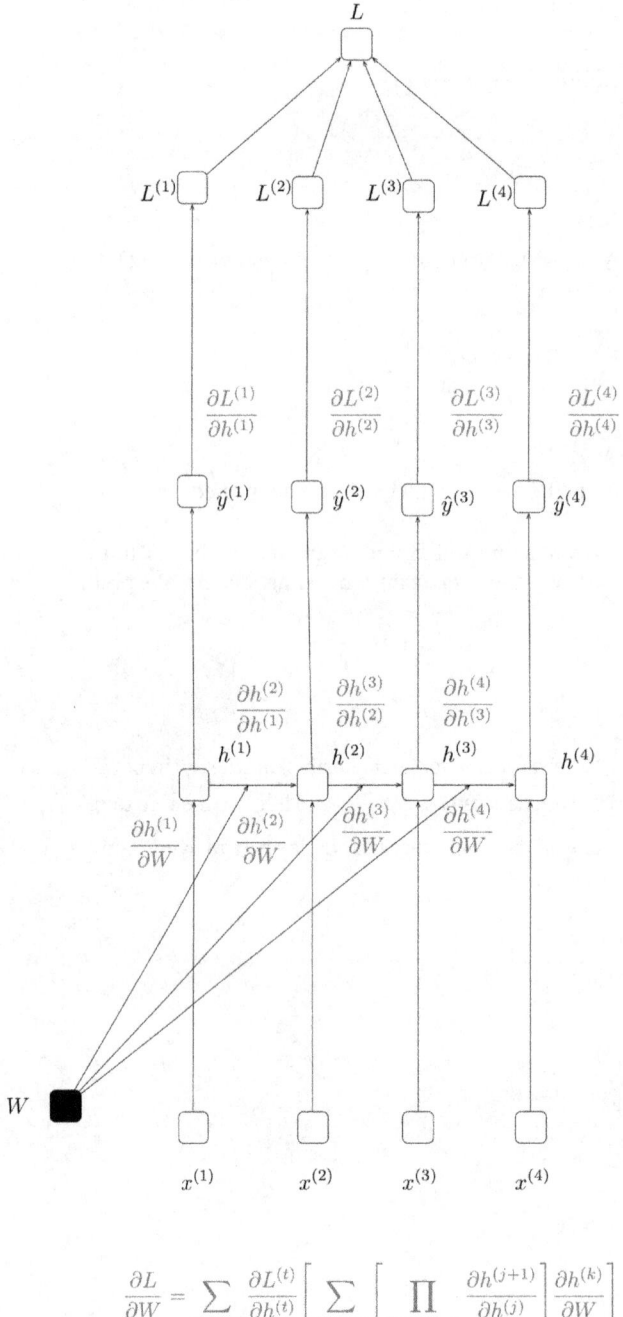

$$\frac{\partial L}{\partial W} = \sum_{1 \leq t \leq \tau} \frac{\partial L^{(t)}}{\partial h^{(t)}} \left[\sum_{1 \leq k \leq t} \left[\prod_{k \leq j \leq t-1} \frac{\partial h^{(j+1)}}{\partial h^{(j)}} \right] \frac{\partial h^{(k)}}{\partial W} \right]$$

Figure 6-10. *Vanishing and Exploding Gradients*

Long Short Term Memory

Let us now take a look at another variation on RNNs, namely, the Long Short Term Memory (LSTM) Network. An LSTM can be described with the following set of equations. Note that the symbol $\odot$. notes pointwise multiplication of two vectors (if $a = [1,1,2]$ and $b = [0.5, 0.5, 0.5]$, then $a \odot b = [0.5, 0.5, 1]$, the functions σ, g and h are non-linear activation functions, all W and R are weight matrices, and all the b terms are bias terms).

$$z^{(t)} = g\left(W_z x^{(t)} + R_z \hat{y}^{(t-1)} + b_z\right)$$

$$i^{(t)} = \sigma\left(W_i x^{(t)} + R_i \hat{y}^{(t-1)} + p_i \odot c^{(t-1)} + b_i\right)$$

$$f^{(t)} = \sigma\left(W_f x^t + R_f \hat{y}^{(t-1)} + p_f \odot c^{(t-1)} + b_f\right)$$

$$c^{(t)} = i^{(t)} \odot z^{(t)} + f^{(t)} \odot c^{(t-1)}$$

$$o^{(t)} = \sigma\left(W_o x^{(t)} + R_o \hat{y}^{(t-1)} + p_o \odot c^{(t)} + b_o\right)$$

$$\hat{y}^{(t)} = o^{(t)} \odot h\left(c^{(t)}\right)$$

The following points are to be noted:

1. The most important element of the LSTM is the cell state denoted by $c^{(t)} = i^{(t)} \odot z^{(t)} + f^{(t)} \odot c^{(t-1)}$. The cell state is updated based on the block input $z^{(t)}$ and the previous cell state $c^{(t-1)}$. The input gate $i^{(t)}$ determines what fraction of the block input makes it into the cell state (hence called a gate). The forget gate $f^{(t)}$ determines how much of the previous cell state to retain.

2. The output $\hat{y}^{(t)}$ is determined based on the cell state $c^{(t)}$ and the output gate $o^{(t)}$, which determines how much the cell state affects the output.

3. The $z^{(t)}$ term is referred to as the block input and it produces a value based on the current input and the previous output.

4. The $i^{(t)}$ term is referred to as the input gate. It determines how much of the input to retain in the cell state $c^{(t)}$.

5. All the p terms are peephole connections, which allow for a faction of the cell state to factor into the computation of the term in question.

6. The computation of the cell state $c^{(t)}$ does not encounter the issue of the vanishing gradient (this is referred to as the constant error carousal). However, LSTMs are affected by exploding gradients and gradient clipping is used while training.

CHAPTER 6 ■ RECURRENT NEURAL NETWORKS

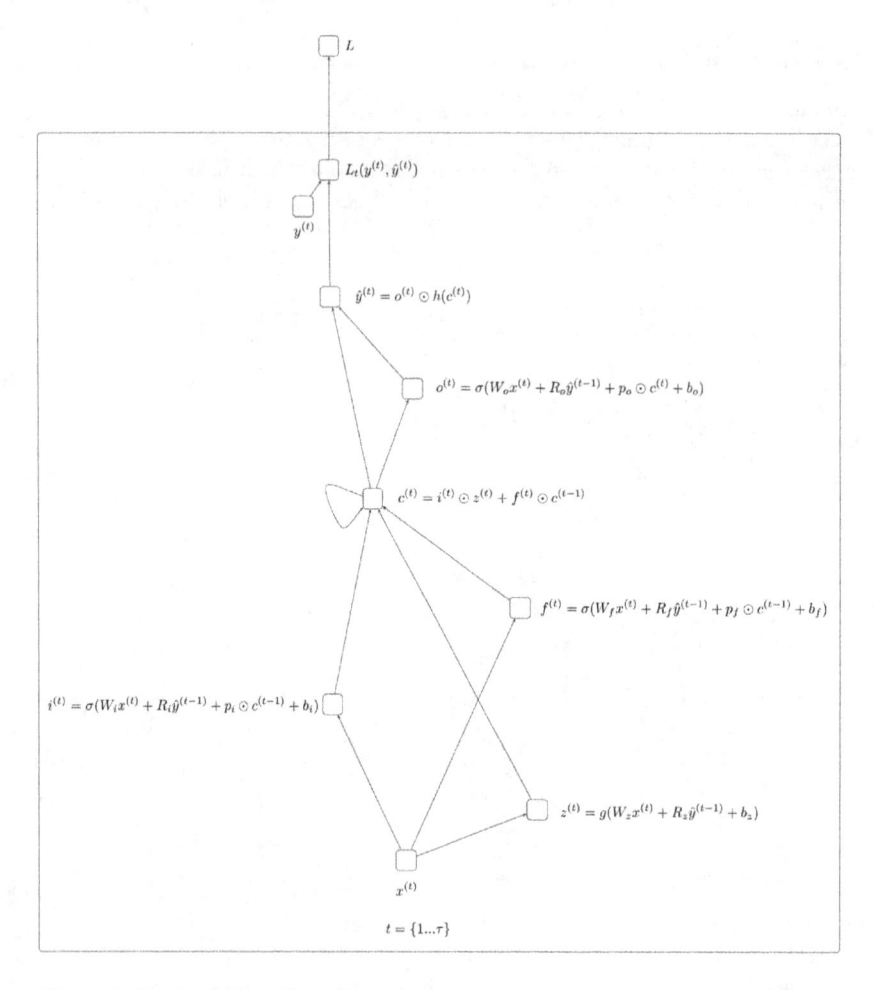

Figure 6-11. *Long Short Term Memory*

Summary

In this chapter we covered the basics of Recurrent Neural Networks (RNN). The key take-home points from this chapter are the notion of the hidden state, training RNNs via unrolling (backpropagation through time), the problem of vanishing and exploding gradients, and long short term memory networks. It is important to internalize how RNNs contain internal/hidden states that allow them to make predictions on a sequence of inputs, an ability that goes beyond conventional neural networks.

CHAPTER 7

Introduction to Keras

This chapter introduces the reader to Keras, which is a library that provides highly powerful and abstract building blocks to build deep learning networks. The building blocks Keras provides are built using Theano (covered earlier) as well as TensorFlow (which is an alternative to Theano for building computational graphs, automatically deriving gradients, etc.). Keras supports both CPU and GPU computation and is a great tool for quickly prototyping ideas.

We will introduce a number of key building blocks Keras provides, and then build a CNN and LSTM using Keras.

Let us start with a simple, single layer neural network. Listing 7-1 provides the code and Figure 7-1 gives the computational graph. The following points are to be noted:

1. A model is defined using the Sequential construct, which allows the user to add/configure layers.

2. Using this functionality, a user can add one or more layers and build the network. The Dense layer is basically a fully connected layer (leading to a vector-matrix or vector-vector product), which we have seen earlier.

3. The input and output dimensionality needs to be specified when the first layer is defined. In this case the model will take an input of dimensionality 500 and produce an output of dimensionality 1.

4. After this layer we add an activation function, in this case a sigmoid.

5. The model once defined needs to be explicitly compiled and, at this time, we provide the loss function, the optimization algorithm, and other metrics we want to calculate.

6. An appropriate loss function needs to be picked given the task at hand; in this case, given that we have a binary classification problem, we select binary cross-entropy.

7. An appropriate optimization algorithm needs to be picked, which typically is a variant of Stochastic Gradient Descent (coved in later chapters).

8. Once compiled we can fit the model by providing the data and evaluate the model.

CHAPTER 7 ■ INTRODUCTION TO KERAS

Listing 7-1. Single Layer Neural Network

```
import numpy as np
from keras.models import Sequential
from keras.layers import Dense, Activation
from keras.utils.visualize_util import plot

model = Sequential()
model.add(Dense(1, input_dim=500))
model.add(Activation(activation='sigmoid'))
model.compile(optimizer='rmsprop', loss='binary_crossentropy', metrics=['accuracy'])

data = np.random.random((1000, 500))
labels = np.random.randint(2, size=(1000, 1))

score = model.evaluate(data,labels, verbose=0)
print "Before Training:", zip(model.metrics_names, score)

model.fit(data, labels, nb_epoch=10, batch_size=32, verbose=0)

score = model.evaluate(data,labels, verbose=0)
print "After Training:", zip(model.metrics_names, score)
plot(model, to_file='s1.png', show_shapes=True)

# Before Training: [('loss', 0.76832762384414677), ('acc', 0.50700000000000001)]
# After Training: [('loss', 0.67270196056365972), ('acc', 0.56299999999999994)]
```

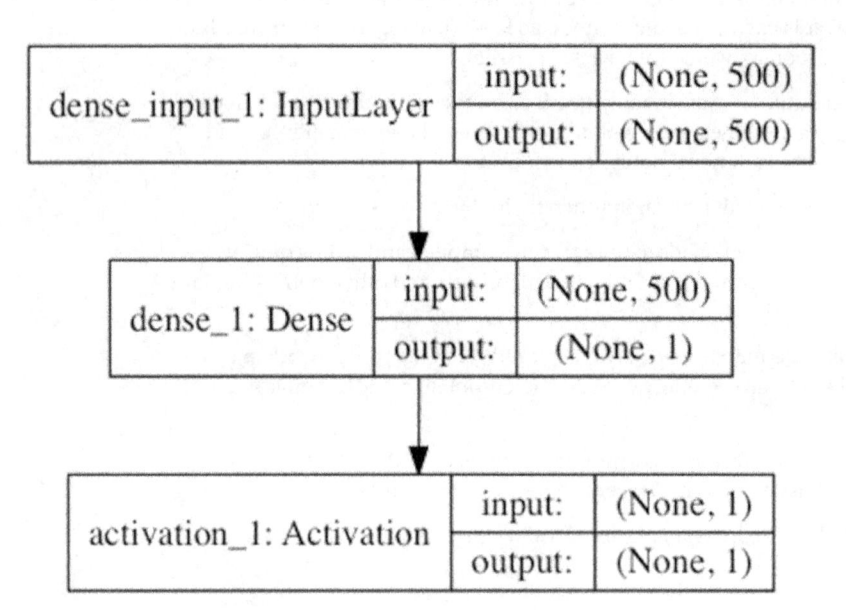

dense_input_1: InputLayer	input:	(None, 500)
	output:	(None, 500)

dense_1: Dense	input:	(None, 500)
	output:	(None, 1)

activation_1: Activation	input:	(None, 1)
	output:	(None, 1)

Figure 7-1. Single Layer Neural Network (Binary Classification)

Listing 7-2. Two Layer Neural Network

```
import numpy as np
from keras.models import Sequential
from keras.layers import Dense, Activation
from keras.utils.visualize_util import plot

model = Sequential()
model.add(Dense(32, input_dim=500))
model.add(Activation(activation='sigmoid'))
model.add(Dense(1))
model.add(Activation(activation='sigmoid'))
model.compile(optimizer='rmsprop', loss='binary_crossentropy', metrics=['accuracy'])

data = np.random.random((1000, 500))
labels = np.random.randint(2, size=(1000, 1))

score = model.evaluate(data,labels, verbose=0)
print "Before Training:", zip(model.metrics_names, score)

model.fit(data, labels, nb_epoch=10, batch_size=32, verbose=0)

score = model.evaluate(data,labels, verbose=0)
print "After Training:", zip(model.metrics_names, score)

plot(model, to_file='s2.png', show_shapes=True)

# Before Training: [('loss', 0.73012506151199341), ('acc', 0.51200000000000001)]
# After Training: [('loss', 0.6588478517532349), ('acc', 0.52700000000000002)]
```

Let us now look at a two-layer neural network. Listing 7-2 provides the code and Figure 7-2 gives the computational graph. The following points are to be noted:

1. A model is defined using the Sequential construct.

2. We add the first layer, using Dense, and specify the input dimensionality. In this case the model will take an input of dimensionality 500 and produce an output of dimensionality 32.

3. We define an activation function, selecting sigmoid.

4. We then define the second layer using Dense. Here we define the output dimensionality to be 1. Note, however, that we do not need to define the input dimensionality, as it is the same as the dimensionality of the output of the previous layer.

5. As before, we define the optimize and loss function, compile, train, and evaluate.

CHAPTER 7 ■ INTRODUCTION TO KERAS

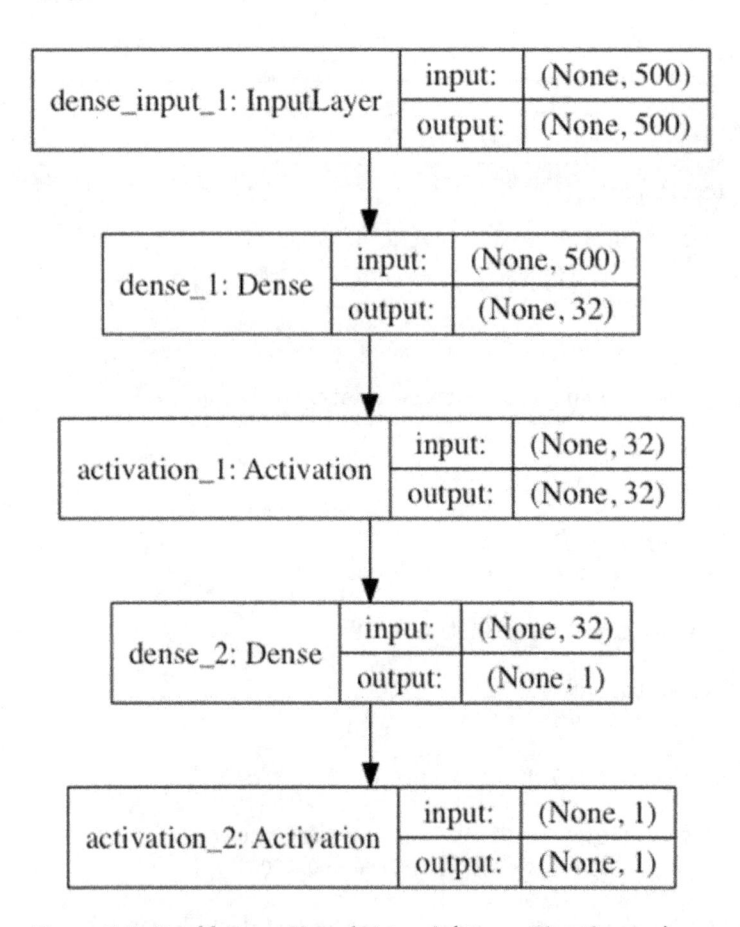

dense_input_1: InputLayer	input:	(None, 500)
	output:	(None, 500)

dense_1: Dense	input:	(None, 500)
	output:	(None, 32)

activation_1: Activation	input:	(None, 32)
	output:	(None, 32)

dense_2: Dense	input:	(None, 32)
	output:	(None, 1)

activation_2: Activation	input:	(None, 1)
	output:	(None, 1)

Figure 7-2. Double Layer Neural Network (Binary Classification)

Let us now look at a two-layer neural network for multiclass classification. Listing 7-3 provides the code and Figure 7-3 gives the computational graph. The following points are to be noted:

1. A model is defined using the Sequential construct.

2. We add the first layer, using Dense, and specify the input dimensionality. In this case the model will take an input of dimensionality 500 and produce an output of dimensionality 32.

3. We define an activation function, selecting sigmoid.

4. We then define the second layer using Dense. Here we define the output dimensionality to be 10. Note that this is exactly equal to the number of classes we have in our dataset.

5. Next we use the softmax activation and the categorical entropy as the loss function (an earlier chapter covers why this is a good choice).

6. We compile, train, and evaluate the model as before.

Listing 7-3. Multiclass Classification

```
import numpy as np
from keras.models import Sequential
from keras.layers import Dense, Activation
from keras.utils.np_utils import to_categorical
from keras.utils.visualize_util import plot

model = Sequential()
model.add(Dense(32, input_dim=500))
model.add(Activation(activation='relu'))
model.add(Dense(10))
model.add(Activation(activation='softmax'))
model.compile(optimizer='rmsprop', loss='categorical_crossentropy', metrics=['categorical_accuracy'])

data = np.random.random((1000, 500))
labels = to_categorical(np.random.randint(10, size=(1000, 1)))

score = model.evaluate(data,labels, verbose=0)
print "Before Training:", zip(model.metrics_names, score)

model.fit(data, labels, nb_epoch=10, batch_size=32, verbose=0)

score = model.evaluate(data,labels, verbose=0)
print "After Training:", zip(model.metrics_names, score)

plot(model, to_file='s3.png', show_shapes=True)

# Before Training: [('loss', 2.4697211952209472), ('categorical_accuracy', 0.092999999999999999)]
# After Training: [('loss', 2.1891849689483642), ('categorical_accuracy', 0.19400000000000001)]
```

CHAPTER 7 ■ INTRODUCTION TO KERAS

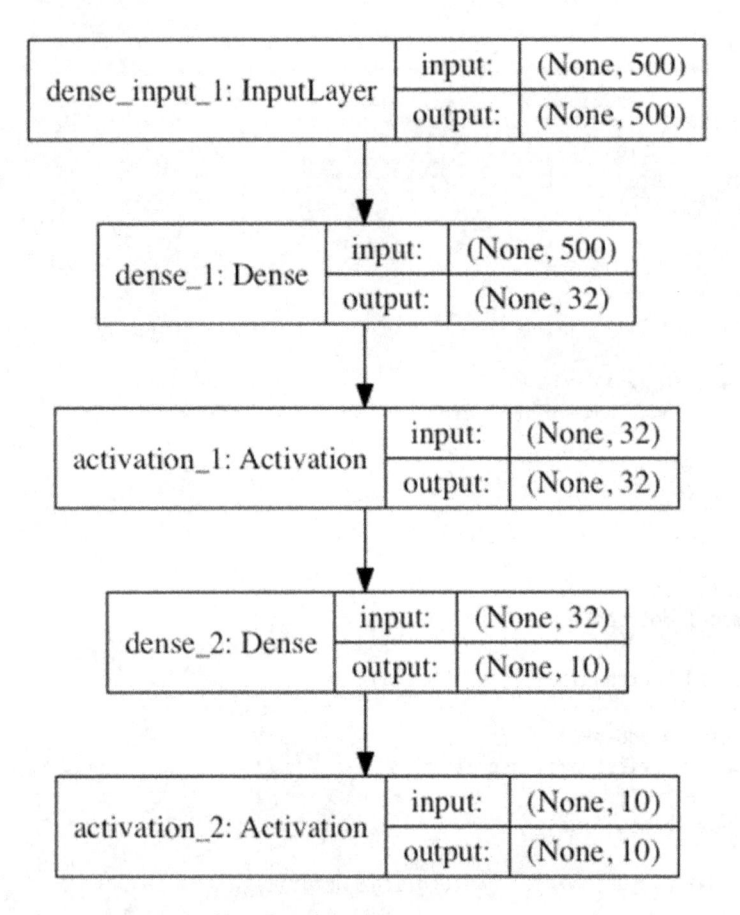

dense_input_1: InputLayer	input:	(None, 500)
	output:	(None, 500)

dense_1: Dense	input:	(None, 500)
	output:	(None, 32)

activation_1: Activation	input:	(None, 32)
	output:	(None, 32)

dense_2: Dense	input:	(None, 32)
	output:	(None, 10)

activation_2: Activation	input:	(None, 10)
	output:	(None, 10)

Figure 7-3. Multiclass Classification

Let us now look at a two-layer neural network for regression. Listing 7-4 provides the code and Figure 7-4 gives the computational graph. The following points are to be noted:

1. A model is defined using the Sequential construct.
2. We add the first layer, using Dense, and specify the input dimensionality. In this case the model will take an input of dimensionality 500 and produce an output of dimensionality 32.
3. We define an activation function, selecting sigmoid.
4. We then define the second layer using Dense, producing an output of dimensionality 1.
5. We select the activation as sigmoid and select mean squared error, which is appropriate for regression.
6. We compile, train, and evaluate the model.

Listing 7-4. Regression

```python
import numpy as np
from keras.models import Sequential
from keras.layers import Dense, Activation
from keras.utils.visualize_util import plot

model = Sequential()
model.add(Dense(32, input_dim=500))
model.add(Activation(activation='sigmoid'))
model.add(Dense(1))
model.add(Activation(activation='sigmoid'))
model.compile(optimizer='rmsprop', loss='mse', metrics=['mean_squared_error'])

data = np.random.random((1000, 500))
labels = np.random.randint(2, size=(1000, 1))

score = model.evaluate(data,labels, verbose=0)
print "Before Training:", zip(model.metrics_names, score)

model.fit(data, labels, nb_epoch=10, batch_size=32, verbose=0)

score = model.evaluate(data,labels, verbose=0)
print "After Training:", zip(model.metrics_names, score)

plot(model, to_file='s4.png', show_shapes=True)

# Before Training: [('loss', 0.26870122766494753), ('mean_squared_error',
0.26870122766494753)]
# After Training: [('loss', 0.22180086207389832), ('mean_squared_error',
0.22180086207389832)]
```

Let us now take a pause and look at how Keras allows for quick iteration of ideas.

1. New models can be quickly defined, trained, and evaluated using the sequential construct.
2. The parameters of the layers input/output dimensionality can be easily modified.
3. We can compare multiple choices of activation functions easily. Listing 7-6 illustrates how we can compare the effects of activation functions.
4. We can compare multiple choices of optimization algorithms easily. Listing 7-5 illustrates how we can compare the effects of different choices of activation algorithms.

CHAPTER 7 ■ INTRODUCTION TO KERAS

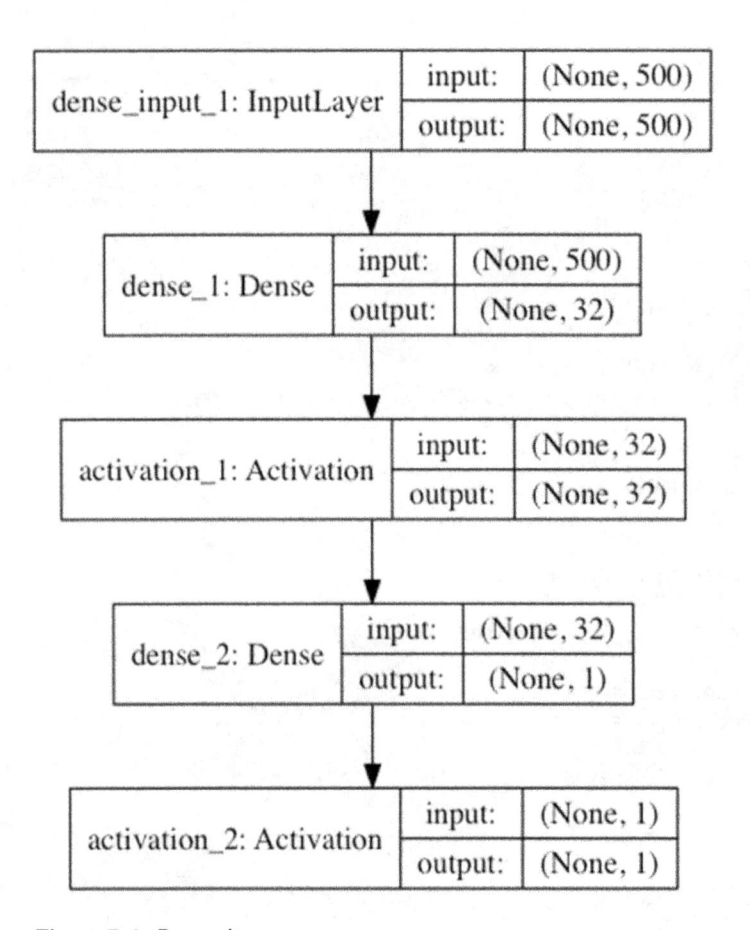

dense_input_1: InputLayer	input:	(None, 500)
	output:	(None, 500)

dense_1: Dense	input:	(None, 500)
	output:	(None, 32)

activation_1: Activation	input:	(None, 32)
	output:	(None, 32)

dense_2: Dense	input:	(None, 32)
	output:	(None, 1)

activation_2: Activation	input:	(None, 1)
	output:	(None, 1)

Figure 7-4. Regression

Listing 7-5. Optimisers

```
import numpy as np
from keras.models import Sequential
from keras.layers import Dense, Activation

def train_given_optimiser(optimiser):
    model = Sequential()
    model.add(Dense(1, input_dim=500))
    model.add(Activation(activation='sigmoid'))
    model.compile(optimizer=optimiser, loss='binary_crossentropy', metrics=['accuracy'])

    data = np.random.random((1000, 500))
    labels = np.random.randint(2, size=(1000, 1))

    score = model.evaluate(data,labels, verbose=0)
    print "Optimiser: ", optimiser
    print "Before Training:", zip(model.metrics_names, score)
```

```
    model.fit(data, labels, nb_epoch=10, batch_size=32, verbose=0)

    score = model.evaluate(data,labels, verbose=0)
    print "After Training:", zip(model.metrics_names, score)

train_given_optimiser("sgd")
train_given_optimiser("rmsprop")
train_given_optimiser("adagrad")
train_given_optimiser("adadelta")
train_given_optimiser("adam")
train_given_optimiser("adamax")
train_given_optimiser("nadam")

# Optimiser:  sgd
# Before Training: [('loss', 0.76416229248046874), ('acc', 0.51800000000000002)]
# After Training: [('loss', 0.6759231286048889), ('acc', 0.56899999999999995)]
# Optimiser:  rmsprop
# Before Training: [('loss', 0.77773557662963866), ('acc', 0.52600000000000002)]
# After Training: [('loss', 0.727150842666626), ('acc', 0.53500000000000003)]
# Optimiser:  adagrad
# Before Training: [('loss', 0.9275067367553711), ('acc', 0.49099999999999999)]
# After Training: [('loss', 0.66770141410827633), ('acc', 0.57599999999999996)]
# Optimiser:  adadelta
# Before Training: [('loss', 0.765235853319519039), ('acc', 0.48799999999999999)]
# After Training: [('loss', 0.70753741836547857), ('acc', 0.51700000000000002)]
# Optimiser:  adam
# Before Training: [('loss', 0.76974405097961429), ('acc', 0.51100000000000001)]

# After Training: [('loss', 0.66079518222808842), ('acc', 0.59399999999999997)]
# Optimiser:  adamax
# Before Training: [('loss', 0.76244759178161625), ('acc', 0.49399999999999999)]
# After Training: [('loss', 0.67273861455917361), ('acc', 0.58499999999999996)]
# Optimiser:  nadam
# Before Training: [('loss', 0.71690645027160649), ('acc', 0.50600000000000001)]
# After Training: [('loss', 0.62006913089752203), ('acc', 0.68799999999999994)]
```

Keras implements a number of optimisers, namely Stocastic Gradient Descent (SGD), RMSProp, AdaGrad, AdataDelta, Adam, Adamax, and Nadam. Chapter 8 covers these (SGD and its variants) in much detail, explaining the intuition for each. For the context of this chapter it suffices to say that Keras makes it easy for users to experiment with these optimisers with very little coding effort.

Listing 7-6. Activation Functions

```
import numpy as np
from keras.models import Sequential
from keras.layers import Dense, Activation

def train_given_activation(activation):
    model = Sequential()
    model.add(Dense(1, input_dim=500))
    model.add(Activation(activation=activation))
    model.compile(optimizer="sgd", loss='binary_crossentropy', metrics=['accuracy'])
```

CHAPTER 7 ■ INTRODUCTION TO KERAS

```
    data = np.random.random((1000, 500))
    labels = np.random.randint(2, size=(1000, 1))

    score = model.evaluate(data,labels, verbose=0)
    print "Activation: ", activation
    print "Before Training:", zip(model.metrics_names, score)

    model.fit(data, labels, nb_epoch=10, batch_size=32, verbose=0)

    score = model.evaluate(data,labels, verbose=0)
    print "After Training:", zip(model.metrics_names, score)

train_given_activation("relu")
train_given_activation("tanh")
train_given_activation("sigmoid")
train_given_activation("hard_sigmoid")
train_given_activation("linear")

# Activation:  relu
# Before Training: [('loss', 2.6973885402679443), ('acc', 0.48899999999999999)]
# After Training: [('loss', 7.7373054656982418), ('acc', 0.505)]
# Activation:  tanh
# Before Training: [('loss', 5.0640698051452633), ('acc', 0.41699999999999998)]
# After Training: [('loss', 7.6523446731567386), ('acc', 0.52000000000000002)]
# Activation:  sigmoid
# Before Training: [('loss', 0.70816111516952518), ('acc', 0.52500000000000002)]
# After Training: [('loss', 0.67464308834075926), ('acc', 0.58199999999999996)]
# Activation:  hard_sigmoid
# Before Training: [('loss', 0.70220352411270137), ('acc', 0.52100000000000002)]
# After Training: [('loss', 0.672945969104766893), ('acc', 0.58099999999999996)]
# Activation:  linear
# Before Training: [('loss', 3.5439299507141113), ('acc', 0.47799999999999998)]
# After Training: [('loss', 8.2581552581787108), ('acc', 0.0)]
```

Keras implements a number of activation functions, namely, tanh, sigmoid, hard_sigmoid, linear, and relu (rectified linear unit). Activation functions and their appropriateness given a task (classification, multiclassification, regression, etc.) are covered in much detail in Chapter 3. For the context of this chapter, it suffices to say that Keras makes it easy for users to experiment with these activation functions with very little coding effort.

Let us now look at the constructs Keras provides to build the Convolution Neural Networks introduced in Chapter 5. The data set we will be using is the MNIST data set, which is a commonly used benchmark data set for deep learning. The data set consists of handwritten digits (60,000 training examples and 10,000 test examples). The task at hand is to predict the digit given the image, so this is a multiclassifcation problem with ten classes.

Listing 7-7. CNN

```
import numpy as np
from keras.datasets import mnist
from keras.models import Sequential
from keras.layers import Dense, Dropout, Activation, Flatten
from keras.layers import Convolution2D, MaxPooling2D
```

```python
from keras.utils import np_utils
from keras.utils.visualize_util import plot

# Image Size
img_rows, img_cols = 28, 28

# Filter
nb_filters = 32

# Pooling
pool_size = (2, 2)

# Kernel
kernel_size = (3, 3)

# Prepare dataset
(X_train, y_train), (X_test, y_test) = mnist.load_data()
X_train = X_train.reshape(X_train.shape[0], img_rows, img_cols, 1)
X_test = X_test.reshape(X_test.shape[0], img_rows, img_cols, 1)
input_shape = (img_rows, img_cols, 1)
X_train = X_train.astype('float32')
X_test = X_test.astype('float32')
X_train /= 255
X_test /= 255
nb_classes = 10
Y_train = np_utils.to_categorical(y_train, nb_classes)
Y_test = np_utils.to_categorical(y_test, nb_classes)

# CNN
model = Sequential()
model.add(Convolution2D(nb_filters, kernel_size[0], kernel_size[1], border_mode='valid',
input_shape=input_shape))
model.add(Activation('relu'))
model.add(Convolution2D(nb_filters, kernel_size[0], kernel_size[1]))
model.add(Activation('relu'))
model.add(MaxPooling2D(pool_size=pool_size))
model.add(Dropout(0.25))
model.add(Flatten())
model.add(Dense(128))
model.add(Activation('relu'))
model.add(Dropout(0.5))
model.add(Dense(nb_classes))
model.add(Activation('softmax'))

# Compilation
model.compile(loss='categorical_crossentropy', optimizer='adadelta', metrics=['accuracy'])

# Training
batch_size = 128
nb_epoch = 1
model.fit(X_train, Y_train, batch_size=batch_size, nb_epoch=nb_epoch, verbose=1, validation_data=(X_test, Y_test))
```

CHAPTER 7 ■ INTRODUCTION TO KERAS

```
# Evaluation
score = model.evaluate(X_test, Y_test, verbose=0)
print "Test Metrics:", zip(model.metrics_names, score)
plot(model, to_file='s7.png', show_shapes=True)

# Output
# Train on 60000 samples, validate on 10000 samples
# Epoch 1/1
# 60000/60000 [==============================] - 128s - loss: 0.3964 - acc: 0.8776 - val_loss: 0.0929 - val_acc: 0.9712
# Test Metrics: [('loss', 0.092853568810969594), ('acc', 0.97119999999999995)]
```

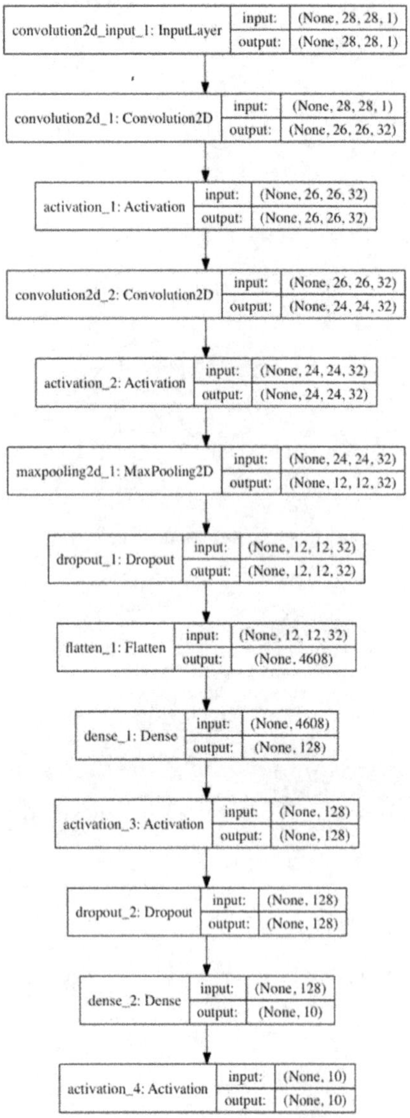

Figure 7-5. CNN

CHAPTER 7 ■ INTRODUCTION TO KERAS

Listing 7-7 presents the source code for the convolution neural network and Figure 7-5 illustrates the computation graph. The following points are to be noted:

1. The overall network consists of two convolution-detector blocks, followed by a max pooling layer which in turn is followed by a two layer fully connected network (refer to Chapter 5).
2. The size of the kernel is 3×3.
3. The pooling operation is done over sections of dimensionality 2×2.
4. There are a number of dropout layers, which are basically a form of regularization (refer to Chapter 1) and operate by randomly turning off a certain number of units. The parameter 0.25 indicates the faction of inputs that will be randomly dropped.
5. The flatten layers convert the input of any dimensionality to a dimensionality of $1 \times n$. So, for instance, an input of dimensionality $2 \times 2 \times 3$ gets converted to a directionality of 1×12.
6. The output layer is softmax and the loss function is categorical entropy, as is appropriate for a multiclassification problem (refer to Chapter 3).
7. The model is fit using adadelta (refer to Chapter 8) and, for the purposes of illustration, we set the epochs to 1 (ideally it's set to much more than that).

Listing 7-8. LSTM

```
import numpy as np
from keras.preprocessing import sequence
from keras.utils import np_utils
from keras.models import Sequential
from keras.layers import Dense, Dropout, Activation, Embedding
from keras.layers import LSTM
from keras.datasets import imdb
from keras.utils.visualize_util import plot

max_features = 20000
maxlen = 80
batch_size = 32

# Prepare dataset
(X_train, y_train), (X_test, y_test) = imdb.load_data(nb_words=max_features)
X_train = sequence.pad_sequences(X_train, maxlen=maxlen)
X_test = sequence.pad_sequences(X_test, maxlen=maxlen)

# LSTM
model = Sequential()
model.add(Embedding(max_features, 128, dropout=0.2))
model.add(LSTM(128, dropout_W=0.2, dropout_U=0.2))
model.add(Dense(1))
model.add(Activation('sigmoid'))

# Compile
model.compile(loss='binary_crossentropy', optimizer='adam', metrics=['accuracy'])
```

CHAPTER 7 ■ INTRODUCTION TO KERAS

```
# Training
model.fit(X_train, y_train, batch_size=batch_size, verbose=1, nb_epoch=1, validation_
data=(X_test, y_test))

# Evalaution
score = model.evaluate(X_test, y_test, batch_size=batch_size)
print "Test Metrics:", zip(model.metrics_names, score)
plot(model, to_file='s8.png', show_shapes=True)

# Output
# Train on 25000 samples, validate on 25000 samples
# Epoch 1/1
# 25000/25000 [==============================] - 165s - loss: 0.5286 - acc: 0.7347 - val_
loss: 0.4391 - val_acc: 0.8076
# 25000/25000 [==============================] - 33s
# Test Metrics: [('loss', 0.43908300422668456), ('acc', 0.80759999999999998)]
```

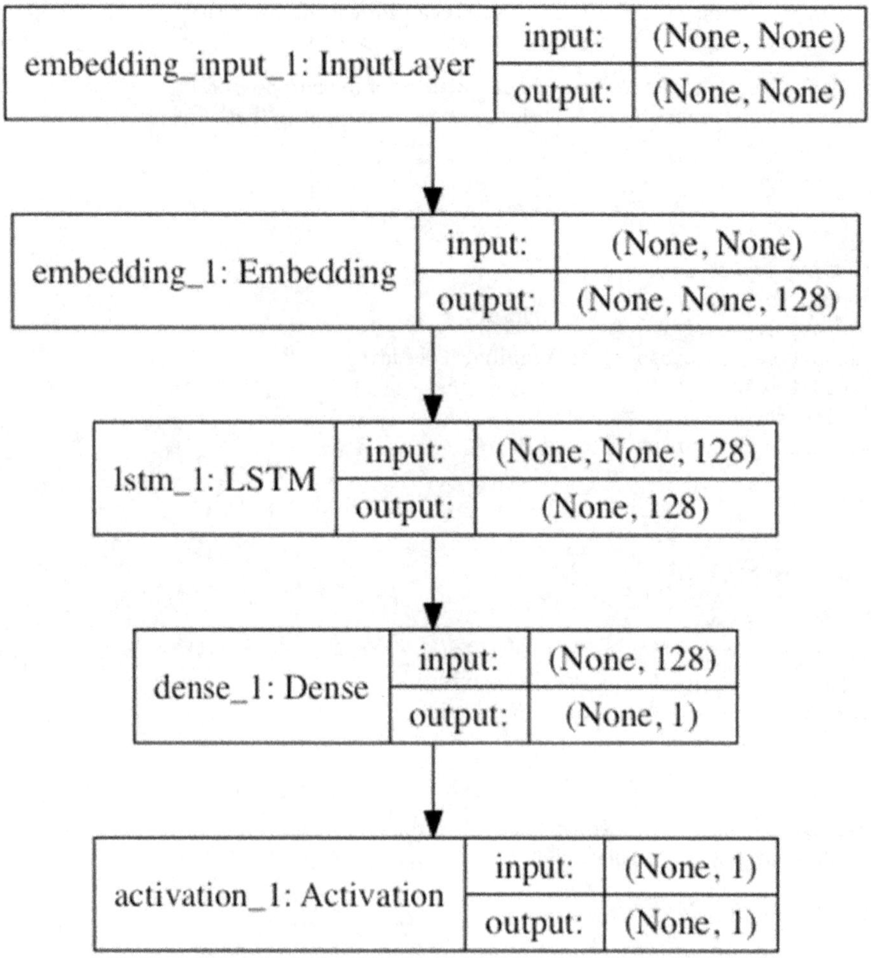

embedding_input_1: InputLayer	input:	(None, None)
	output:	(None, None)

embedding_1: Embedding	input:	(None, None)
	output:	(None, None, 128)

lstm_1: LSTM	input:	(None, None, 128)
	output:	(None, 128)

dense_1: Dense	input:	(None, 128)
	output:	(None, 1)

activation_1: Activation	input:	(None, 1)
	output:	(None, 1)

Figure 7-6. LSTM

Let us now look at the construct Keras provides to build LSTM Networks, introduced in Chapter 6 (refer to Listing 7-8 and Figure 7-6). The data set we will be using is from IMDB and represents 25,000 reviews from IMDB categorized as positive or negative, making this a binary sequence classification problem. The data is preprocessed to contain only frequent words (the words are actually represented as integers). Listing 7-8 presents the source code and Figure 7-6 illustrates the computational graph. Keras provides a fairly high-level construct for LSTMs, which allows users to construct LSTM models.

Summary

In this chapter we covered the basics of using Keras, using a number of small and simple examples. We encourage the reader to experiment with the examples. Keras has extensive documentation, which is recommended further reading.

CHAPTER 8

Stochastic Gradient Descent

An essential step in building a deep learning model is solving the underlying optimization problem, as defined by the loss function. This chapter covers Stochastic Gradient Descent (SGD), which is the most commonly used algorithm for solving such optimization problems. We also cover a breadth of algorithmic variations published in academic literature which improve on the performance of SGD, and present a bag of largely undocumented tricks which will allow the user to go an extra mile. Lastly, we cover some ground on parallel/distributed SGD and touch on Second Order Methods for completeness.

Most of the examples presented in the accompanying code for this chapter are based on a Python package called downhill. Downhill implements SGD with many of its variations and is an excellent choice for experimenting.

Optimization Problems

Simply put, an optimization problem involves finding the parameters which minimize a mathematical function.

For example, given the function $f(x) = 2x$, finding the value of x which minimizes the function is an optimization problem (refer to Figure 8-1).

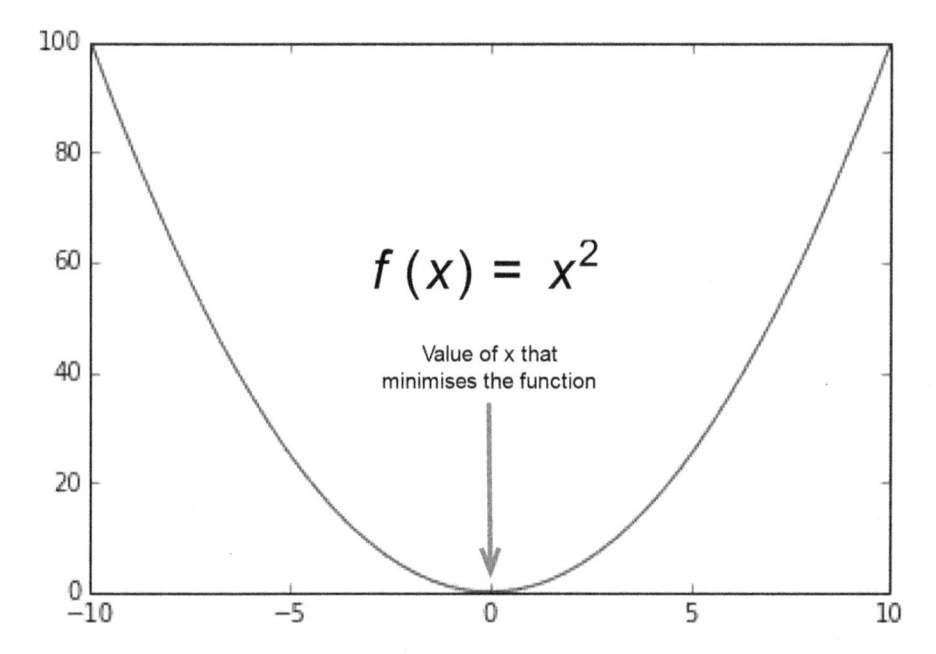

Figure 8-1. *An optimization problem involves finding the parameters that minimize a given function*

While the functions we want to minimize while building deep learning models are way more complicated (involving multiple parameters which may be scalars, vectors, or matrices), conceptually it's simply finding the parameters that minimize the function.

The function one wants to optimize for while building a deep learning model is referred to as the loss function. The loss function may have a number of scalar/vector/matrix-valued parameters but always has a scalar output. This scalar output represents the goodness of the model. Goodness, typically, means a combination of how well the model predicts and how simple the model is.

Note For now, we will stay away from the statistical/machine learning aspects of a loss function (covered elsewhere in the book) and focus purely on solving such optimization problems. That is, we assume that we have been presented with a loss function $L(x)$ where x represents the parameters of the model and the job at hand is to find the values for x which minimize $L(x)$.

Method of Steepest Descent

Let us now look at a simple mathematical idea, which is the intuition behind SGD. For the sake of simplicity, let us assume that x is just one vector. Given that we want to minimize $L(x)$, we want to change or update x such that $L(x)$ reduces. Let u represent the unit vector or direction in which x should be ideally changed and let α denote the magnitude (scalar) of this step. A higher value of α implies a larger step in the direction u, which is not desired. This is because u is evaluated for the current value of x and it will be different for a different x.

Thus, we want to find a u such that

$$\lim_{\alpha \to 0} L(x + \alpha u)$$

is minimized. It follows that

$$\lim_{\alpha \to 0} L(x + \alpha u) = u^T \nabla_x L(x).$$

Thus, we basically want to find a u such that

$$u^T \nabla_x L(x)$$

is minimized. Note that $\nabla_x L(x)$ is the gradient of $L(x)$.

Given that both u^T and $\nabla_x L(x)$ are vectors, it follows that

$$u^T \nabla_x L(x) = |u| \cdot |\nabla_x L(x)| \cos \theta,$$

where θ is the angle between the two vectors (refer to Figure 8-2).

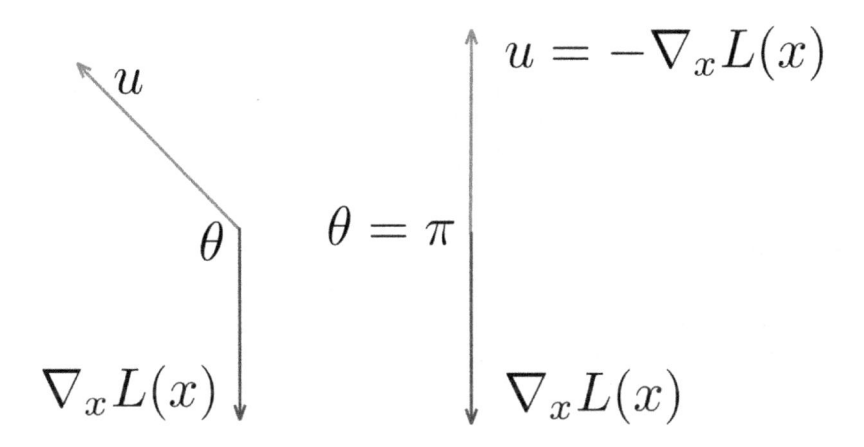

Figure 8-2. *Finding the desired direction of update*

The value of cos θ would be minimized at $\theta = \pi$, that is to say the vectors are pointing in the opposite direction. Thus, it follows that setting the direction $u = -\nabla_x L(x)$ would achieve our desired objective. This leads to a simple iterative algorithm as follows:

Input: α, n

Initialize x to a random value.
For n steps do:

   Update $x = x - \alpha \nabla_x L(x)$

   Output: x

Batch, Stochastic (Single and Mini-batch) Descent

So far, we were denoting our loss function as $L(x)$. The training data (examples) were implicit in this notation. For the purpose of this discussion, we need to make them explicit. Let us denote our training data as $D = \{d_1, d_2, \ldots d_n\}$. Our loss function should now be denoted as $L_D(x)$. This simply means that the loss function is being evaluated with parameters x and with respect to a set of data points D. Let T be a subset of examples in D; then $L_T(x)$ denotes the loss function evaluated over the set of examples T. Similarly, $\nabla_x L_D(x)$ and $\nabla_x L_T(x)$ denote the gradients of the loss function $L(x)$ computed over the sets of training data D and T, respectively.

Note For now, we will stay away from the computation of gradients of loss functions over subsets of data. These can be generated using automatic differentiation (covered elsewhere in the book) quite easily (even for arbitrary complicated loss functions) and need not be derived manually.

Armed with this notation, we can now discuss three variants of the steepest descent approach we discussed earlier.

Batch

In this approach, the entire dataset D is used in the update step. That is, x is updated as $x = x - \nabla_x L_D(x)$. Two things are apparent about this approach. First, that it is expensive as it requires a computation over the entire dataset. Second, the update direction is the most accurate one, given our entire dataset.

Stochastic Single Example

In this approach, only a single example from D is used in the update step. That is, x is updated as $x = x - \nabla_x L_S(x)$ where $|S| = 1$. Note that we use a different example in each iteration chosen randomly (hence the term stochastic, which simply means having a random nature). Two things are apparent about this approach, too. First, that it is quite cheap as it requires a computation of the gradient over only a single example. Second, the update direction is not as accurate as we are only using a very small fraction of the training dataset.

Stochastic Mini-batch

In this approach, only a small subset of examples from D is used in the update step. That is, x is updated as $x = x - \nabla_x L_S(x)$ where $|S| < |D|$. Note that we use a different set of examples in each iteration chosen randomly (hence the term stochastic).

Batch vs. Stochastic

In practice, stochastic approaches dominate over batch approaches and are much more commonly used. A seemingly nonintuitive fact about stochastic approaches is that not only is the gradient over few examples cheaper to compute, not getting the exact direction (using only a small number of examples) actually leads to better solutions. This is particularly true for large datasets with redundant information wherein the examples are not too different from each other. Another reason for stochastic approaches performing better is the presence of multiple local minima with different depths. In a sense, the noise in the direction allows for jumping across the trenches while a batch approach will converge in the trench it started with.

Challenges with SGD

Having covered the conceptual description of SGD, let us now consider the challenges of applying it to solving real world problems while build deep learning models.

Local Minima

Local minima are suboptimal solutions (refer to Figure 8-3) that trap any steepest descent approach and prevent the iterative procedure for making progress towards a better solution.

CHAPTER 8 STOCHASTIC GRADIENT DESCENT

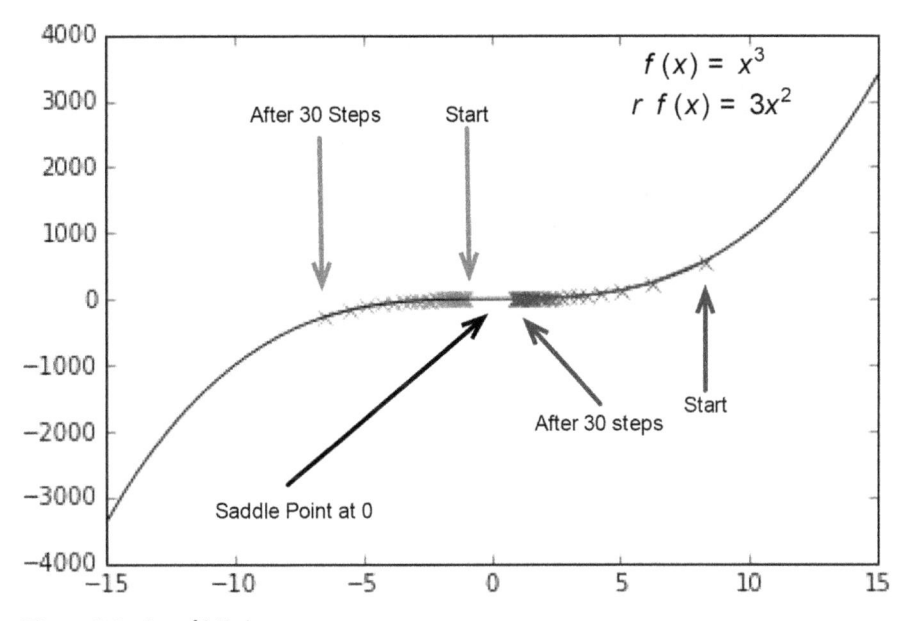

Figure 8-3. Local Minima

Saddle Points

Saddle points are points (refer to Figure 8-4) where the gradient evaluates to zero but the point is not a local minimum. Saddle points are any steepest descent approach and prevent the iterative procedure for making progress towards a better solution. There is good empirical evidence that saddle points are much more common than local minima when it comes to optimization problems in a high number of dimensions (which is always the case when it comes to building deep learning models).

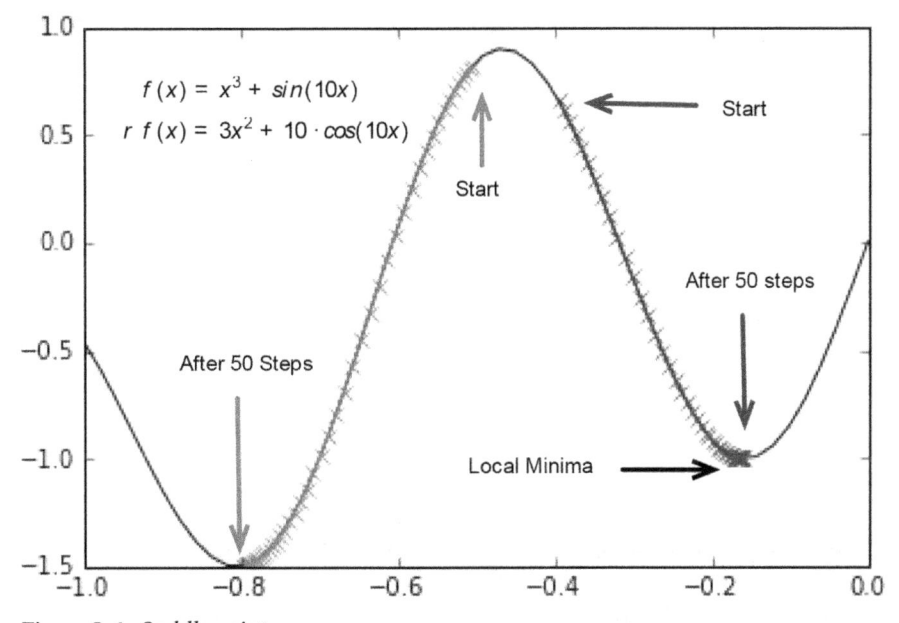

Figure 8-4. Saddle point

117

CHAPTER 8 ■ STOCHASTIC GRADIENT DESCENT

Selecting the Learning Rate

The α is the earlier discussion which represents the magnitude (scalar) of the step (in the direction u) is taken in each iteration so as to update x. This α is commonly referred to as the learning rate and it has a big impact on finding good solutions to the optimization problem (refer to Figure 8-5). Too high a learning rate can cause the solution to bounce around and too low a learning rate means slow convergence (implying not getting to a good solution in a given number of iterations). When it comes to loss functions with many parameters trained on sparse datasets, a single global learning rate for all parameters makes the problem of choosing a learning rate even more challenging.

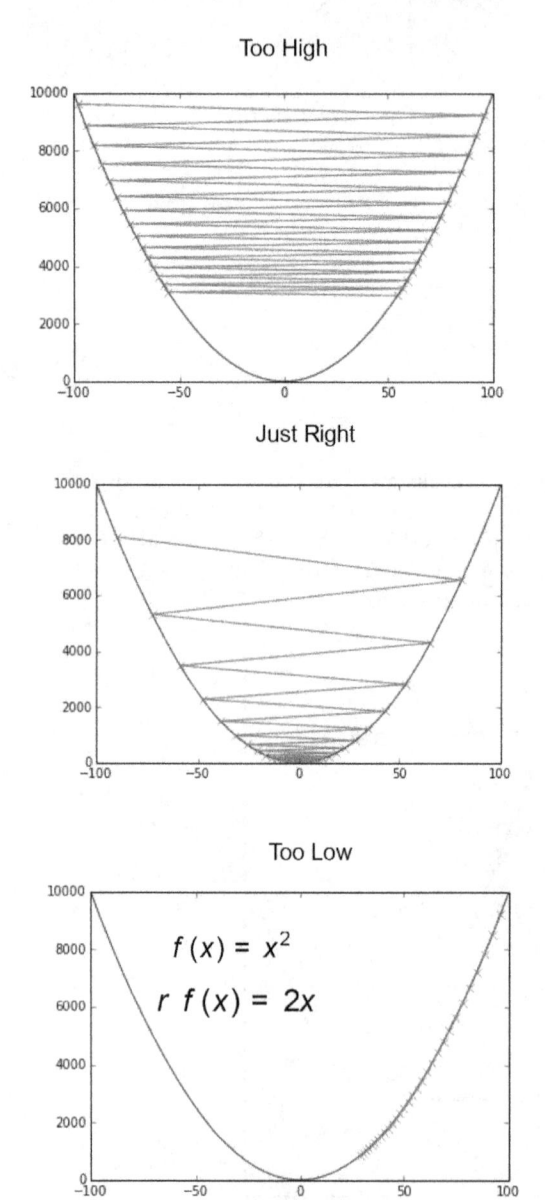

Figure 8-5. Learning rate needs to be set properly

118

Slow Progress in Narrow Valleys

Another problem inherent to steepest descent is the slow progress in narrow valleys generated due to badly scaled datasets. Progress slows down drastically as we get closer to the solution (refer to Figure 8-6).

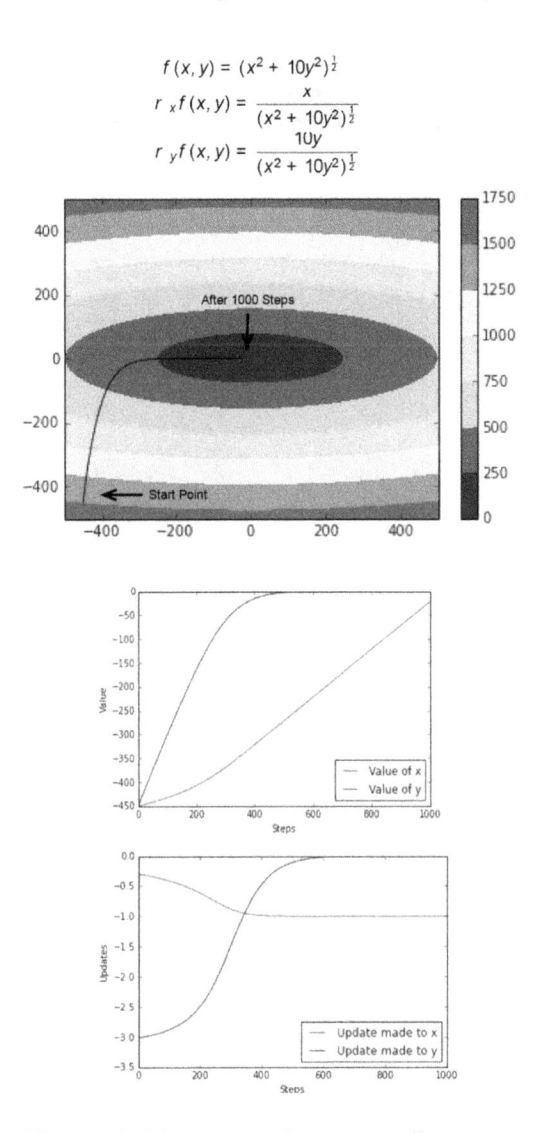

$$f(x, y) = (x^2 + 10y^2)^{\frac{1}{2}}$$
$$\nabla_x f(x, y) = \frac{x}{(x^2 + 10y^2)^{\frac{1}{2}}}$$
$$\nabla_y f(x, y) = \frac{10y}{(x^2 + 10y^2)^{\frac{1}{2}}}$$

Figure 8-6. Slow progress in narrow valleys

Algorithmic Variations on SGD

We will now cover a number of algorithmic variations for SGD proposed in academic literature that address the challenges discussed earlier.

CHAPTER 8 ■ STOCHASTIC GRADIENT DESCENT

Momentum

Consider the update step for SGD described earlier,

$$x = x - \alpha \nabla_x L(x).$$

The intuition behind momentum is to use a fraction of the previous update for the current update. That is, let u_s denote the update to the parameters x in step s. Similarly, let u_{s-1} denote the update in the previous step. Now, let us update x with

$$u_s = \gamma u_{s-1} + \alpha \nabla_x L(x).$$

That is, we update

$$x = x - u_s$$

instead of

$$x = x - \alpha \nabla_x L(x).$$

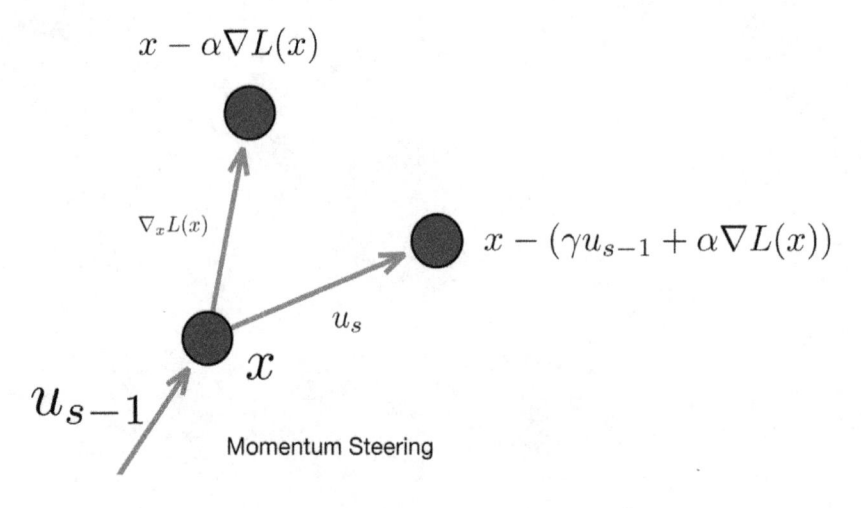

Figure 8-7. Momentum steering

Simply put, we have used a faction of the update in the previous step for the current update. This idea is referred to as momentum, as it is akin to the momentum acquired by a ball rolling downhill. A ball that has picked up momentum will bounce out of small ditches (local minima) along the way and reach the bottom of the hill. It will also keep up somewhat with the speed of previous downhill movement even if the hill has a much reduced slope (because it has picked up momentum). The momentum term basically causes new step direction to be biased by the step previous direction (refer to Figure 8-7). Use of momentum has been empirically shown to cause reduced oscillation and faster convergence.

Nesterov Accelerated Gradient (NAS)

Using the same notation as before, the Nesterov accelerated gradient is basically updating x with

$$u_s = \gamma u_{s-1} + \alpha \nabla_x L(x - \gamma u_{s-1}).$$

That is, we update $x = x - u_s$.

The intuition behind this is looking one step ahead. That is, we first take a step in the direction of the accumulated gradient and do an adaptation. The intuition behind NAS is looking ahead and anticipating, which leads to better solutions (refer to Figure 8-8).

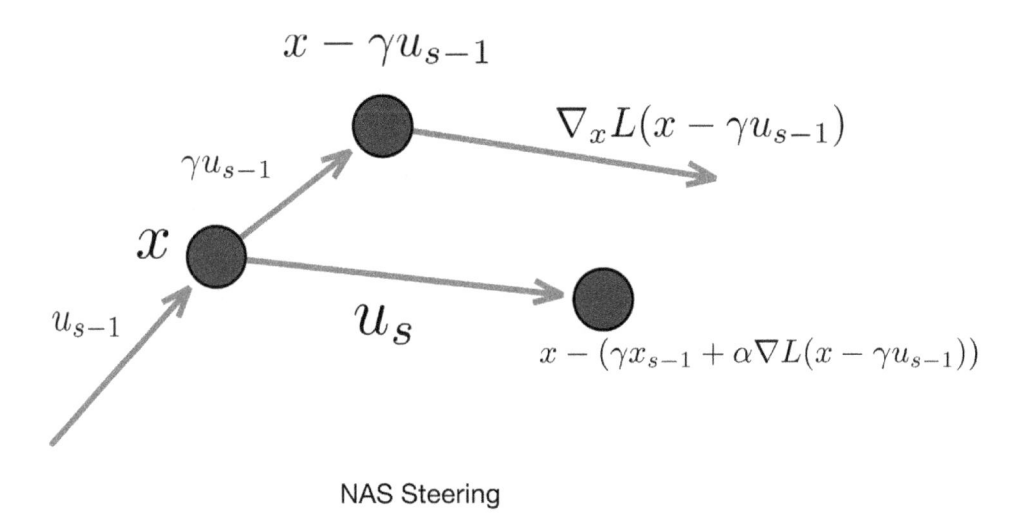

Figure 8-8. NAS steering

Annealing and Learning Rate Schedules

When gradient descent approaches a minimum, we have seen how a bad learning rate can cause it to oscillate around the minima (see Figure 8-5). Annealing refers to reducing the learning rate as it approaches the minima. This can be done manually (stopping the gradient descent and restarting from the same point with a reduced learning rate) or via learning rate schedules which introduce a number of user-controlled hyper parameters which dictate how the learning rate is reduced based on the number of steps taken. However, it must be noted that we are using the same learning rate for all the parameters, which may not be appropriate; a per-parameter learning rate adjustment is desired.

Adagrad

The Adagrad algorithm adjusts the learning rate for each parameter. So far, we have been denoting the parameters of the loss function as x. Note that x is actually a large number of parameters, each of which is being updated with the same learning rate. Let x_i denote one of the parameters and let g_i^s denote the gradient for x_i at step s. For steps $0, 1, \ldots, S-1$ we have a corresponding series of gradients $g_i^0, g_i^1, \ldots, g_i^s$.

CHAPTER 8 ■ STOCHASTIC GRADIENT DESCENT

Let

$$G = \left(g_i^0\right)^2 + \left(g_i^1\right)^2 + \ldots + \left(g_i^{S-1}\right)^2,$$

which is basically the sum of squares of the gradients for each step up to the previous step. The update rule in Adagrad is

$$x_i = x_i - \frac{\alpha}{G^{\frac{1}{2}}} g_i^s.$$

The α term is the global learning rate, which gets adapted for each parameter based on the previous gradients. It must also be noted that as G accumulates, the learning rate slows down for each parameter and eventually no progress can be made, which is a weakness of Adagrad.

RMSProp

The RMSProp algorithm improves on the Adagarad algorithm's weakness of completely halted progress beyond a certain number of iterations. The intuition here is to use a window of fixed size over the gradients computed at each step rather than use the full set of gradients. That is, compute G over only the past W steps. Now, it's conceptually equivalent but computationally cheaper to treat the computation of

$$G = \frac{\left(g_i^{S-W}\right)^2 + \left(g_i^{S-w+1}\right)^2 + \ldots + \left(g_i^{S-1}\right)^2}{W}$$

as the accumulation of exponentially decaying average of square of gradients rather than store all values of

$$g_i^{-w}, g_i^{-w+1}, \ldots, g_i^{-2}, g_i^{-1}$$

and compute G at each step. That is, we compute

$$E\left[\left(g_i\right)^2\right]^S = \rho E\left[\left(g_i\right)^2\right]^{S-1} + (1-\rho)\left(g_i^s\right)^2$$

where ρ is the decay.

Now, note that in Adagrad we were computing the update as
$x_i = x_i - \frac{\alpha}{G^{\frac{1}{2}}} g_i^s$. Consider the value of $G^{\frac{1}{2}}$. We can see that this is simply the root-mean-square of g_i, that is

$$RMS[g_i] = G^{\frac{1}{2}} = \sqrt{E\left[\left(g_i\right)^2\right]^S}.$$

Thus, we can compute the update as

$$x_i = x_i - \frac{\alpha}{RMS[g_i]} g_i^s.$$

Adadelta

The intuition behind Adadelta is to consider whether the unit of the parameter and the update to the parameter is the same. The author of the Adadelta argues that this is not the same in the case of any first order methods like steepest descent (but is the same in the case of second order methods like Newton's method). In order to fix this issue, the proposed update rule of Adadelta is

$$x_i = x_i - \frac{RMS[\Delta x_i]^{S-1}}{RMS[g_i]^S} g_i^S$$

where $RMS[\Delta x]^{S-1}$ is the root-mean-square of the actual updates to x. Note that $RMS[\Delta x_i]^{S-1}$ lags behind $RMS[g_i]^S$ by one step.

Adam

Adam computes the updates by maintaining the exponentially weighted averages of both g_i and $(g_i)^2$ for each parameter (denoted by the subscript i). The update rule for Adam is

$$x_i = x_i - \frac{\alpha}{E\left[\left(g_i^{S-1}\right)\right]^2} E\left[g_i^{S-1}\right].$$

It is important to note that $E\left[g_i^{S-1}\right]$ and $E\left[(g_i^{S-1})^2\right]$ are biased towards zero in the initial steps for small decay rates (there are two decay rates here—one for $E\left[g_i^{S-1}\right]$ and one for $E\left[(g_i^{S-1})^2\right]$—which we denote by ρ_1 and ρ_2 respectively). This bias can be corrected by computing

$$E\left[g_i^{S-1}\right] = \frac{E\left[g_i^{S-1}\right]}{1-\rho_1}$$

and

$$E\left[(g_i^{S-1})^2\right] = \frac{E\left[(g_i^{S-1})^2\right]}{1-\rho_2}$$

respectively.

Resilient Backpropagation

The intuition behind Resilient Backpropagation is that the sign of the gradient switches back and forth between positive and negative when the learning rate is too high (refer to Figure 7). The key idea is to keep track of the sign of the previous gradient and match it with the current gradient. If the sign is the same, use a higher learning rate and, if different, use a lower learning rate. Note that this is done for every parameter. The hyper parameters include the amounts to increase and decrease the learning rate (in case the sign matches or does not match, respectively).

Equilibrated SGD

Equilibrated SGD aims to address issues SGD experiences with saddle points. The key idea here is that we need second order information (second derivatives of the loss function) to get out of the trap of a saddle point. The update rule for Equilibrated SGD is given by $x_i = x_i - \dfrac{\alpha}{\sqrt{D_i^s}} g_i^s$ where $D_i^s = \rho D_i^{s-1} + (1-\rho)(H_d)^2$ (exponentially weighted average) and H_d is the diagonal of the Hessian matrix of $L(x)$ (computed symbolically) evaluated at $x \in \mathcal{N}(0,1)$ (normal distribution with 0 mean and standard deviation of 1).

Tricks and Tips for using SGD

We will now cover a number of tricks and tips for SGD proposed in academic literature that address the challenges discussed earlier.

Preprocessing Input Data

It is of utmost importance that data is scaled well so as to ease the optimization (refer to Figure 8-6). A good rule of thumb is to standardize the data by subtracting the mean and divide by the standard deviation to scale the data. So, if $X = \{X_1, X_2 \ldots X_n\}$ is one of the input variables, we transform the data so that

$$X_i = \dfrac{X_i - \mu}{\sigma}.$$

In case of sparse data (most of X_i are equal to zero), the standardization process will cause the data to become dense, max-abs scaling where

$$X_i = \dfrac{|X_i|}{\max(X)}.$$

Scaling the feature to have a unit norm

$$X_i = \dfrac{X_i}{|X_{i2}|}$$

is another approach to scaling data.

It is also a good practice to remove linear correlations amongst input variables from input data using Principal Component Analysis.

Choice of Activation Function

Common examples of activation function are the standard logistic function $f(x) = \dfrac{1}{1+e^{-x}}$ and the hyperbolic tangent function $f(x) = \tanh(x)$. A recommended approach is to use an activation function that is symmetrical around 0 (rather than only positive or negative), for instance, $f(x) = 1.7159 \tanh\left(\dfrac{2}{3}x\right)$. It is also recommended that a small linear term be added to prevent flat sports, $f(x) = \tanh(x) + ax$.

Preprocessing Target Value

While target values can be binary (0,1) in many cases, it is advisable to transform the target variable to values that lie within the range (not asymptotically, but practically) of the activation functions used to define the loss function. Not doing so leads to parameters being updated to higher and higher values without achieving any effect (on the output label). However, if the value of the target label is being used as a measure of confidence, then the labels which have been unnecessarily pushed to higher values are bad estimates of the confidence. While 0 and 1 may be extreme values for the activation function, it is also important not to choose targets that lie in the linear region of the activation function. A recommended approach is to choose values that maximize the second derivative of the activation function, for instance, ±1 for

$$f(x) = 1.7159 \tanh\left(\frac{2}{3}x\right).$$

Initializing Parameters

It is a recommended practice to initialize parameters randomly (normal distribution, zero-mean, unit variance). Another recipe for neural networks where the activation function is $f(x) = 1.7159 \tanh\left(\frac{2}{3}x\right)$ (and the data is standardized) is to set weights to $m^{-\frac{1}{2}}$ where m is the fan-in (the number of connections feeding into the node).

Shuffling Data

It is recommended practice to shuffle input data, as it may be in a particular order and hence might bias the SGD. A rare exception to this is Curriculum Learning wherein examples are presented in a meaningful order (increasing difficulty of prediction).

Batch Normalization

While our parameters are initialized in a way such that they are normalized (set randomly, normal distribution, zero-mean, and unit variance), they do not remain normalized over the update steps. Batch normalization renormalizes parameters after each batch (refer to batch SGD).

Early Stopping

Early stopping basically involves measuring the loss on an unseen (unused for SGD) subset of training data (called validation data) and stopping when there is no change observed in the loss. Typically, there are two hyper parameters introduced: one which determines whether the change is significant (any change in loss less than this value is treated as not a change) and a patience parameter, which is the number of times a no change step can be taken before the iterative procedure terminates.

Gradient Noise

The gradient noise trick introduces a mean centered noise, $\mathcal{N}(0, \sigma)$, in every update step. Here, σ is a hyper parameter and the gradient is computed as $g_i = g_i + \mathcal{N}(0, \sigma)$.

Parallel and Distributed SGD

We now cover two parallel and distributed approaches for SGD. SGD in its basic form is a sequential algorithm and convergence can be very slow on large data sets and models with a large number of parameters. Parallel and distributed approaches have a great impact when it comes to dealing with large volumes of training data (in the order of billions) and a large number of model parameters (in the order of millions).

Hogwild

Consider the update step of the SGD procedure. What makes the algorithm inherently sequential is update step $x = x - \alpha \nabla_x L(x)$. Let's say that we want to employ multiple threads of computation to make the iteration faster. Since we want only one thread to do this (do the update one step at a time), we would place a lock around this step (to prevent a race condition). Once we do that, this essentially becomes a sequential algorithm; no matter how many cores and threads we devote to the process, only one thread is actually doing the work, while all others are waiting on a lock.

The intuition behind Hogwild is that the race condition caused by not placing a lock on the update step does not lead to much inconsistency in updates when the optimization problem is sparse. This is simply because each update step touches only a few parameters. The authors of Hogwild provide strong theoretical and empirical evidence for this finding and the gains on large datasets are significant. Hogwild is easy to implement on multi-core CPUs and GPUs.

Downpour

Downpour is a distributed algorithm for SGD that consists of two key moving parts: model replica and parameter server (refer to Figure 8-9). A model replica is a set of machines that operates on a subset of data, where every machine operates only on a subset of parameters. There are many such model replicas, each operating on a different subset of a large dataset. The parameter server is a set of machines that maintains a common global state of the model. Model replicas retrieve the global state from the parameter server, update the model based on the subset of data and update the global state. Note that the fetch and update of the global state does not happen at every iteration. There are two levels of distribution with Downpour. First, the model parameters (what we have been denoting as x so far) are split across multiple machines in each model replica. Second, the data is split amongst model replicas. So, essentially, each machine is doing the gradient update step on a subset of model parameters, using a subset of data. The global state is updated asynchronously. In spite of the apparent inconsistencies introduced by Downpour, it has been found to be very effective when it comes to training a large model with large amounts of data.

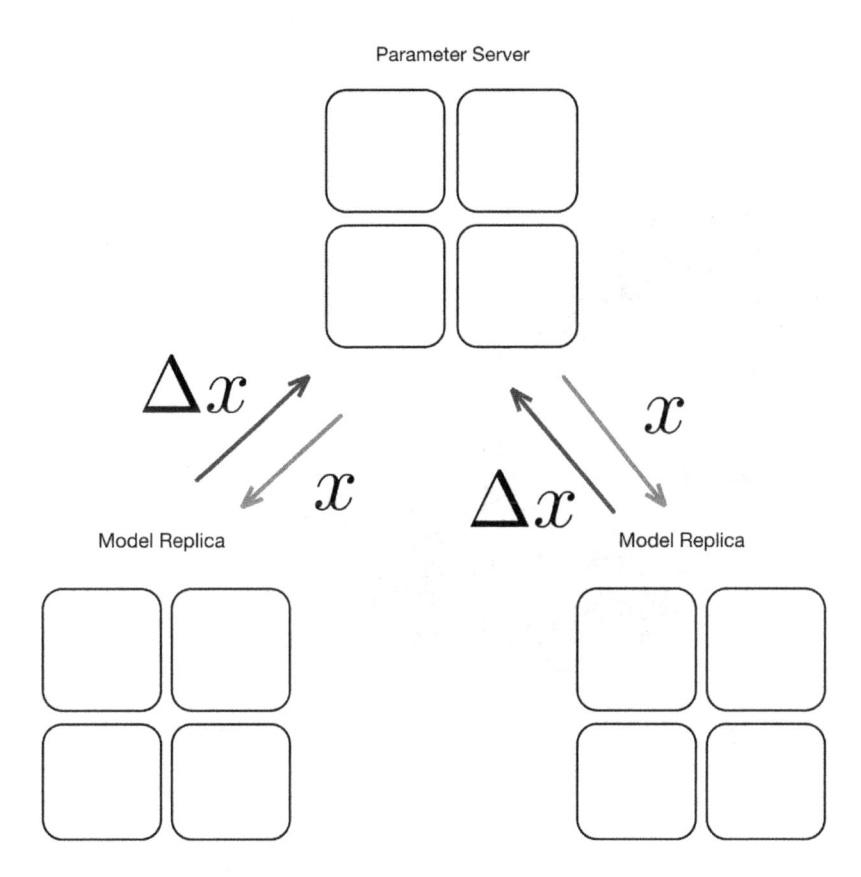

Figure 8-9. Downpour

Hands-on SGD with Downhill

We will now a hands-on exercise with SGD using a Python package called Downhill. Downhill implements SGD with many of its variants. It operates on loss functions defined in Theano, which makes it a very convenient tool to play with SGD variants on arbitrary loss functions defined in Theano. Let us start with generating a dataset for our exercise (Listing 8-1, Figure 8-10).

Listing 8-1. Generating data for our excercise

```
#Specifiy the number of examples we need (5000) and the noise level
train_X, train_y = sklearn.datasets.make_moons(5000, noise=0.1)

#One hot encode the target values
train_y_onehot = numpy.eye(2)[train_y]

#Plot the data
pylab.scatter(train_X[:-1000, 0], train_X[:-1000, 1], c=train_y[:-1000], cmap=pylab.
cm.Spectral)
```

CHAPTER 8 ■ STOCHASTIC GRADIENT DESCENT

This should produce a plot of the dataset we generated. The objective at hand is to train a model to distinguish between the red and blue dots.

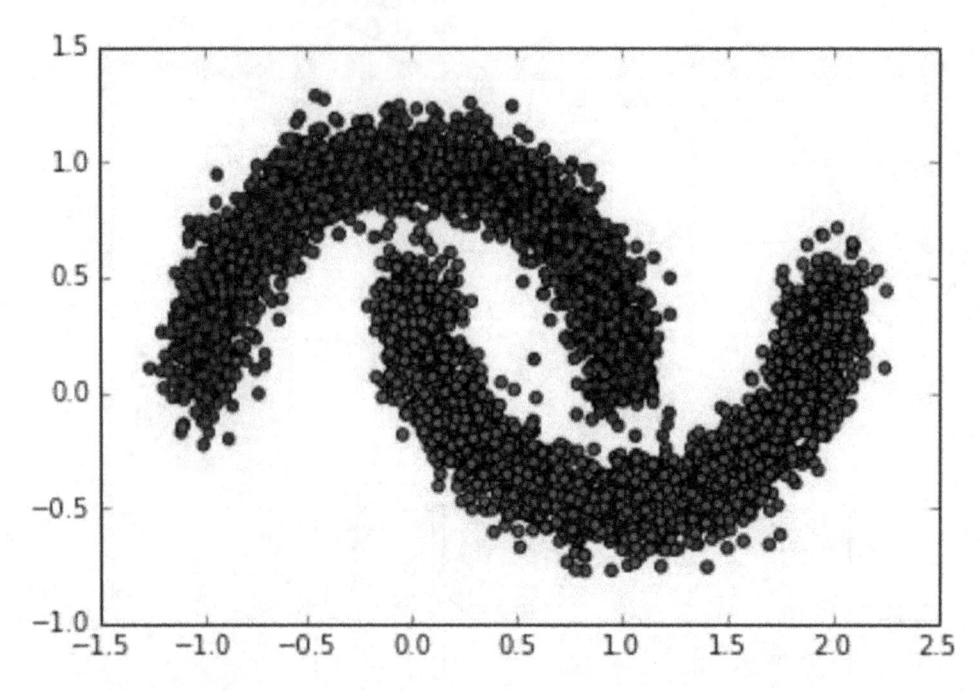

Figure 8-10. Dataset for our experiments

Next let's define a loss function with Theano.

Listing 8-2. Defining the loss function

```
#Set Seed
numpy.random.seed(0)

num_examples = len(train_X)

#Our Neural Network
nn_input_dim = 2
nn_hdim = 1000
nn_output_dim = 2

#Regularization
reg_lambda = numpy.float64(0.01)

#Weights and bias terms
W1_val = numpy.random.randn(nn_input_dim, nn_hdim)
b1_val = numpy.zeros(nn_hdim)
W2_val = numpy.random.randn(nn_hdim, nn_output_dim)
b2_val = numpy.zeros(nn_output_dim)

X = T.matrix('X')
```

CHAPTER 8 ■ STOCHASTIC GRADIENT DESCENT

```python
y = T.matrix('y')
W1 = theano.shared(W1_val, name='W1')
b1 = theano.shared(b1_val, name='b1')
W2 = theano.shared(W2_val, name='W2')
b2 = theano.shared(b2_val, name='b2')

batch_size = 1

#Our Loss function
z1 = X.dot(W1) + b1
a1 = T.tanh(z1)
z2 = a1.dot(W2) + b2
y_hat = T.nnet.softmax(z2)
loss_reg = 1./batch_size * reg_lambda/2 * (T.sum(T.sqr(W1)) + T.sum(T.sqr(W2)))
loss = T.nnet.categorical_crossentropy(y_hat, y).mean() + loss_reg

prediction = T.argmax(y_hat, axis=1)
predict = theano.function([X], prediction)
```

■ **Note** For now, we will stay away from the details of defining loss functions with Theano (covered elsewhere in the book).

Next we set up a simple SGD using Downhill. We use all default parameters and want do 10K iterations. The patience parameter is set to 10K also so that early stopping (described earlier in the chapter) does not kick in.

Listing 8-3. SGD

```python
#Store the training and vlidation loss
train_loss = []
validation_loss = []

opt = downhill.build('sgd', loss=loss)

#Set up training and validation dataset splits, use only one example in a batch #and use
only one batch per step/epoc

#Use everything except last 1000 examples for training
train = downhill.Dataset([train_X[:-1000], train_y_onehot[:-1000]], batch_size=batch_size,
iteration_size=1)

#Use last 1000 examples for valudation
valid = downhill.Dataset([train_X[-1000:], train_y_onehot[-1000:]])

#SGD
iterations = 0
for tm, vm in opt.iterate(train, valid, patience=10000):
    iterations += 1

    # Record the training and validation loss
    train_loss.append(tm['loss'])
    validation_loss.append(vm['loss'])
```

CHAPTER 8 ■ STOCHASTIC GRADIENT DESCENT

```
if iterations > 10000:
    break
```

We can now visualize the decision boundary over the training (Figure 8-11) and validation (Figure 8-12) sets, and the loss (Figure 8-13).

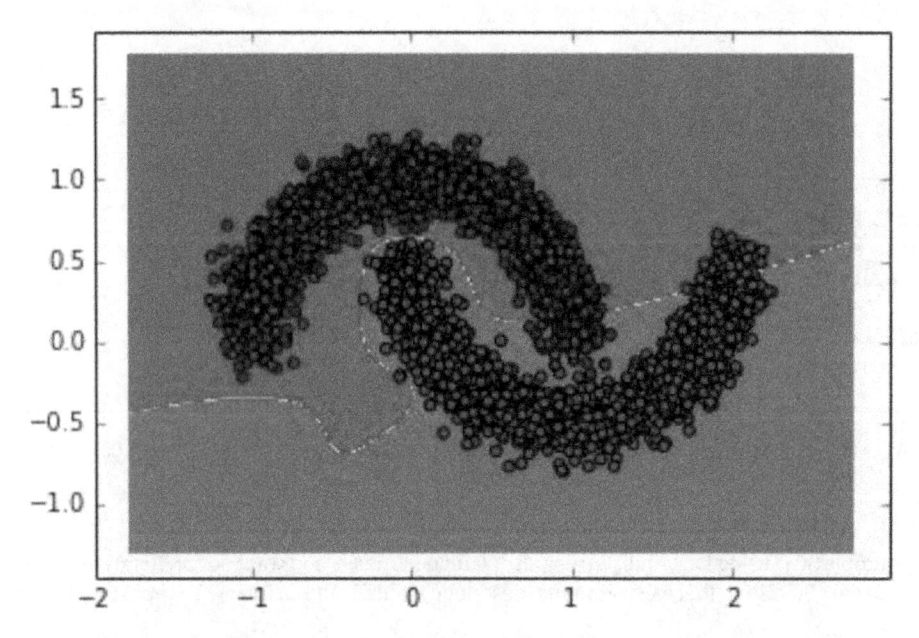

Figure 8-11. Decision boundary over training set

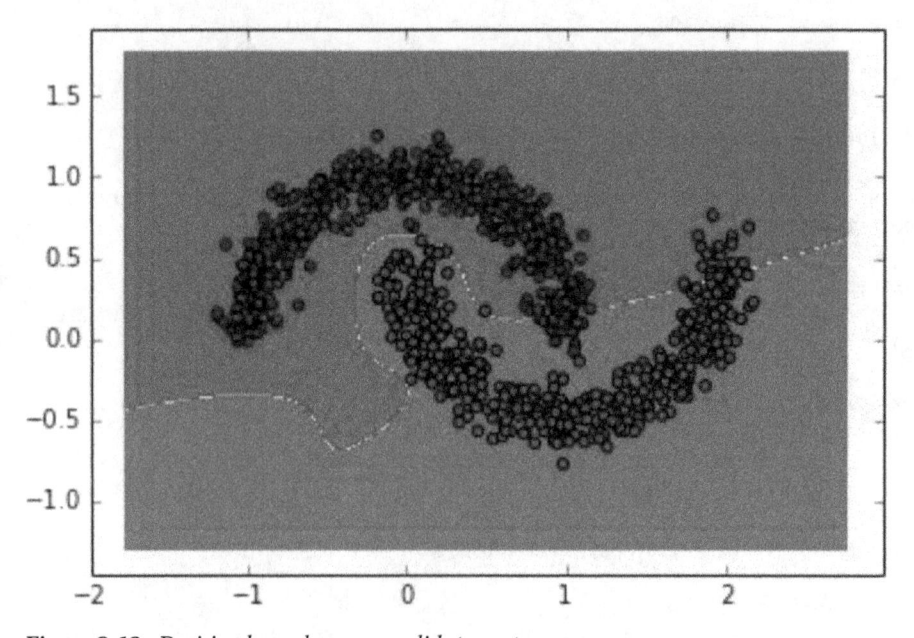

Figure 8-12. Decision boundary over validaton set

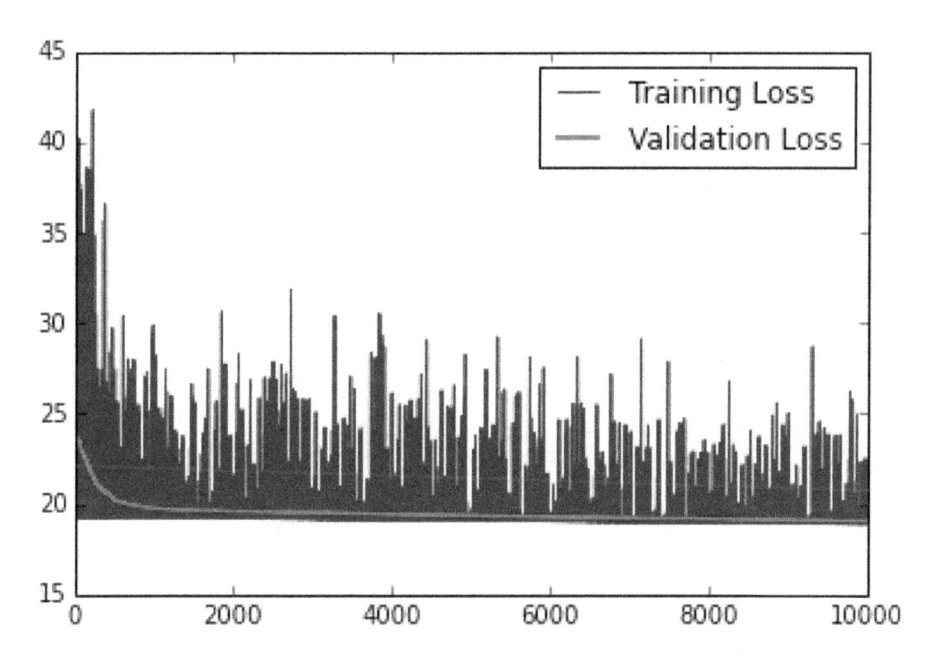

Figure 8-13. Training and Validation Loss over 10K iterations

Listing 8-4. Using SGD variants implemented in Downhill

```
def build_model(algo):
    loss_value = []

    W1.set_value(W1_val)
    b1.set_value(b1_val)
    W2.set_value(W2_val)
    b2.set_value(b2_val)

    opt = downhill.build(algo, loss=loss)

    train = downhill.Dataset([train_X[:-1000], train_y_onehot[:-1000]], batch_size=1,
    iteration_size=1)
    valid = downhill.Dataset([train_X[-1000:], train_y_onehot[-1000:]])
    iterations = 0
    for tm, vm in opt.iterate(train, valid, patience=1000):
        iterations += 1
        loss_value.append(vm['loss'])
        if iterations > 1000:
            break
    return loss_value
```

CHAPTER 8 ■ STOCHASTIC GRADIENT DESCENT

```
algo_names = ['adadelta', 'adagrad', 'adam', 'nag', 'rmsprop', 'rprop', 'sgd']
losses = []
for algo_name in algo_names:
    print algo_name
    vloss = build_model(algo_name)
    losses.append(numpy.array(vloss))
```

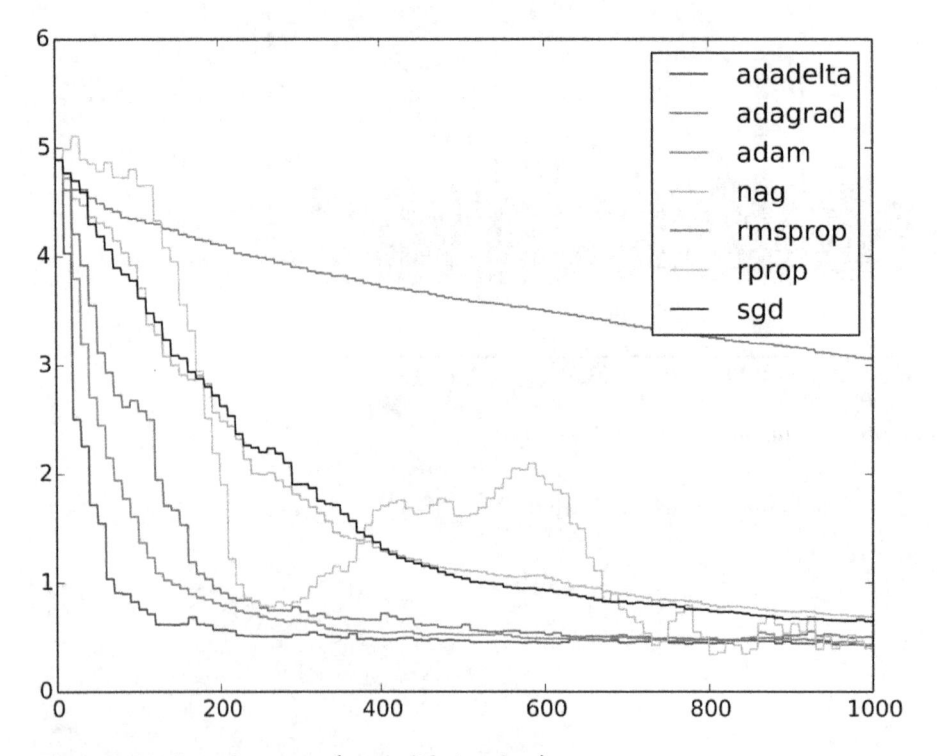

Figure 8-14. Learning curves (over validation data)

Let us now try out a number of SGD variants implemented in Downhill (Listing 8-4) and visualize the learning curves (Figure 8-14). We will be running Adadelta, Adagrad, Adam, Nesterov Accelerated Gradient (NAG), RMSProp, Resilient Backpropagation, and vanilla SGD as before. We run all these algorithms with default parameters for 1000 steps.

Summary

In this chapter we covered Stochastic Gradient Descent (SGD), the weaknesses of SGD, a number of algorithmic variations to address these weaknesses, and a number of tricks to make SGD effective. SGD is the most common approach to train deep learning models. The reader is advised to go over the examples in the source code listings and also look at the implementations of SGD and its variants in the Downhill package for further clarity and perspective.

One important aspect that we did not cover in this chapter is how gradients for arbitrary loss functions (required for SGD) are computed. This is covered in the next chapter on automatic differentiation.

CHAPTER 9

Automatic Differentiation

In the chapter on Stochastic Gradient Descent, we treated the computation of gradients of the loss function $\nabla_x L(x)$ as a black box. In this chapter we open this black box and cover the theory and practice of automatic differentiation. Automatic differentiation is a mature technology that allows for the effortless and efficient computation of gradients of arbitrarily complicated loss functions. This is critical when it comes to minimizing loss functions of interest; at the heart of building any deep learning model lies an optimization problem, which is invariably solved using stochastic gradient descent, which in turn requires one to compute gradients.

Most of the applications in this chapter are based on the Python package Autograd, which provides a mature set of capabilities for automatic differentiation.

Automatic differentiation is distinct from both numerical and symbolic differentiation, and we start by covering enough about both of these so that distinction becomes clear. For the purposes of illustration, assume that our function of interest is $f : \mathbb{R} \to \mathbb{R}$ and we intend to find the derivative of f denoted by $f'(x)$.

Numerical Differentiation

Numerical differentiation in its basic form follows from the definition of derivative/gradient. So, given that

$$f'(x) = \frac{df}{dx} = \lim_{\Delta x \to 0} \frac{f(x+\Delta x) - f(x)}{\Delta x}$$

we can compute the $f'(x)$ using the forward difference method as

$$f'(x) = D_+(h) = \frac{f(x+h) - f(x)}{h},$$

setting a suitably small value for h. Similarly, we can compute $f'(x)$ using the backward difference method as

$$f'(x) = D_-(h) = \frac{f(x) - f(x-h)}{h},$$

again by setting a suitably small value for h. A more symmetric form is the central difference approach, which computes f' as

$$f'(x) = D_0(h) = \frac{f(x+h) - f(x-h)}{2h}.$$

A further development over this idea is Richardson's extrapolation

$$f'(x) = \frac{4D_0(h) - D_0(2h)}{3}.$$

The approximation errors for forward and backward differences are in the order of h, that is, $O(h)$, while those for central difference and Richardson's approximation are $O(h^2)$ and $O(h^4)$ respectively.

The key problems with numerical differentiation are the computational cost, which grows with the number of parameters in the loss function, the truncation errors, and the round off errors. The truncation error is the inaccuracy we have in the computation of $f'(x)$ due to h not being zero. The round off error is inherent to using floating point numbers and floating point arithmetic (as against using infinite precision numbers, which would be prohibitive expensive).

Numerical differentiation is thus not a feasible approach for computing gradients while building deep learning models. The only place where numerical differentiation comes in handy is quickly checking if gradients are being computed correctly. This is highly recommended when you have computed gradients manually or with a new/unknown automatic differentiation library. Ideally, this check should be put in as an automated check/assertion before staring SGD.

Note Numerical differentiation is implemented in a Python package called Scipy. We do not cover it here, as it is not directly relevant to deep learning.

Symbolic Differentiation

Symbolic differentiation in its basic form is a set of symbol rewriting rules applied to the loss function to arrive at the derivatives/gradients. Consider two of such simple rules:

$$\frac{d}{dx}(f(x) + g(x)) = \frac{d}{dx}f(x) + \frac{d}{dx}g(x)$$

and

$$\frac{d}{dx}x^n = nx^{(n-1)}.$$

Now, given a function like $f(x) = 2x^3 + x^2$, we can successively apply the symbol writing rules to first arrive at

$$f'(x) = \frac{d}{dx}(2x^3) + \frac{d}{dx}(x^2)$$

by applying the first rewriting rule and $f'(x) = 6x^2 + 2x$ by applying the second rule. Symbolic differentiation is thus automating what we do when we derive gradients manually. Of course, the number of such rules can be large, and more sophisticated algorithms can be leveraged to make this symbol rewriting more efficient. However, in its essence, symbolic differentiation is simply the application of a set of symbol rewriting rules. The key advantage of symbolic differentiation is that it generates a legible mathematical expression for the derivative/gradient that can be understood and analyzed.

The key problem with symbolic differentiation is that it is limited to the symbolic differentiation rules already defined, which can cause us to hit roadblocks when trying to minimize complicated loss functions. An example of this is when your loss function involves an if-else clause or a for/while loop. In a sense, symbolic differentiation is differentiating a (closed form) mathematical expression; it is not differentiating a given computational procedure.

Another problem with automatic differentiation is that a naïve application of symbol rewriting rules, in some cases, can lead to an explosion of symbolic terms (expression swell) and make the process computationally unfeasible. Typically, a fair amount of compute effort is required to simplify such expressions and produce a closed form expression of the derivative.

Note Symbolic differentiation is implemented in a Python package called SymPy. We do not cover it here, as it is not directly relevant to deep learning.

Automatic Differentiation Fundamentals

The first key intuition behind automatic differentiation is that all functions of interest (which we intend to differentiate) can be expressed as compositions of elementary functions for which corresponding derivative functions are known. Composite functions, thus can be differentiated by applying the chain rule for derivatives. This intuition is also at the basis of symbolic differentiation.

The second key intuition behind automatic differentiation is that, rather than storing and manipulating intermediate symbolic forms of derivatives of primitive functions, one can simply evaluate them (for a specific set of input values) and thus address the issue of expressions well. Since intermediate symbolic forms are being evaluated, we do not have the burden of simplifying the expression. Note that this prevents us from getting a closed form mathematical expression of the derivate like the one symbolic differentiation gives us; what we get via automatic differentiation is the evaluation of the derivative for a given set of values.

The third key intuition behind automatic differentiation is that, because we are evaluating derivatives of primitive forms, we can deal with arbitrary computational procedures and not just closed form mathematical expressions. That is, our function can contain if-else statements, for-loops, or even recursion. The way automatic differentiation deals with any computational procedure is to treat a single evaluation of the procedure (for a given set of inputs) as a finite list of elementary function evaluations over the input variables to produce one or more output variables. While there might be control flow statements (if-else statements, for-loops, etc.), ultimately, there is a specific list of function evaluations that transform the given input to the output. Such a list/evaluation trace is referred to as a Wengert list.

CHAPTER 9 ■ AUTOMATIC DIFFERENTIATION

Let us set the stage for discussing automatic differentiation by introducing a simple function $f(x_1, x_2) = (x_1^2 + x_2^2)^{\frac{1}{2}}$. Figure 9-1 shows the computational graph for the function. Note that we also introduce some intermediate variables for convenience.

x_1

x_2

Square

Square

$v_1 = x_1^2$

$v_2 = x_2^2$

$$f(x_1, x_2) = (x_1^2 + x_2^2)^{\frac{1}{2}}$$

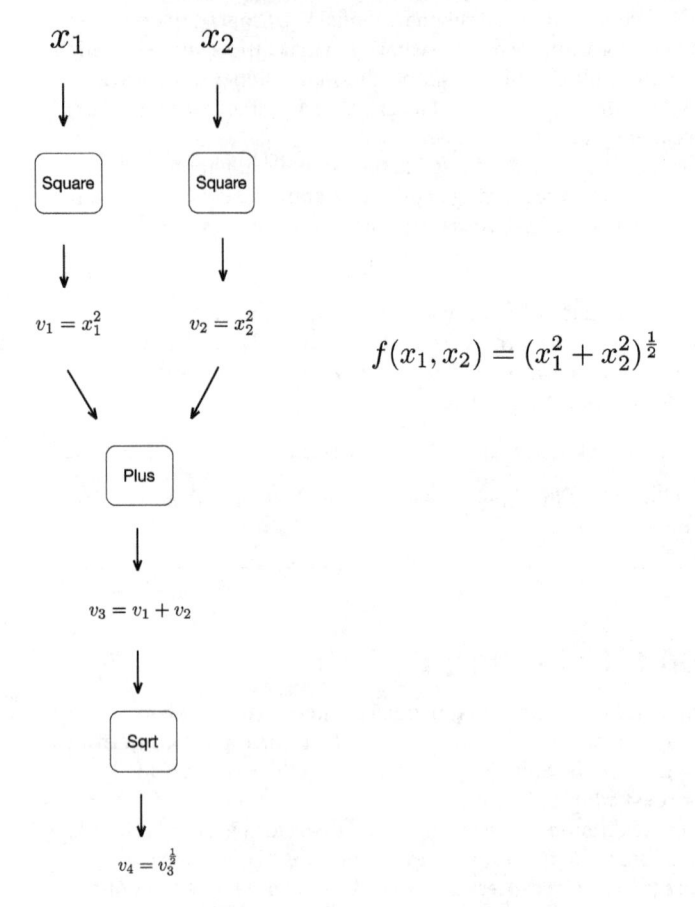

Plus

$v_3 = v_1 + v_2$

Sqrt

$v_4 = v_3^{\frac{1}{2}}$

Figure 9-1. *A simple function and its computational graph*

Forward/Tangent Linear Mode

The forward mode (also called tangent linear mode) of automatic differentiation associates each intermediate variable in the computational graph with a derivative. More formally, we have $\dot{v}_i = \frac{\partial v_i}{\partial x}$ for all values of *i* where $\dot{v}_i$ is the derivative of the intermediate variable v_i with respect to an input variable/other intermediate variable *x*. Figure 9-2 illustrates this for the example function we introduced earlier.

CHAPTER 9 ■ AUTOMATIC DIFFERENTIATION

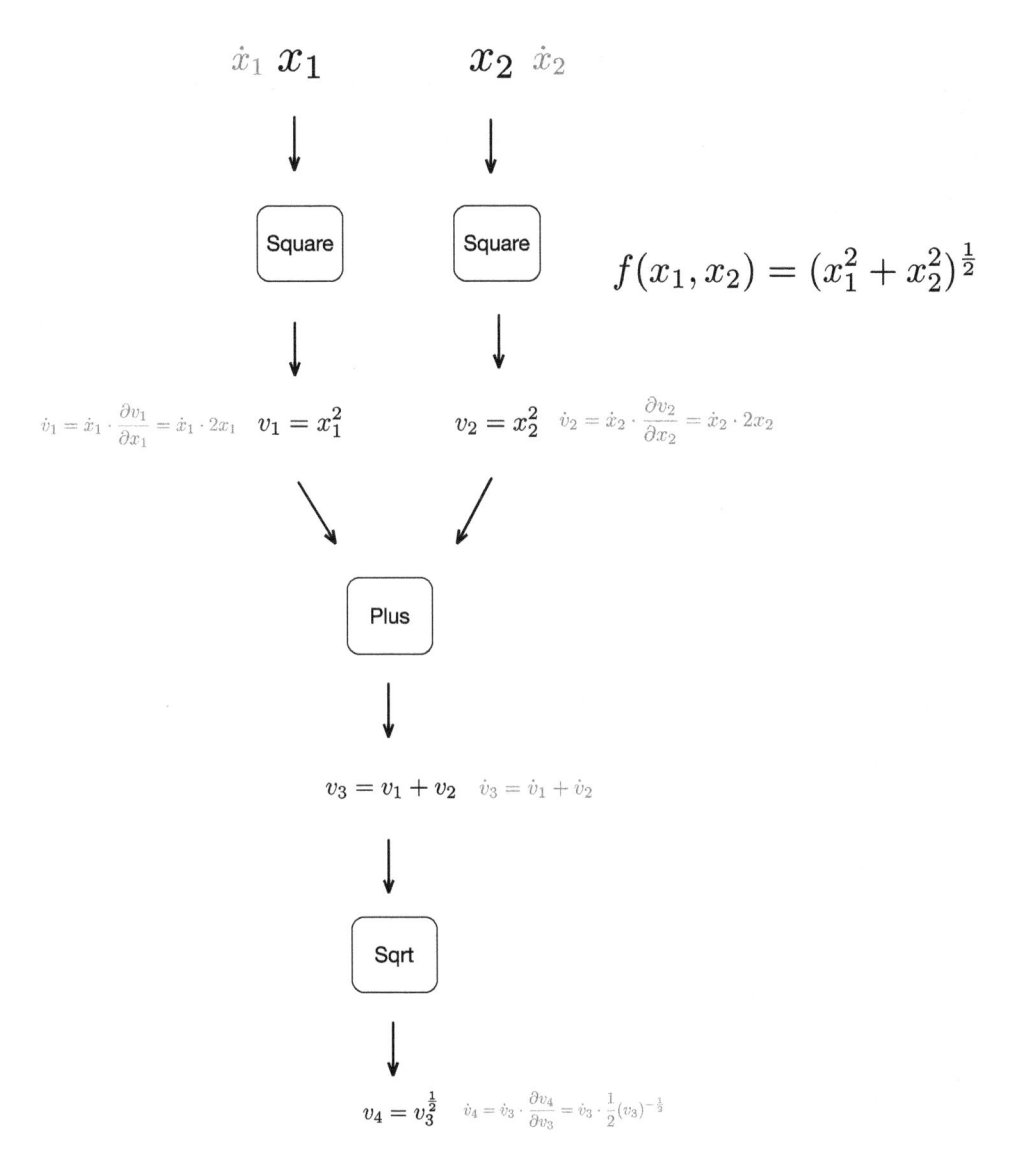

```
     ẋ₁ x₁              x₂ ẋ₂
      ↓                  ↓
   ┌──────┐           ┌──────┐
   │Square│           │Square│     f(x₁, x₂) = (x₁² + x₂²)^(1/2)
   └──────┘           └──────┘
      ↓                  ↓
```

$\dot{v}_1 = \dot{x}_1 \cdot \frac{\partial v_1}{\partial x_1} = \dot{x}_1 \cdot 2x_1$ $v_1 = x_1^2$ $v_2 = x_2^2$ $\dot{v}_2 = \dot{x}_2 \cdot \frac{\partial v_2}{\partial x_2} = \dot{x}_2 \cdot 2x_2$

```
         ↘          ↙
          ┌──────┐
          │ Plus │
          └──────┘
             ↓
```

$v_3 = v_1 + v_2$ $\dot{v}_3 = \dot{v}_1 + \dot{v}_2$

```
          ↓
       ┌──────┐
       │ Sqrt │
       └──────┘
          ↓
```

$v_4 = v_3^{\frac{1}{2}}$ $\dot{v}_4 = \dot{v}_3 \cdot \frac{\partial v_4}{\partial v_3} = \dot{v}_3 \cdot \frac{1}{2}(v_3)^{-\frac{1}{2}}$

Figure 9-2. *Associating every intermediate variable with a derivative in forward mode automatic differentation*

Note that there are a number of ways by which such a computational graph can be constructed and the derivatives for the intermediate variables can be associated to the nodes. This can be done explicitly by parsing the given function (to be differentiated) or implicitly by using operator overloading. For the purposes of this discussion it suffices to say that the given function can be decomposed into its elementary functions and, using the derivatives of the elementary functions and the chain rule, we can associate intermediate variables with their corresponding derivatives.

137

CHAPTER 9 ■ AUTOMATIC DIFFERENTIATION

Given such an augmented computational graph, we can evaluate the value of the (partial) derivative of the given function with respect to a particular variable (and a set of inputs) by evaluating the expressions associated with the augmented computational graph. For this evaluation, we have values for all the input variables and we set all the values of the derivatives of the input variables to 0, except for the variable for which we intend to evaluate the partial derivative, which we set to 1. Figures 9-3 and 9-4 illustrate such an evaluation of the computational graph.

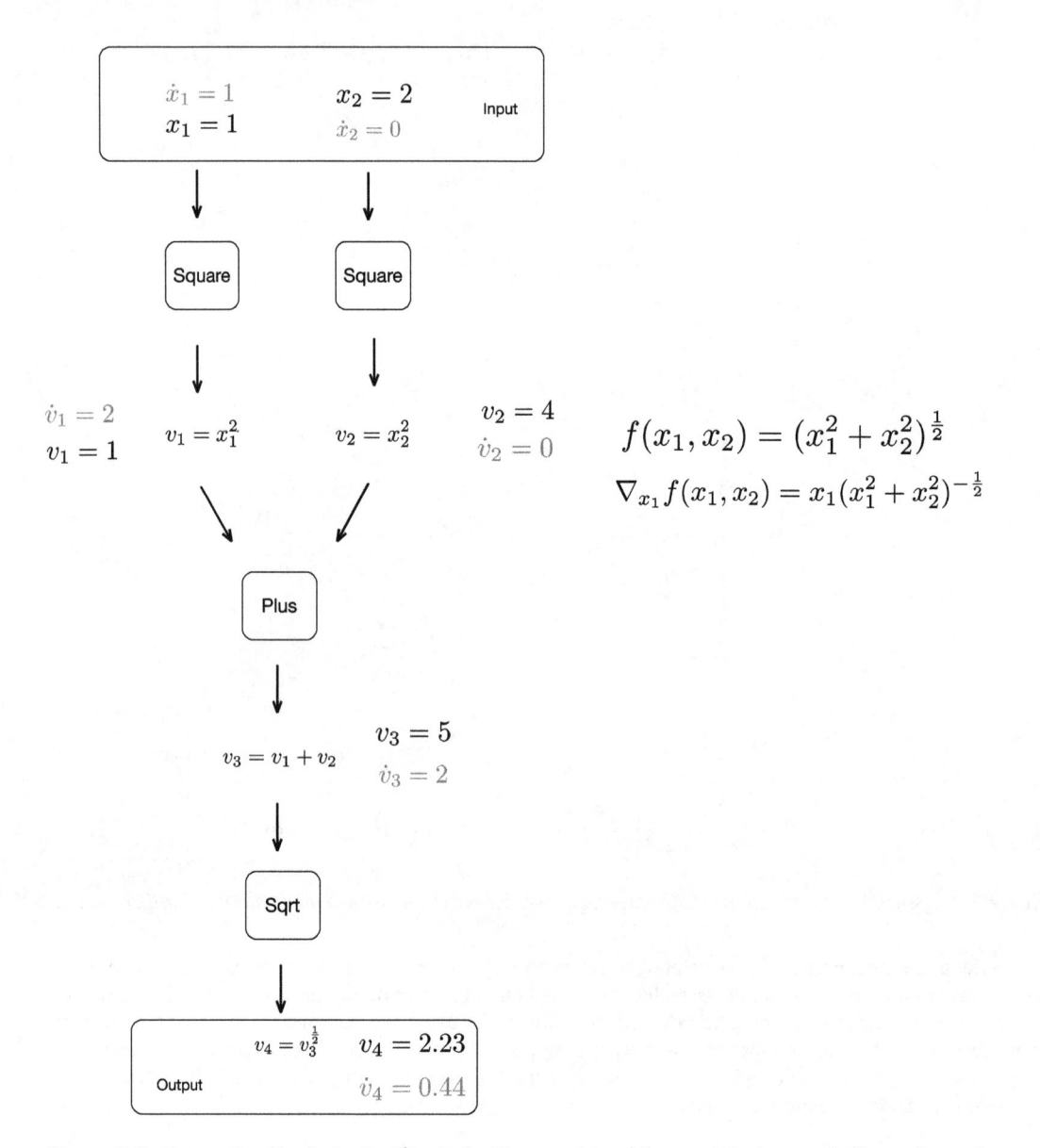

$$f(x_1, x_2) = (x_1^2 + x_2^2)^{\frac{1}{2}}$$

$$\nabla_{x_1} f(x_1, x_2) = x_1(x_1^2 + x_2^2)^{-\frac{1}{2}}$$

Figure 9-3. *Computing the derivative (partial with respect to x_1) for a particular set of values of x_1 and x_2*

[Input]
$$\dot{x}_1 = 0 \quad x_2 = 2$$
$$x_1 = 1 \quad \dot{x}_2 = 1$$

↓ ↓

Square Square

↓ ↓

$\dot{v}_1 = 0$ $v_1 = x_1^2$ $v_2 = x_2^2$ $v_2 = 4$
$v_1 = 1$ $\dot{v}_2 = 4$

$$f(x_1, x_2) = (x_1^2 + x_2^2)^{\frac{1}{2}}$$
$$\nabla_{x_1} f(x_1, x_2) = x_1(x_1^2 + x_2^2)^{-\frac{1}{2}}$$

Plus

↓

$v_3 = v_1 + v_2 \quad v_3 = 5$
$\dot{v}_3 = 4$

↓

Sqrt

↓

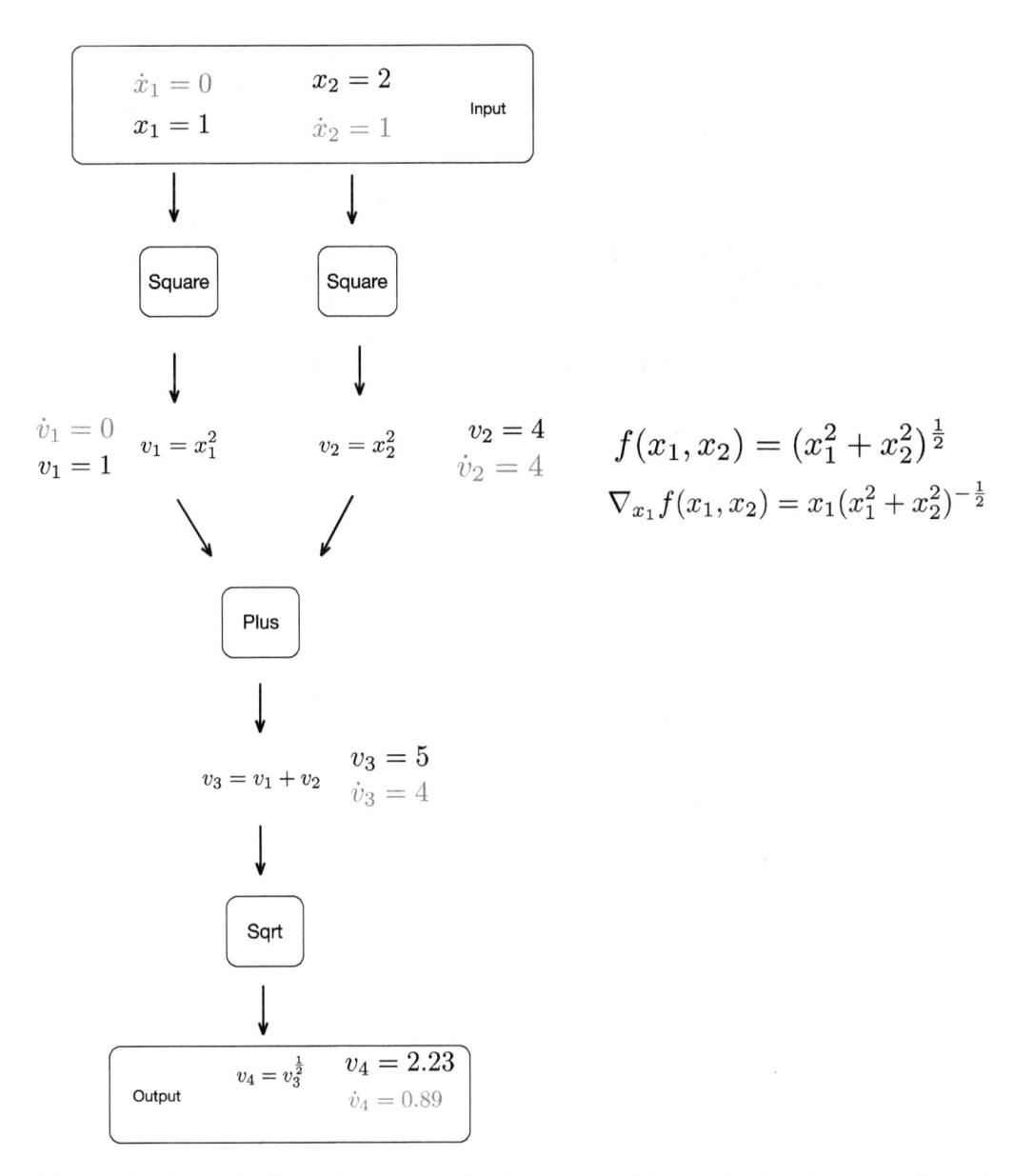

[Output] $v_4 = v_3^{\frac{1}{2}} \quad v_4 = 2.23$
$\dot{v}_4 = 0.89$

Figure 9-4. *Computing the derivative (partial with respect to x_2) for a particular set of values of x_1 and x_2*

CHAPTER 9 ■ AUTOMATIC DIFFERENTIATION

It must be noted that with forward mode automatic differentiation we need to perform one evaluation of the augmented computational graph for computing the partial derivative with respect to each input variable. It follows that for computing the gradient for a function with respect to n input variable we would require n evaluations. Thus, forward mode automatic differentiation is expensive when it comes to computing gradients for functions with a lot of input variables, which is a common case in deep learning where loss functions consist of many input variables and a single output variable.

It is also clear that forward mode automatic differentiation is a fairly straightforward application of the chain rule and can be implemented easily using operator overloading. Forward mode automatic differentiation is often implemented by the use of dual numbers, which are defined as a truncated Taylor series of the form $v + \dot{v}\epsilon$. Arithmetic on dual numbers can be defined using $\epsilon^2 = 0$ and treating a non-dual number as $v + 0\dot{v}$. Dual numbers, in a sense, carry the derivative with them throughout their lifetime. Thus, given that we have a complete implementation of dual numbers, the derivatives can simply be computed as a side/parallel effect of the operations on the dual component.

Reverse/Cotangent/Adjoint Linear Mode

The reverse mode (also called cotangent linear mode or adjoint mode) of automatic differentiation also associates each intermediate variable in the computational graph with a derivative computed backward from the output. This bears a striking resemblance to backpropagation. More formally, we have $\bar{v}_i = \frac{\partial y_i}{\partial v_i}$ for all values of i where $\bar{v}_i$ is the derivative of the output/intermediate variable y_i for all values of i. Figure 9-5 illustrates this for the example function we introduced earlier.

To evaluate the derivative, we first do a forward pass over the augmented computational graph as shown in Figure 9-6. This is followed by a reverse pass in which the derivatives are computed, which is illustrated in Figure 9-7.

Reverse mode automatic differentiation computes all the partial derivatives in a single forward pass and a single reverse pass and thus scales well with respect to functions with many input variables common to loss functions in deep learning.

CHAPTER 9 ■ AUTOMATIC DIFFERENTIATION

$\bar{x}_1 = \bar{v}_1 \cdot \frac{\partial v_1}{\partial x_1} = \bar{v}_1 \cdot 2x_1$ x_1 x_2 $\bar{x}_2 = \bar{v}_2 \cdot \frac{\partial v_2}{\partial x_2} = \bar{v}_2 \cdot 2x_2$

↓   ↓

[Square]   [Square] $f(x_1, x_2) = (x_1^2 + x_2^2)^{\frac{1}{2}}$

↓   ↓

$\bar{v}_1 = \bar{v}_3 \cdot \frac{\partial v_3}{\partial v_1} = \bar{v}_3 \cdot 1$ $v_1 = x_1^2$ $v_2 = x_2^2$ $\bar{v}_2 = \bar{v}_3 \cdot \frac{\partial v_3}{\partial v_2} = \bar{v}_3 \cdot 1$

↘   ↙

[Plus]

↓

$v_3 = v_1 + v_2$ $\bar{v}_3 = \bar{v}_4 \cdot \frac{\partial v_4}{\partial v_3} = \bar{v}_4 \cdot \frac{1}{2}(v_3)^{-\frac{1}{2}}$

↓

[Sqrt]

↓

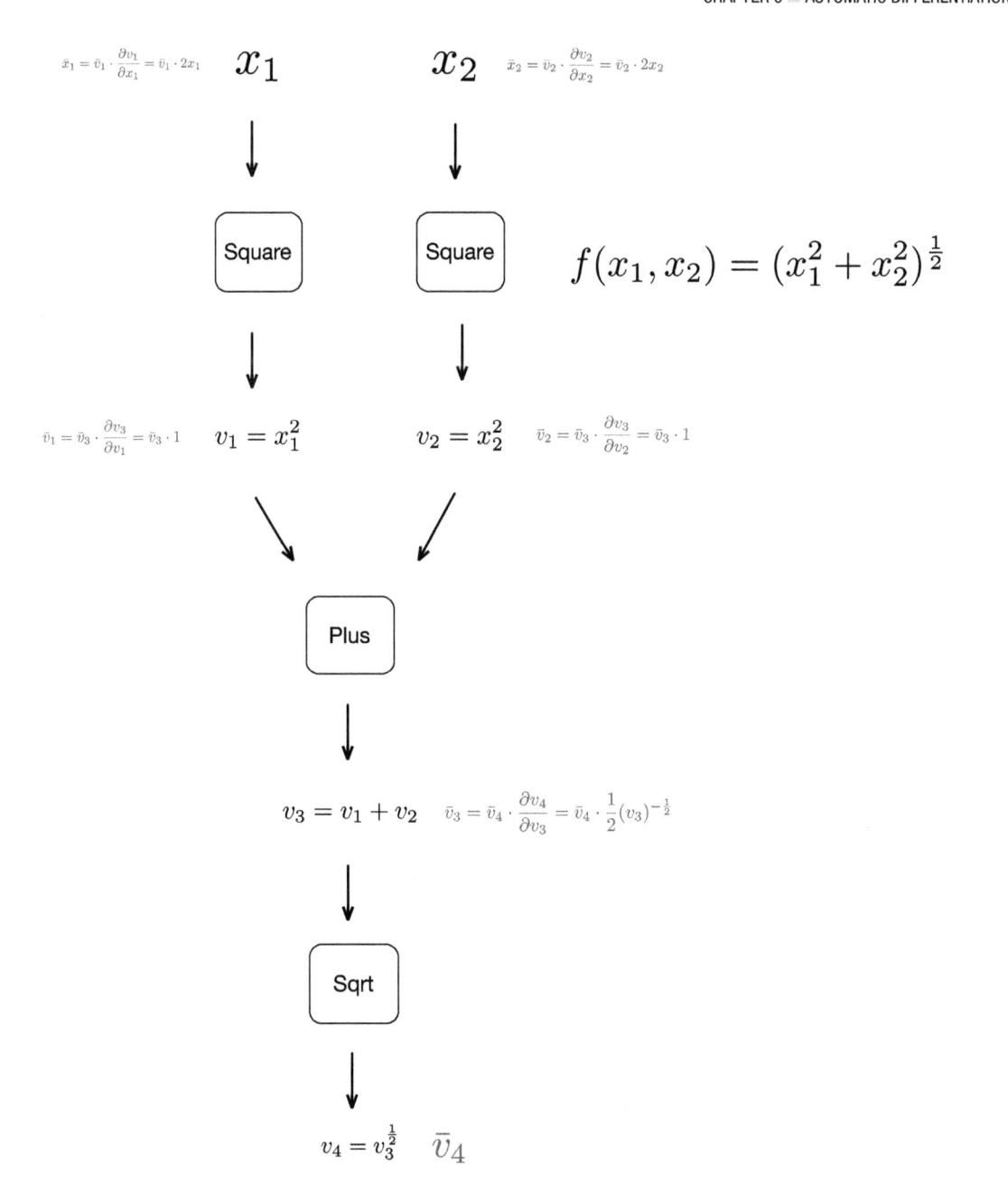

$v_4 = v_3^{\frac{1}{2}}$ $\bar{v}_4$

Figure 9-5. *Associating every intermediate variable with a derivative in reverse mode automatic differentiation*

CHAPTER 9 ■ AUTOMATIC DIFFERENTIATION

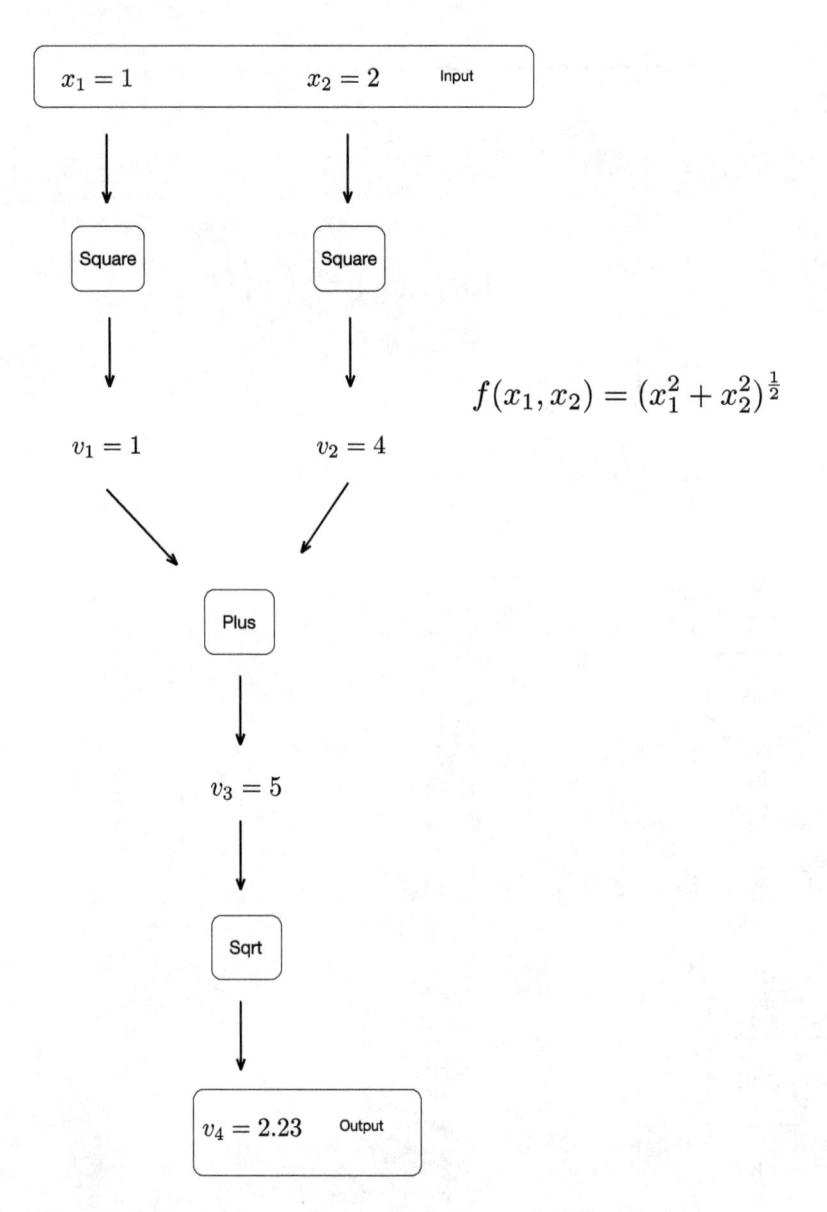

Figure 9-6. *Forward pass of reverse mode automatic differentiation*

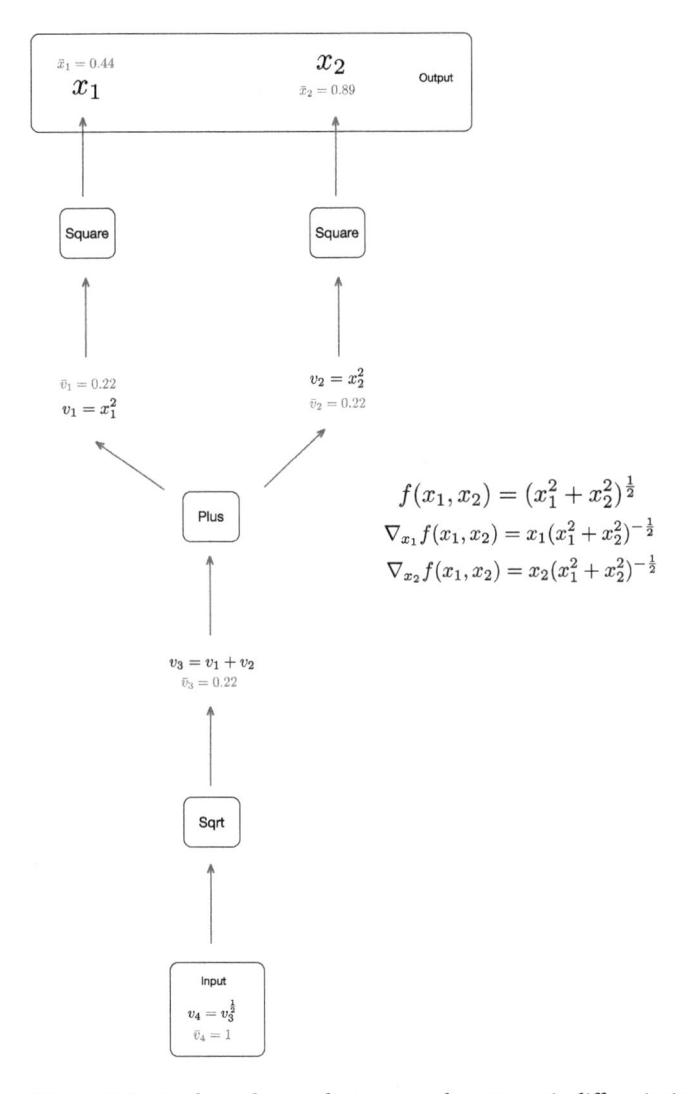

Figure 9-7. Backward pass of reverse mode automatic diffrentiation

Implementation of Automatic Differentiation

Let us now take a look at how Automatic Differentiation is commonly implemented. The three key approaches are using source code transformation and operator overloading (explicit or implicit dual number implementation).

Source Code Transformation

The source code transformation approach involves the user implementing the loss function in a regular programming language and then using an automatic differentiation tool to generate the corresponding gradient function. These two can then be compiled by the standard build tool chain to be used as part of a larger application. Refer to Figure 9-8.

CHAPTER 9 ■ AUTOMATIC DIFFERENTIATION

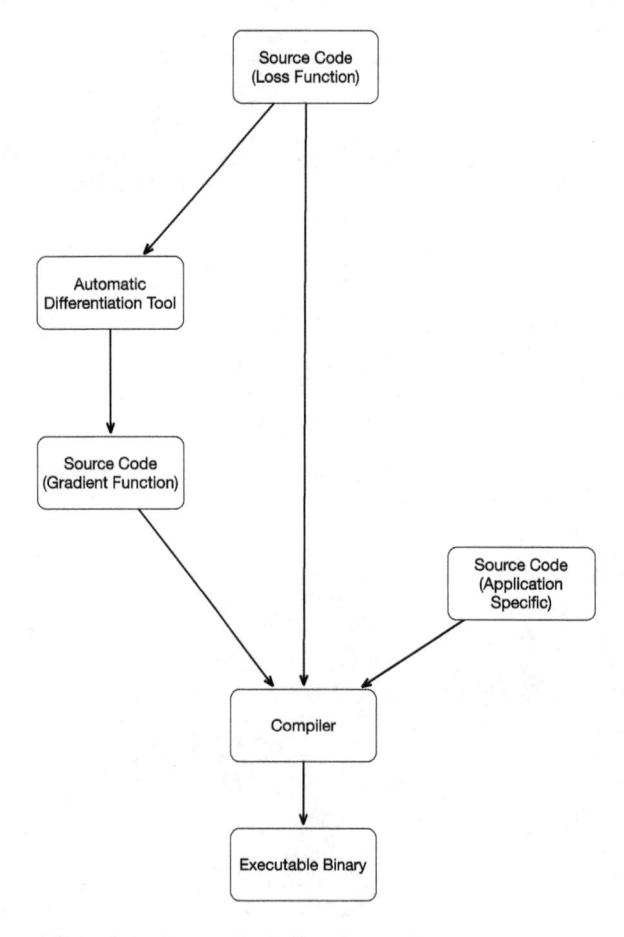

Figure 9-8. Source Code Transformation

Operator Overloading

The operator overloading approach basically is an explicit/implicit implementation of the dual number approach wherein the corresponding differentiation operation is implemented for every primitive operation of interest. Users implement their loss functions using the primitive operations and the computation of the gradients happen by the invocation of the overloaded method implementing the differentiation operation. Refer to Figure 9-9.

CHAPTER 9 ■ AUTOMATIC DIFFERENTIATION

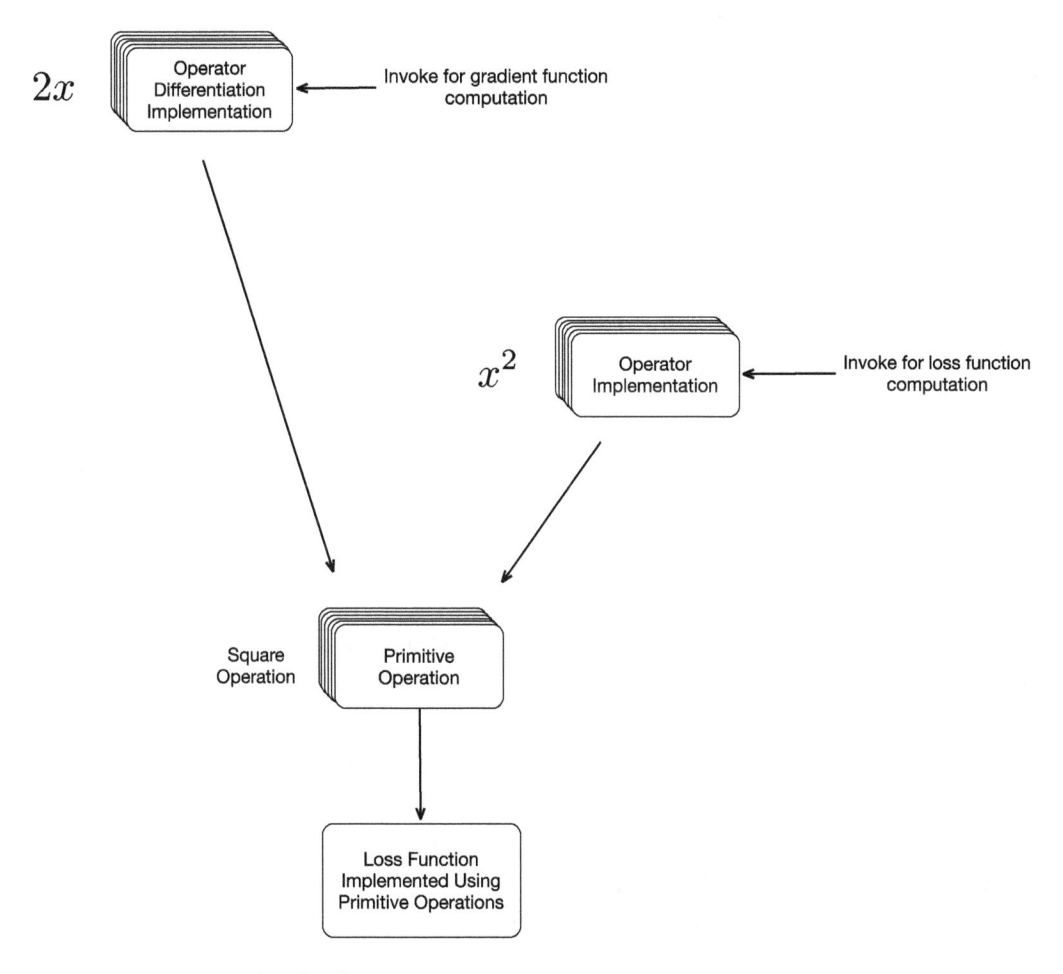

Figure 9-9. Operator Overloading

■ **Note** One key implementation detail surrounding the operator overloading approach is whether the operators in question are those already implemented in established library/core language or if the automatic differentiation tool provides its own operators. Autograd is an example an automatic differentiation tool that overloads the established Numpy Library whereas Theano provides its own operators for which corresponding differential operations are implemented.

Hands-on Automatic Differentiation with Autograd

We will now do a hands-on exercise with Automatic Differentiation using a Python package called Autograd. Autograd implements Reverse mode automatic differentiation and can compute derivatives for arbitrary Python and Numpy code.

Listing 9-1. Finding gradient for $f(x_1, x_2) = (x_1^2 + x_2^2)^{\frac{1}{2}}$

```
#Wrapper Around Numpy
import autograd.numpy as numpy

#Function to generate gradients
from autograd import grad

#Define the function
def f(x1, x2): return numpy.sqrt(x1 * x1 + x2 * x2)

#Compute the gradient w.r.t the first input variable x1
g_x1_f = grad(f,0)

#Compute the gradient w.r.t the second input variable x2
g_x2_f = grad(f,1)

#Evaluate and print the value of the function at x1=1, x2=2
print f(1,2)
#Produces 2.23

#Evaluate and print the value of the gradient w.r.t x1 at x1=1, x2=2
print g_x1_f(1,2)
#Produces 0.44

#Evaluate and print the value of the gradient w.r.t x2 at x1=1, x2=2
print g_x2_f(1,2)
#Produces 0.89
```

Let us get started by taking the function that we have used for discussion throughout this chapter, $f(x_1, x_2) = (x_1^2 + x_2^2)^{\frac{1}{2}}$, and finding the gradient. As will be apparent, Autograd makes this really easy. Listing 9-1 illustrates this.

Autograd provides a utility function to check the correctness of the computed gradients. Listing 9-2 illustrates this. It is a good idea to conduct such checks, especially when we are computing gradients for complicated loss functions involving control flow statements.

Listing 9-2. Checking the gradient for $f(x_1, x_2) = (x_1^2 + x_2^2)^{\frac{1}{2}}$

```
from autograd.util import quick_grad_check

#Define the function
def f(x1, x2): return numpy.sqrt(x1 * x1 + x2 * x2)

#Computes and checks the gradient for the given values

quick_grad_check(f,1.0,extra_args=[2.0])

#Output
#
#Checking gradient of <function f at 0x10504bed8> at 1.0
#Gradient projection OK
#(numeric grad: 0.447213595409, analytic grad: 0.4472135955)
```

CHAPTER 9 ■ AUTOMATIC DIFFERENTIATION

Listing 9-3. Logistic Regression using Autograd

```
import pylab
import sklearn.datasets
import autograd.numpy as np
from autograd import grad

# Generate the data
train_X, train_y = sklearn.datasets.make_moons(500, noise=0.1)

# Define the activation, prediction and loss functions for Logistic Regression
def activation(x):
    return 0.5*(np.tanh(x) + 1)

def predict(weights, inputs):
    return activation(np.dot(inputs, weights))

def loss(weights):
    preds = predict(weights, train_X)
    label_probabilities = preds * train_y + (1 - preds) * (1 - train_y)
    return -np.sum(np.log(label_probabilities))

# Compute the gradient of the loss function
gradient_loss = grad(loss)

# Set the initial weights
weights = np.array([1.0, 1.0])

# Steepest Descent
loss_values = []
learning_rate = 0.001
for i in range(100):
    loss_values.append(loss(weights))
    step = gradient_loss(weights)
    weights -= step * learning_rate

# Plot the decision boundary
x_min, x_max = train_X[:, 0].min() - 0.5, train_X[:, 0].max() + 0.5
y_min, y_max = train_X[:, 1].min() - 0.5, train_X[:, 1].max() + 0.5
x_mesh, y_mesh = np.meshgrid(np.arange(x_min, x_max, 0.01), np.arange(y_min, y_max, 0.01))
Z = predict(weights, np.c_[x_mesh.ravel(), y_mesh.ravel()])
Z = Z.reshape(x_mesh.shape)
cs = pylab.contourf(x_mesh, y_mesh, Z, cmap=pylab.cm.Spectral)
pylab.scatter(train_X[:, 0], train_X[:, 1], c=train_y, cmap=pylab.cm.Spectral)
pylab.colorbar(cs)

# Plot the loss over each step
pylab.figure()
pylab.plot(loss_values)
pylab.xlabel("Steps")
pylab.ylabel("Loss")
pylab.show()
```

CHAPTER 9 ■ AUTOMATIC DIFFERENTIATION

Let us now compute gradient for something a bit more complicated, the loss function for logistic regression. Let's also fit the model using steepest descent. Listing 9-1 shows the code for the same, and Figures 9-10 and 9-11 show the decision boundary and the loss over the steepest descent steps.

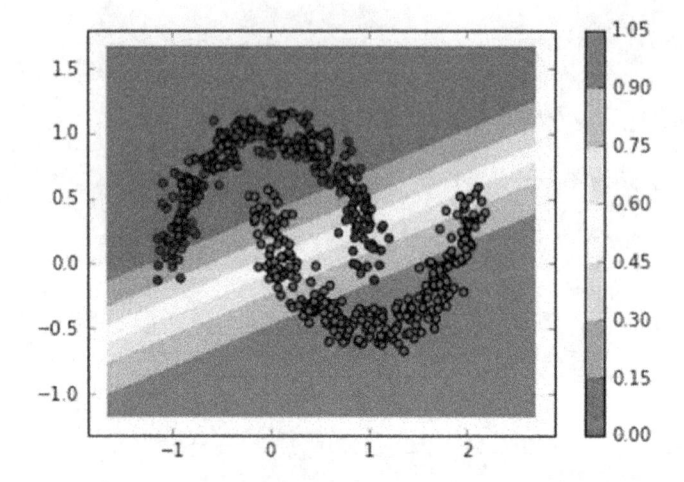

Figure 9-10. *Decision boundary and training data for Logistic Regression*

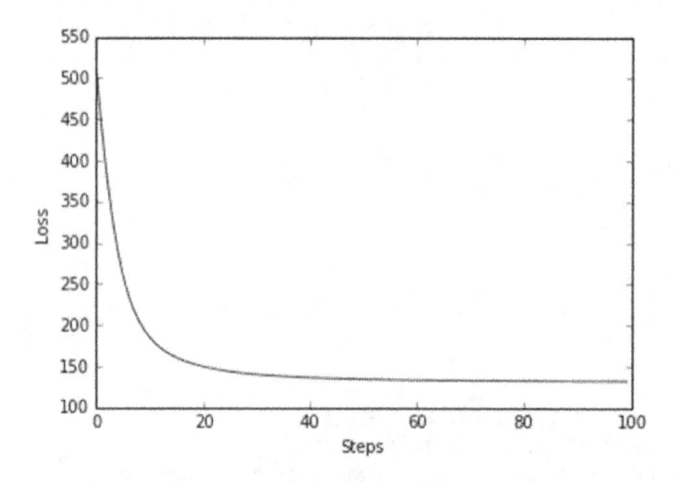

Figure 9-11. *Loss over steps for Logistic Regression*

Summary

In this chapter we covered the basics of Automatic Differentiation, which is commonly referred to as backpropagation in the Neural Network Community. The key take-away for the reader in this chapter is that automatic differentiation enables the computation of gradients for arbitrarily complex loss functions and is one of the key enabling technologies for Deep Learning. The reader should also internalize the concepts of automatic differentiation and how it is different from both symbolic and numerical differentiation.

CHAPTER 10

Introduction to GPUs

This chapter introduces the reader to GPU (Graphics Processing Unit)-based computation, which has played and will continue to play a big role in the successful application of Deep Learning in a variety of application domains. Typically, a Deep Learning practitioner is working with high-level libraries like Keras or Theano, which automatically translates the computation to be performed seamlessly to CPU or GPU. While in a majority of the cases, a practitioner of Deep Learning is not required to understand the internal workings of the GPU (as many high-level libraries are available), it is essential to be aware of the basics.

The essence of GPU-based computation is the notion of Single Instruction, Multiple Data (SIMD), wherein the same computation is being performed in parallel (over may cores) on multiple data points. This computational paradigm is very suitable for compute heavy linear algebra operations. As we have seen in earlier chapters, the core computation involved in training deep learning models is the computation of gradients and updating the parameters based on these gradients. At the heart of this lie basic linear algebraic operations (dot products, vector matrix multiplications, etc.) and this GPU-based computation is quite suitable for training (and making predictions) using the same.

Let us start by describing the key elements of such a GPU-based computation. Figure 10-1 schematically illustrates these key elements.

CHAPTER 10 ■ INTRODUCTION TO GPUS

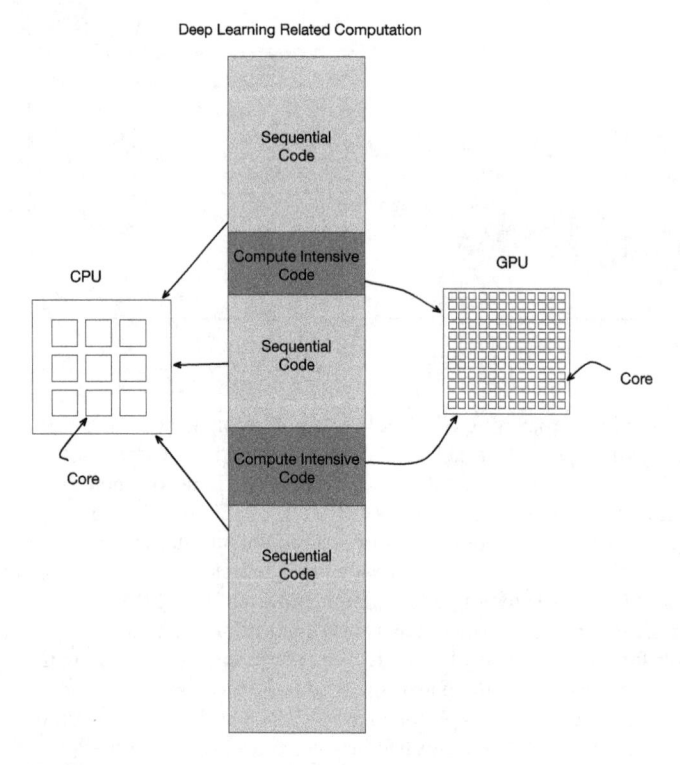

Figure 10-1. GPU-based Computation

The following points are to be noted:

1. Deep learning-related computation involves some code to be executed sequentially and some compute-intensive code which can be parallelized.

2. Typically, the sequential code involves loading the data from disk, etc., which is handled by the CPU.

3. The computationally heavy code typically involves computing the gradients and updating the parameters. Data for this computation is first transferred to the GPU memory, and this computation then happens on the GPU.

4. Next, the results are brought back to the main memory for further sequential processing.

5. There might be multiple blocks of such computationally heavy code interlaced with sequential code.

■ **Note** There are two main ecosystems built around GPUs: one is CUDA, which is specific to Nvidia, and OpenCL, which is vendor-neutral. We will be covering concepts around GPU computation in the context of OpenCL.

Let us start by looking at the overall programming model for GPU-based computation as described by OpenCL. OpenCL is a vendor neural framework for heterogeneous computation involving CPUs, GPUs, DSPs (Digital Signal Processors), and FPGAs (Field Programmable Gate Arrays), etc. Figure 10-2 illustrates the physical view of the system.

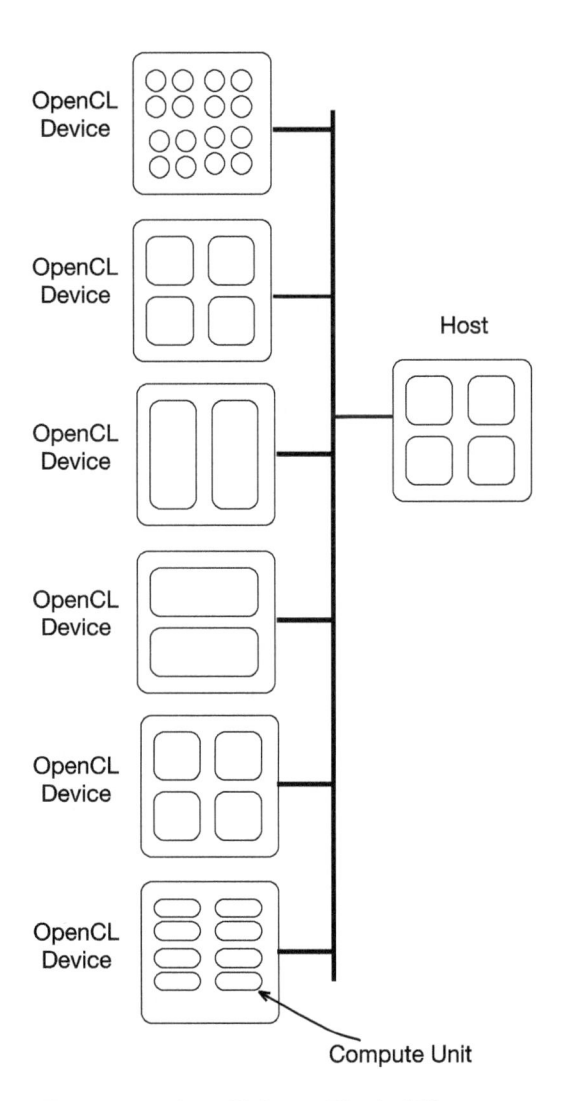

Figure 10-2. OpenCL System Physical View

The following points are to be noted:

1. The overall system consists of the Host and a number of OpenCL devices.
2. The host refers to the CPU running the OS, which can communicate with a number of OpenCL devices.
3. OpenCL devices are heterogeneous, as in, different. They might be involving CPUs, GPUs, DSPs (Digital Signal Processors), and FPGAs (Field Programmable Gate Arrays), etc.
4. OpenCL devices contain one or more compute units.

Let's now look at the logical view of an OpenCL system illustrated in Figure 10-3.

CHAPTER 10 ▪ INTRODUCTION TO GPUS

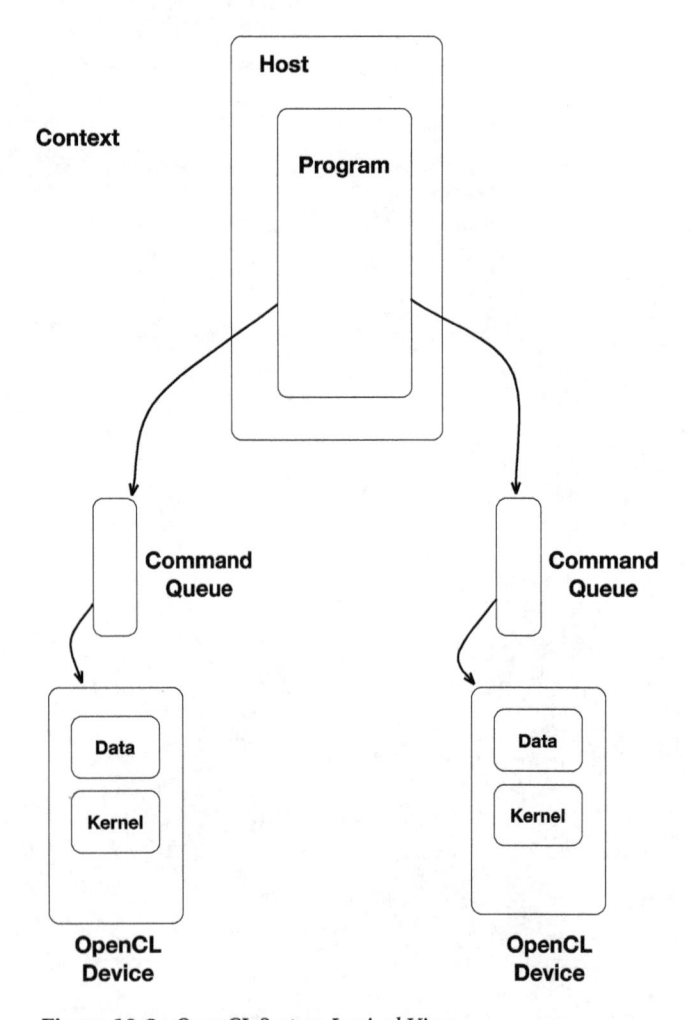

Figure 10-3. *OpenCL System Logical View*

The following points are to be noted:

1. An OpenCL program runs on the host system.
2. The OpenCL program communicates with OpenCL devices using command queues. Each OpenCL device has a separate command queue.
3. Each OpenCL device houses data in its memory, sent to it by the program running on the host.
4. Each OpenCL device runs code sent to it by the host program, referred to as the kernel.
5. The host program, the command queues, the data, and the kernels together constitute an execution context.
6. The execution context essentially is the logical envelopment of the heterogeneous computation. The host program orchestrates this computation by sending data and code to be executed to the OpenCL devices and getting the results.

CHAPTER 10 ■ INTRODUCTION TO GPUS

Let's now take a look at the logical memory layout on an OpenCL device. Figure 10-4 illustrates the same.

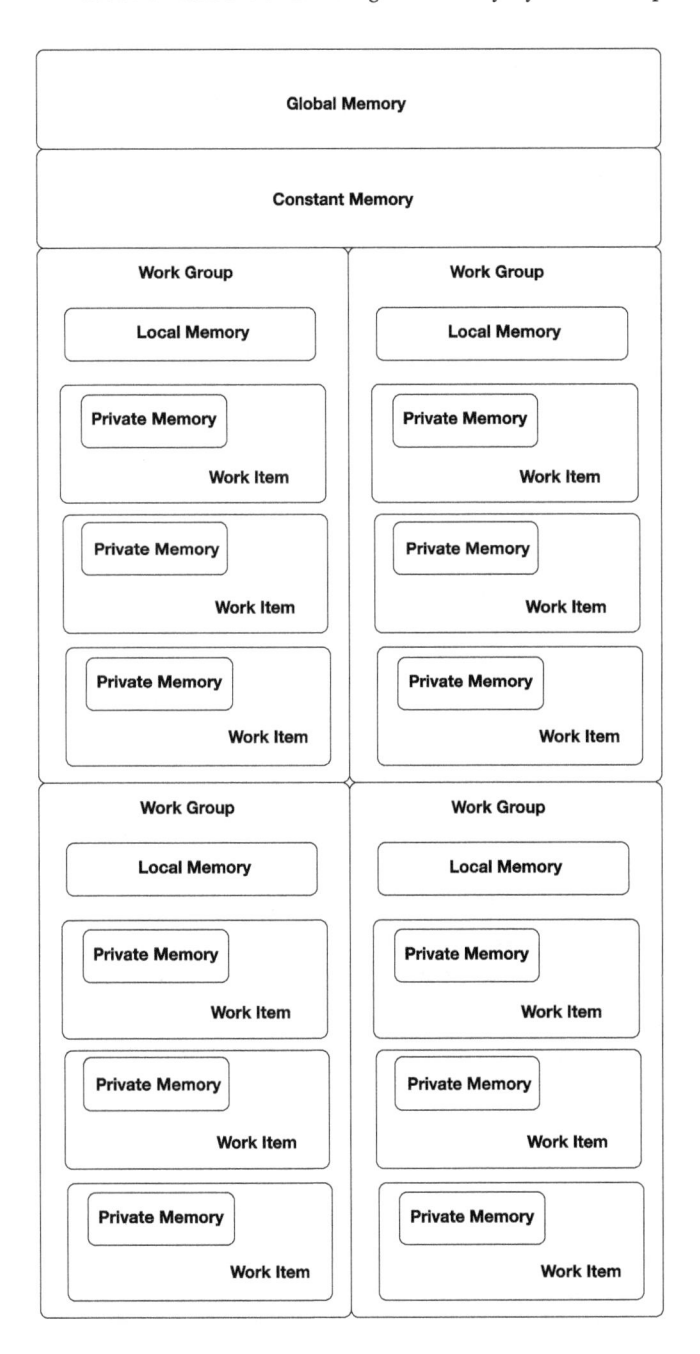

Figure 10-4. Device Memory

The following points are to be noted:

1. An OpenCL device has a global memory, which is accessible to the host program as well as all the running kernels on the device.

153

CHAPTER 10 ■ INTRODUCTION TO GPUS

2. An OpenCL device has a constant memory, which is just like global memory but it is read-only for an executing kernel.

3. A Work Item is the logical unit of parallelism and it has its own private memory. Only the kernel code corresponding to this particular work item is aware of this memory.

4. A Work Group is the logical unit of synchronization and it contains a number of Work Items. Note that any synchronization can only be done within a Work Group.

5. A Work group has its own Local Memory that can only be accessed from within the Work Group.

Let us now take a look at the programming model with respect to an OpenCL Device (Figure 10-5).

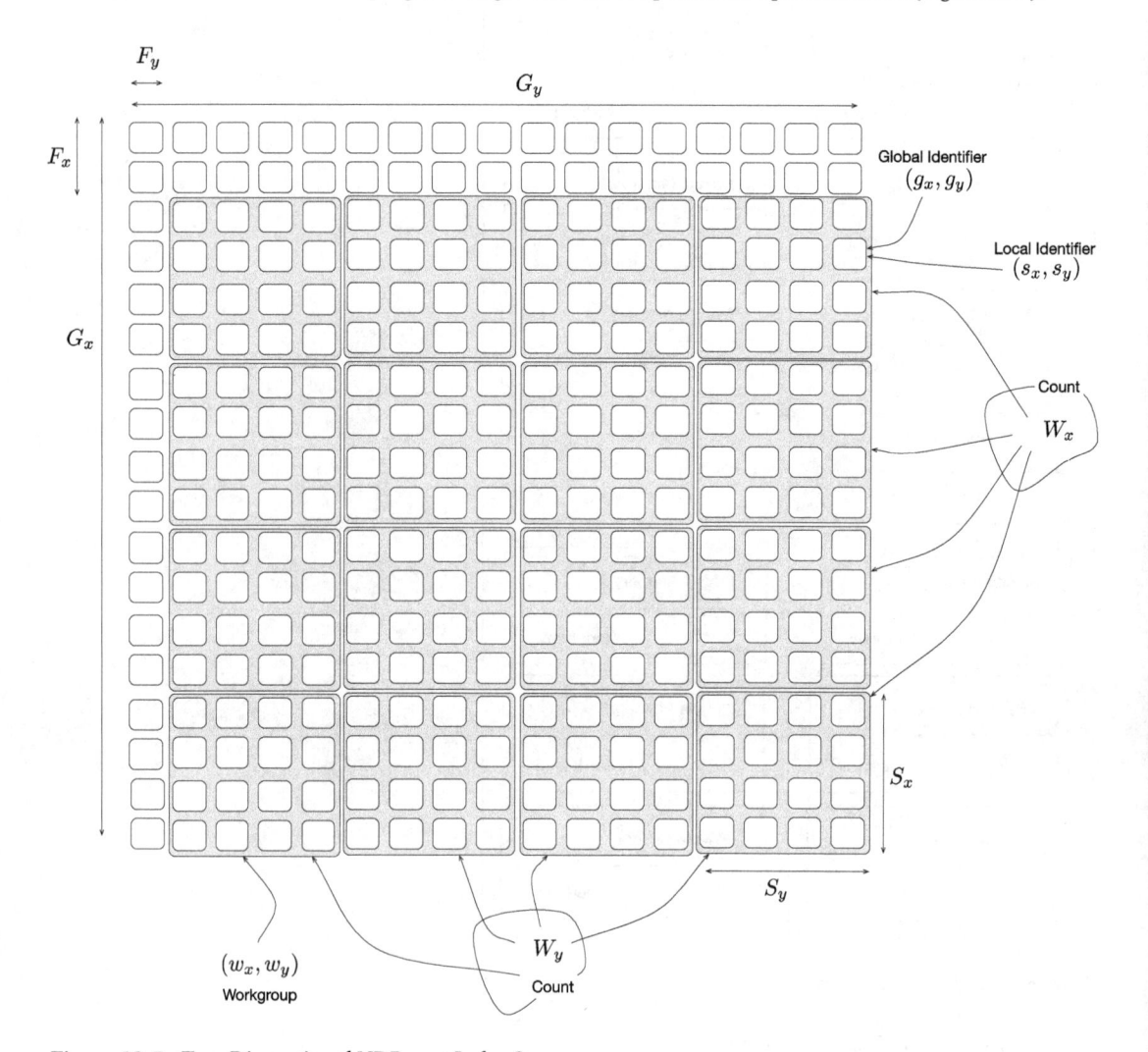

Figure 10-5. Two-Dimensional NDRange Index Space

The following points are to be noted:

1. An OpenCL kernel is launched to perform work on data already transferred to the device memory. While launching, the number of work groups and the numbers of work items in each work group is logically specified.

2. The kernel is invoked in parallel for each work item in a work group. Work groups execute in no particular order and a kernel can find out the current work item identifier and work group identifier.

3. Synchronization can happen only within a work group.

4. A work item identifier can be 1-, 2-, or 3- dimensional (NDRange). This basically makes it easy to write kernels for 1-D (time series), 2-D (images), and 3-D (volumes) data sets.

Let us now introduce some notation that will allow us to describe the indexing. We will assume the indexing is 2-D, but the same reasoning applies to 1-D or 3-D data. We denote by (G_x, G_y) the global indexing space. Let us now look at how this global indexing space gets broken into work groups and work items. For convenience, we define offsets (F_x, F_y) which define the portion of the indexing that is not broken into work items and work groups. Let (S_x, S_y) define the size of the work group and (W_x, W_y) define the number of work groups. Along similar lines, let (g_x, g_y) denote the global identifiers, (s_x, s_y) denote the local identifiers, and let (w_x, w_y) denote the work group identifiers. Then, the relationship between local and global identifiers is described as $(g_x, g_y) = (w_x S_x + s_x + F_x, w_y S_y + s_y + F_y)$.

Writing a kernel for a given computation basically involves leveraging this identifier mechanism and the parallel invocations of the kernels over work items and work groups to perform the task at hand. Listings 10-2 and 10-3 illustrate this for vector addition and matrix multiplication, respectively. Listing 10-1 simply prints out the details of the OpenCL system that the reader can use to determine the details of their system.

Listing 10-1. Getting Information on GPUs

```
import pyopencl as cl

print "OpenCL Platforms and Devices"
for platform in cl.get_platforms():
    print "Platform Name: ", platform.name
    print "Platform Vendor", platform.vendor
    print "Platform Version:", platform.version
    print "Platform Profile:", platform.profile
    for device in platform.get_devices():
        print "\n"
        print "\tDevice Name ", device.name
        print "\tDevice Type ",  cl.device_type.to_string(device.type)
        print "\tDevice Max Clock Speed ", "{0} Mhz".format(device.max_clock_frequency)
        print "\tDevice Compute Units ",  "{0}".format(device.max_compute_units)
        print "\tDevice Local Memory ",   "{0:.0f} KB".format(device.local_mem_size/1024.0)
        print "\tDevice Constant Memory ", "{0:.0f} KB".format(device.max_constant_buffer_size/1024.0)
        print "\tDevice Global Memory " "{0:.0f} GB".format(device.global_mem_size/(1024*1024*1024.0))

# OpenCL Platforms and Devices
# Platform Name:  Apple
# Platform Vendor Apple
```

CHAPTER 10 ■ INTRODUCTION TO GPUS

```
# Platform Version: OpenCL 1.2 (Nov 18 2015 20:45:47)
# Platform Profile: FULL_PROFILE
#
#
#       Device Name   Intel(R) Core(TM) i7-4770HQ CPU @ 2.20GHz
#       Device Type   CPU
#       Device Max Clock Speed   2200 Mhz
#       Device Compute Units  8
#       Device Local Memory   32 KB
#       Device Constant Memory   64 KB
#       Device Global Memory  16 GB
#
#
#       Device Name   Iris Pro
#       Device Type   GPU
#       Device Max Clock Speed   1200 Mhz
#       Device Compute Units  40
#       Device Local Memory   64 KB
#       Device Constant Memory   64 KB
#       Device Global Memory  2 GB
```

Listing 10-2. Vector Addition

```
import numpy as np
import pyopencl as cl
import time

vector1 = np.random.random(5000000).astype(np.float32)
vector2 = np.random.random(5000000).astype(np.float32)

cl_context = cl.create_some_context()
queue = cl.CommandQueue(cl_context)
mf = cl.mem_flags
vector1_in_gpu = cl.Buffer(cl_context, mf.READ_ONLY | mf.COPY_HOST_PTR, hostbuf=vector1)
vector2_in_gpu = cl.Buffer(cl_context, mf.READ_ONLY | mf.COPY_HOST_PTR, hostbuf=vector2)
result_in_gpu = cl.Buffer(cl_context, mf.WRITE_ONLY, vector1.nbytes)

cl_program = cl.Program(cl_context, """
__kernel void sum(
    __global const float *vector1, __global const float *vector2, __global float *result)
{
  int i = get_global_id(0);
  result[i] = vector1[i] + vector2[i];
}
""").build()

t0 = time.time()
cl_program.sum(queue, vector1.shape, None, vector1_in_gpu, vector2_in_gpu, result_in_gpu)
t1 = time.time()
gpu_time = t1 - t0
print "GPU Time", gpu_time
```

156

CHAPTER 10 ■ INTRODUCTION TO GPUS

```python
result_in_numpy = np.empty_like(vector1)
cl.enqueue_copy(queue, result_in_numpy, result_in_gpu)

t0 = time.time()
cpu_result = vector1 + vector2
t1 = time.time()
cpu_time = t1 - t0
print "CPU Time", cpu_time

print "Norm of Difference", np.linalg.norm(result_in_numpy - cpu_result)

# GPU Time 0.00202608108521
# CPU Time 0.00995397567749
# Norm of Difference 0.0
```

Listing 10-3. Matrix Multiplication

```python
import numpy as np
import pyopencl as cl
import time

matrix1 = np.random.random((500,500)).astype(np.float32)
matrix2 = np.random.random((500,500)).astype(np.float32)

cl_context = cl.create_some_context()
queue = cl.CommandQueue(cl_context)
mf = cl.mem_flags
matrix1_in_gpu = cl.Buffer(cl_context, mf.READ_ONLY | mf.COPY_HOST_PTR, hostbuf=matrix1)
matrix2_in_gpu = cl.Buffer(cl_context, mf.READ_ONLY | mf.COPY_HOST_PTR, hostbuf=matrix2)
result_in_gpu = cl.Buffer(cl_context, mf.WRITE_ONLY, matrix1.nbytes)

cl_program = cl.Program(cl_context, """
__kernel void product(
    int size, __global const float *matrix1, __global const float *matrix2, __global float *result)
{
    int i = get_global_id(0);
    int j = get_global_id(1);
    result[i + size * j] = 0;
    for (int k = 0; k < size; k++)
    {
        result[i + size * j] += matrix1[k + size * i] * matrix2[j + size * k];
    }
}
""").build()

t0 = time.time()
cl_program.product(queue, matrix1.shape, None, np.int32(len(matrix1)), matrix1_in_gpu,
matrix2_in_gpu, result_in_gpu)
t1 = time.time()
gpu_time = t1 - t0
print "GPU Time", gpu_time
```

```
result_in_numpy = np.empty_like(matrix1)
cl.enqueue_copy(queue, result_in_numpy, result_in_gpu)

t0 = time.time()
cpu_result = np.dot(matrix1, matrix2)
t1 = time.time()
cpu_time = t1 - t0
print "CPU Time", cpu_time

print "Norm of Difference", np.linalg.norm(result_in_numpy - cpu_result.T)

# GPU Time 0.00202608108521
# CPU Time 0.00995397567749
# Norm of Difference 0.0
```

Summary

In this chapter we have introduced the reader to GPU-based computation, which is one of the key enabling technologies for Deep Learning.

One key point to note is that, in this chapter, we have covered the basics of GPU computation using OpenCL, which is vendor-neutral. The concepts apply with minor variation to other vendor-specific GPU computation libraries like CUDA, which is both older and popular as compared to OpenCL. The reader is advised to try out the examples in the source code listings in the chapter following, while reading up on the documentation of CUDA, which would be much easier to follow given that the reader has internalized the foundations. Libraries like cuDNN, which is a CUDA-based library for deep learning, is recommended further reading. It must be noted, however, that in many cases, when it comes to applying Deep Learning to a real-world problem, it suffices to use high-level libraries like Theano and Keras, which generate GPU code.

The second key point to note is the importance of GPU-based computation for Deep Learning. The single instruction, multiple data paradigm (SIMD) is ideal for Deep Learning, as most of computation with respect to deep learning boils down to stochastic gradient descent (SGD). At the heart of SGD we have the computation of gradients, which are essentially linear algebraic (vector/matrix) operations. As data sets and the sizes of the parameters grow, it becomes essential to perform SGD in a scalable way, and GPUs currently are the best suited computational paradigm.

CHAPTER 11

Introduction to Tensorflow

In this chapter we will cover Tensorflow which allows users to define mathematical functions via computational graphs and to compute their gradients. Tensorflow is conceptually similar to Theano, and Keras uses both of them as back ends.

Tensorflow supports training of large models in a multiple Graphical Processing Unit (GPU), distributed setting and while the project is not as mature as Theano, it has strong backing from industry leaders such as Google and hence should be in the toolkit of anyone working on deep learning. Another important characteristic of Tensorflow is that it provides very good facilities to view computational graphs and other metrics/summaries while training a model via a tool called Tensorboard. This comes quite in handy while building, training, and debugging models.

The landscape of tools/libraries in deep learning has evolved rapidly over the recent past and it's important to develop an understanding of where Tensorflow fits within this landscape. At an abstract perspective deep learning frameworks allow a user to define networks either via a config (like Caffe) or programmatically like Theano, Tensorflow, or Torch. Furthermore, the programming language exposed to define networks might vary, like Python in the case of Theano and Tensorflow or Lua in the case of Torch. An additional variation on them is whether the framework provides define-compile-execute semantics or dynamic semantics (as in the case of PyTorch). Tensorflow as a framework provides for a programmatic definition of the network in Python with define-compile-execute semantics. We will be covering the differences between define-compile-execute semantics and dynamic semantics in Chapter 12.

At its essence, Tensorflow allows users to define mathematical functions on tensors (hence the name) using computational graphs and to compute their gradients. A tensor is a multidimensional array of numbers, simply a conceptual extension of matrix/vector to an arbitrary number of dimensions. From a capabilities perspective Tensorflow has the capabilities of Numpy on GPU with automatic differentiation.

The overall flow of using Tensorflow is as follows:

1. Define the network/model using mathematical expressions which define a computational graph.

2. Use the automatic differentiation capabilities of Tensorflow to compute the gradients.

3. Use Stochastic Gradient Descent (or variants) to fit the model.

CHAPTER 11 ■ INTRODUCTION TO TENSORFLOW

Computational graphs defined in Tensorflow run in sessions. Let us start with a simple example in Tensorflow (refer to Listing 11-1 for the source code and Figure 11-1 for the computational graph). The following points are to be noted:

1. Expressions can be defined using predefined constants.

2. Each constant needs to be given a name (in addition to the variable name) to get a properly annotated graph in Tensorboard.

3. The computational graph defined as a result of the mathematical function needs to run in a session.

4. A summary writer object needs to be created to send data over to Tensorboard.

5. We can use the add_graph method to pass on the computational graph to Tensorboard for visualization.

6. Defining the expression is distinct from executing it (using session.run).

Listing 11-1. Computational Graph with Scalar Constants

```
import tensorflow as tf

a = tf.constant(1.0, name='a')
b = tf.constant(2.0, name='b')
c = tf.constant(3.0, name='c')
d = tf.constant(4.0, name='d')
e = tf.constant(5.0, name='e')
f = ((a - b + c) * d )/e

sess = tf.Session()
writer = tf.summary.FileWriter("./temp")
writer.add_graph(sess.graph)

print "Expected: ((1 - 2 + 3) * 4)/5.0 = ", ((1 - 2 + 3) * 4)/5.0
result = sess.run(f)
print "Via Tensorflow: ((1 - 2 + 3) * 4)/5.0 = ", result

# Expected: ((1 - 2 + 3) * 4)/5.0 =  1.6
# Via Tensorflow: ((1 - 2 + 3) * 4)/5.0 =  1.6
```

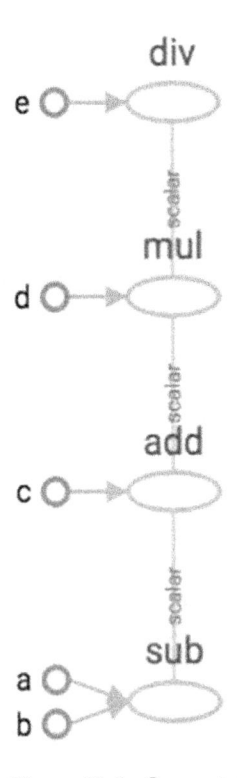

Figure 11-1. Computational graph with scalar constants

Let us now look at the important concept of placeholder. A placeholder in Tensorflow is a variable whose value is defined at runtime by the user (refer to Listing 11-2 for the source code and Figure 11-2 for the computational graph). The following points are to be noted:

1. The data type of the placeholder is defined at declaration time.
2. A name needs to be provided to placeholders for them to be properly annotated in the computational graph.
3. Expressions can be defined with placeholders similar to constants.
4. The values of placeholders are provided when a computational graph corresponding to an expression is run (using session.run) by defining them via a dictionary called deed_dict.

CHAPTER 11 ■ INTRODUCTION TO TENSORFLOW

Listing 11-2. Computational Graph with Scalar Placeholders

```
import tensorflow as tf

a = tf.placeholder(tf.float32, name='a')
b = tf.placeholder(tf.float32, name='b')
c = tf.placeholder(tf.float32, name='c')
d = tf.placeholder(tf.float32, name='d')
e = tf.placeholder(tf.float32, name='e')
f = ((a - b + c) * d )/e

sess = tf.Session()
writer = tf.summary.FileWriter("./temp")
writer.add_graph(sess.graph)

print "Expected: ((1 - 2 + 3) * 4)/5.0 = ", ((1 - 2 + 3) * 4)/5.0
result = sess.run(f,feed_dict = {a:1,b:2,c:3,d:4,e:5})
print "Via Tensorflow: ((1 - 2 + 3) * 4)/5.0 = ", result

# Expected: ((1 - 2 + 3) * 4)/5.0 =   1.6
# Via Tensorflow: ((1 - 2 + 3) * 4)/5.0 =   1.6
```

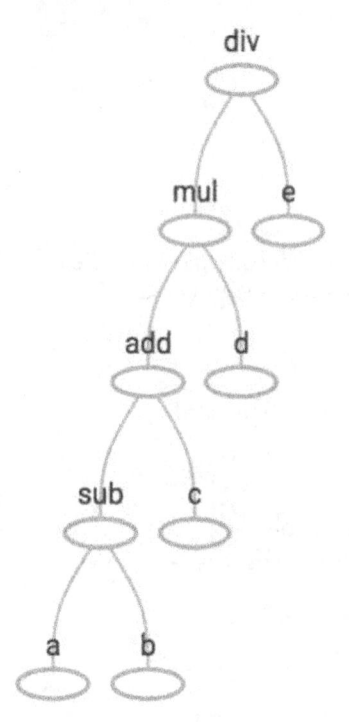

Figure 11-2. Computational graph with scalar placeholders

Computational graphs can contain a mix of constants and placeholders (refer to Listing 11-3 for the source code and Figure 11-3 for the computational graph). Observe carefully how the computational graphs in the three Figures (11-1, 11-2, and 11-3) are different. The Tensorboard visualization of computational graphs is key to debugging large models and it's important to understand this representation. Also, note that all our examples so far are using scalars.

CHAPTER 11 ■ INTRODUCTION TO TENSORFLOW

Listing 11-3. Computational Graph with Constant Scalars and Scalar Placeholders

```
import tensorflow as tf

a = tf.placeholder(tf.float32, name='a')
b = tf.placeholder(tf.float32, name='b')
c = tf.constant(3.0, name='c')
d = tf.constant(4.0, name='d')
e = tf.constant(5.0, name='e')
f = ((a - b + c) * d )/e

sess = tf.Session()
writer = tf.summary.FileWriter("./temp")
writer.add_graph(sess.graph)

print "Expected: ((1 - 2 + 3) * 4)/5.0 = ", ((1 - 2 + 3) * 4)/5.0
result = sess.run(f,feed_dict={a:1,b:2})
print "Via Tensorflow: ((1 - 2 + 3) * 4)/5.0 = ", result

# Expected: ((1 - 2 + 3) * 4)/5.0 =  1.6
# Via Tensorflow: ((1 - 2 + 3) * 4)/5.0 =  1.6
```

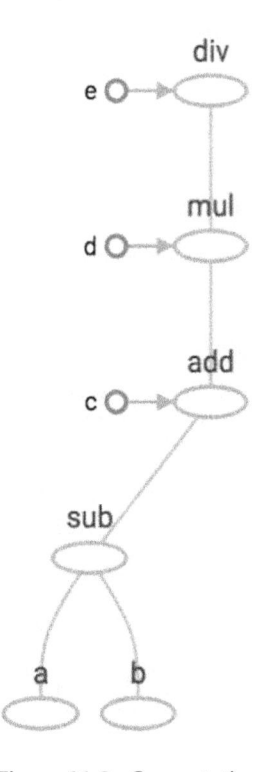

Figure 11-3. Computational graph with constant scalars and scalar placeholders

CHAPTER 11 INTRODUCTION TO TENSORFLOW

Let us now look at the important concept of variable. A variable in Tensorflow is something whose value is defined at declaration time and then updated at runtime (refer to Listing 11-4 for the source code and Figure 11-4 for the computational graph). Typically, variables are using to represent the parameters/weights of the model. The following points are to be noted:

1. The initial value of the variable is defined at declaration time.
2. A name needs to be provided to variables for them to be properly annotated in the computational graph.
3. Expressions can be defined with variables similar to constants and placeholders.
4. During the execution of the computational graph the values of the variables are set (as defined) by calling the global_variable_initialiser method.
5. Computational graphs can be a mix of variables, constants, and placeholders.

Listing 11-4. Computational Graph with Scalar Variables and Scalar Placeholders

```
import tensorflow as tf

a = tf.placeholder(tf.float32, name='a')
b = tf.placeholder(tf.float32, name='b')
c = tf.Variable(initial_value=3.0, name='c')
d = tf.Variable(initial_value=4.0, name='d')
e = tf.constant(5.0, name='e')
f = ((a - b + c) * d )/e

sess = tf.Session()
writer = tf.summary.FileWriter("./temp")
writer.add_graph(sess.graph)

print "Expected: ((1 - 2 + 3) * 4)/5.0 = ", ((1 - 2 + 3) * 4)/5.0
sess.run(tf.global_variables_initializer())
result = sess.run(f,feed_dict={a:1,b:2})
print "Via Tensorflow: ((1 - 2 + 3) * 4)/5.0 = ", result

# Expected: ((1 - 2 + 3) * 4)/5.0 =  1.6
# Via Tensorflow: ((1 - 2 + 3) * 4)/5.0 =  1.6
```

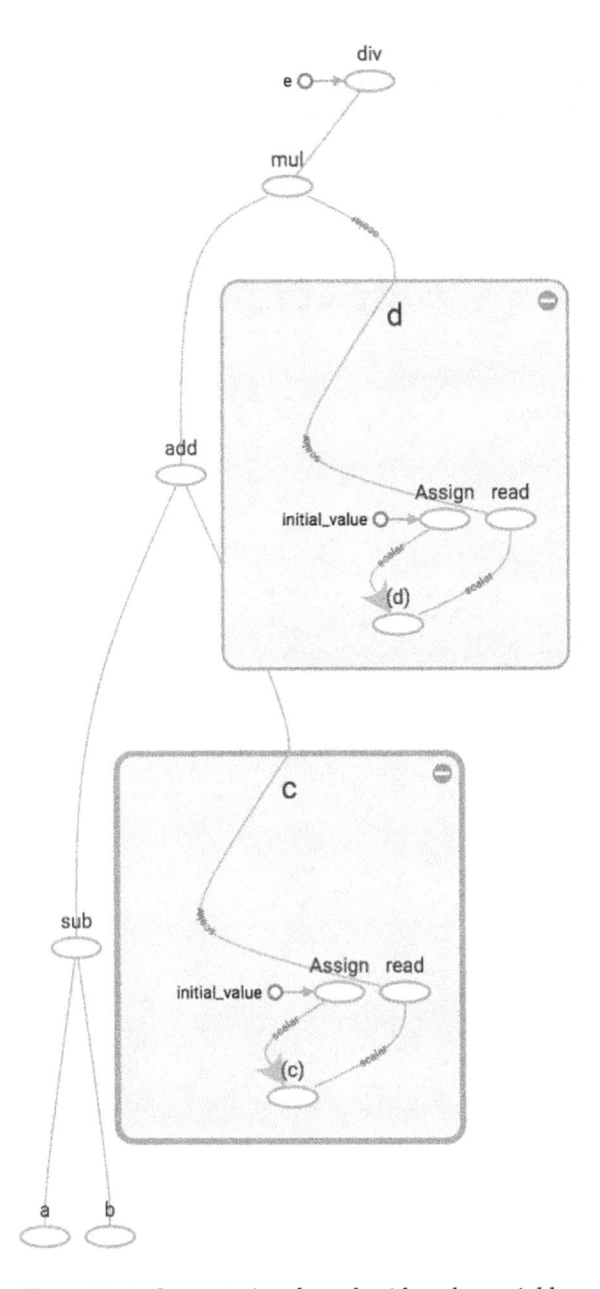

Figure 11-4. Computational graph with scalar variables and scalar placeholders

CHAPTER 11 ■ INTRODUCTION TO TENSORFLOW

The examples we have seen so far consist of scalar placeholders, variables, and constants. Let us now extend this notion to tensors (refer to Listing 11-5 for the source code and Figure 11-5 for the computational graph). Notice how the edges are annotated with the dimensions. The following points are to be noted:

1. Tensors can be initialized with Numpy arrays.
2. A name needs to be provided to constants for them to be properly annotated in the computational graph.
3. Tensor/matrix/vector operations should respect the dimensionality. Errors on this get detected when the computational graph is executed in the session, which makes debugging a bit tricky.

Listing 11-5. Computational Graph with Vector Constants

```
import numpy as np
import tensorflow as tf

a_data = np.array([[1,1],[1,1]])
b_data = np.array([[2,2],[2,2]])
c_data = np.array([[5,5],[5,5]])
d_data = np.array([[3,3],[3,3]])

a = tf.constant([[1,1],[1,1]], name='a')
b = tf.constant([[2,2],[2,2]], name='b')
c = tf.constant([[5,5],[5,5]], name='c')
d = tf.constant([[3,3],[3,3]], name='d')
e = (a + b - c) * d

sess = tf.Session()
writer = tf.summary.FileWriter("./temp")
writer.add_graph(sess.graph)

print "Expected:", (a_data + b_data - c_data) * d_data
result = sess.run(e)
print "Via Tensorflow: ", result

# Expected: [[-6 -6]
#   [-6 -6]]
# Via Tensorflow:    [[-6 -6]
#   [-6 -6]]
```

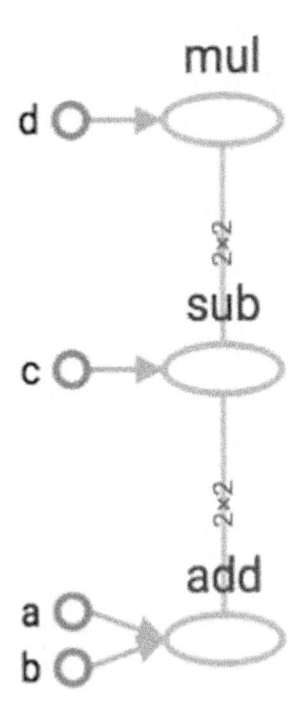

Figure 11-5. Computational graph with vector constants

Our next example illustrates tensor placeholders (refer to Listing 11-6 for the source code and Figure 11-6 for the computational graph). The following points are to be noted:

1. The feed_dict is to be used to define the value of the placeholders when the computational graph is run in the session.

2. A name needs to be provided to placeholders for them to be properly annotated in the computational graph.

Listing 11-6. Computational Graph with Vector Placeholders

```
import numpy as np
import tensorflow as tf

a_data = np.array([[1,1],[1,1]])
b_data = np.array([[2,2],[2,2]])
c_data = np.array([[5,5],[5,5]])
d_data = np.array([[3,3],[3,3]])

a = tf.placeholder(tf.float32, name='a')
b = tf.placeholder(tf.float32, name='b')
c = tf.placeholder(tf.float32, name='c')
d = tf.placeholder(tf.float32, name='d')
e = (a + b - c) * d
```

CHAPTER 11 ■ INTRODUCTION TO TENSORFLOW

```
sess = tf.Session()
writer = tf.summary.FileWriter("./temp")
writer.add_graph(sess.graph)

print "Expected:", (a_data + b_data - c_data) * d_data
result = sess.run(e,feed_dict={a:[[1,1],[1,1]],b:[[2,2],[2,2]],c:[[5,5],[5,5]]
,d:[[3,3],[3,3]]})
print "Via Tensorflow: ", result

# Expected: [[-6 -6]
#  [-6 -6]]
# Via Tensorflow:  [[-6 -6]
#  [-6 -6]]
```

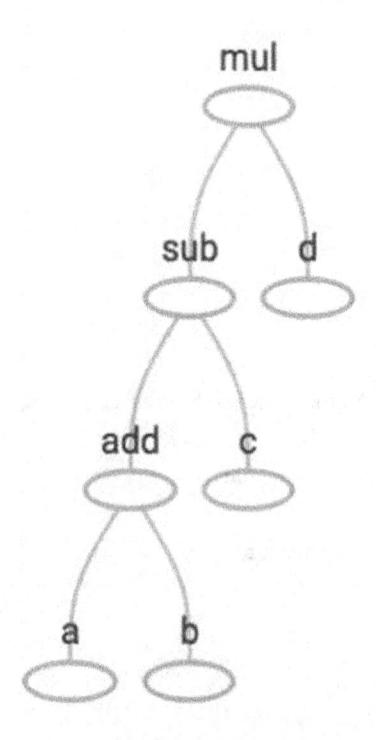

Figure 11-6. Computational graph with vector placeholders

CHAPTER 11 ■ INTRODUCTION TO TENSORFLOW

Our next example illustrates tensor placeholders and constants (refer to Listing 11-7 for the source code and Figure 11-7 for the computational graph).

Listing 11-7. Computational Graph with Vector Constants and Placeholders

```
import numpy as np
import tensorflow as tf

a_data = np.array([[1,1],[1,1]])
b_data = np.array([[2,2],[2,2]])
c_data = np.array([[5,5],[5,5]])
d_data = np.array([[3,3],[3,3]])

a = tf.constant([[1.0,1.0],[1.0,1.0]], name='a')
b = tf.constant([[2.0,2.0],[2.0,2.0]], name='b')
c = tf.placeholder(tf.float32, name='c')
d = tf.placeholder(tf.float32, name='d')
e = (a + b - c) * d

sess = tf.Session()
writer = tf.summary.FileWriter("./temp")
writer.add_graph(sess.graph)

print "Expected:", (a_data + b_data - c_data) * d_data
result = sess.run(e,feed_dict={c:[[5.0,5.0],[5.0,5.0]],d:[[3.0,3.0],[3.0,3.0]]})
print "Via Tensorflow: ", result

# Expected: [[-6 -6]
#  [-6 -6]]
# Via Tensorflow:   [[-6 -6]
#  [-6 -6]]
```

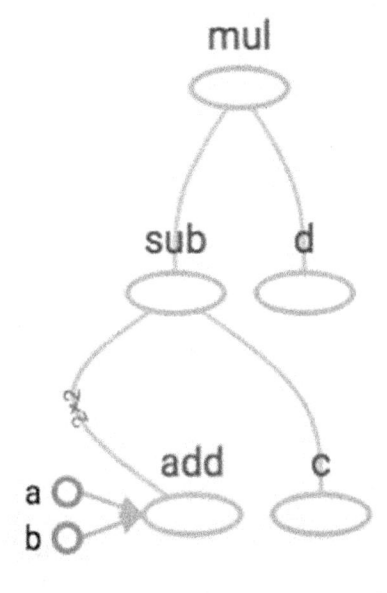

Figure 11-7. Computational graph with vector constants and placeholders

169

CHAPTER 11 ■ INTRODUCTION TO TENSORFLOW

Our next example illustrates tensor placeholders, variables, and constants (refer to Listing 11-8 for the source code and Figure 11-8 for the computational graph). Note carefully the dimensionality indicated on the edges of the computational graph. This can be very useful while debugging computational graphs.

Listing 11-8. Computational Graph with Vector Constants, Variables, and Placeholder

```
import numpy as np
import tensorflow as tf

a_data = np.array([[1,1],[1,1]])
b_data = np.array([[2,2],[2,2]])
c_data = np.array([[5,5],[5,5]])
d_data = np.array([[3,3],[3,3]])

a = tf.constant([[1.0,1.0],[1.0,1.0]], name='a')
b = tf.constant([[2.0,2.0],[2.0,2.0]], name='b')
c = tf.Variable(initial_value=[[5.0,5.0],[5.0,5.0]], name='c')
d = tf.placeholder(tf.float32, name='d')
e = (a + b - c) * d

sess = tf.Session()
writer = tf.summary.FileWriter("./temp")
writer.add_graph(sess.graph)

print "Expected:", (a_data + b_data - c_data) * d_data
sess.run(tf.global_variables_initializer())
result = sess.run(e,feed_dict={d:[[3.0,3.0],[3.0,3.0]]})
print "Via Tensorflow: ", result

# Expected: [[-6 -6]
#  [-6 -6]]
# Via Tensorflow:   [[-6 -6]
#  [-6 -6]]
```

170

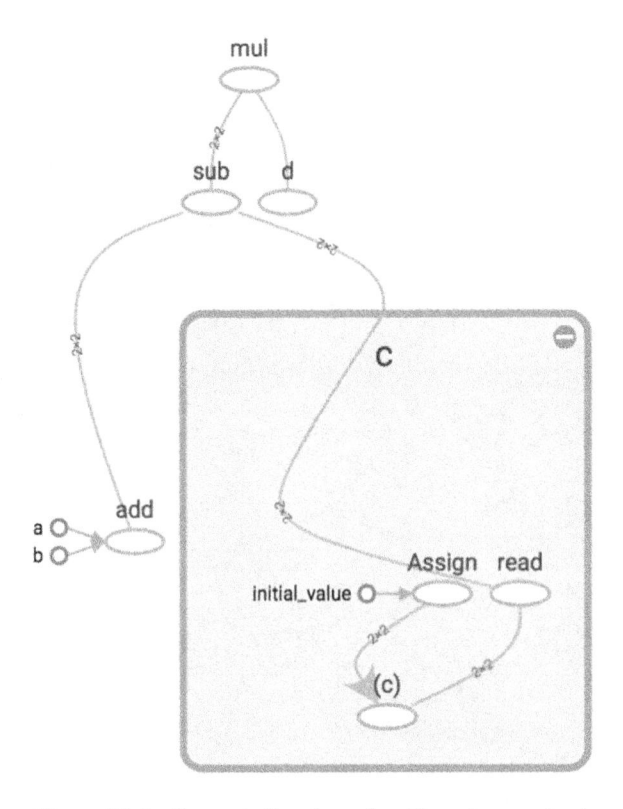

Figure 11-8. Computational graph with vector constants, variables, and placeholders

Our next example illustrates placeholders, variables, and constants, both tensor and scalar (refer to Listing 11-9 for the source code and Figure 11-9 for the computational graph). Note carefully the dimensionality indicated on the edges of the computational graph. This can be very useful while debugging computational graphs.

Listing 11-9. Computational Graph with Scalar/Vector Placeholders, Variables, and Constants

```
import numpy as np
import tensorflow as tf

a = tf.placeholder(tf.float32, name='a')
b = tf.placeholder(tf.float32, name='b')
c = tf.Variable(initial_value=[[5.0,5.0],[5.0,5.0]], name='c')
d = tf.Variable(initial_value=[[3.0,3.0],[3.0,3.0]], name='d')

p = tf.placeholder(tf.float32, name='p')
q = tf.placeholder(tf.float32, name='q')
r = tf.Variable(initial_value=3.0, name='r')
s = tf.Variable(initial_value=4.0, name='s')
u = tf.constant(5.0, name='u')
e = (((a * p) + (b - q) - (c + r )) * d/s) * u

sess = tf.Session()
writer = tf.summary.FileWriter("./temp")
writer.add_graph(sess.graph)
```

CHAPTER 11 ■ INTRODUCTION TO TENSORFLOW

```
a_data = np.array([[1,1],[1,1]])
b_data = np.array([[2,2],[2,2]])
c_data = np.array([[5,5],[5,5]])
d_data = np.array([[3,3],[3,3]])
print "Expected:", (((a_data * 1.0) + (b_data - 2.0) - (c_data + 3.0 )) * d_data/4.0) * 5.0
sess.run(tf.global_variables_initializer())
result = sess.run(e,feed_dict={p:1.0, q:2.0, a:[[1,1],[1,1]],b:[[2,2],[2,2]]})
print "Via Tensorflow: ", result

# Expected: [[-26.25 -26.25]
#  [-26.25 -26.25]]
# Via Tensorflow:  [[-26.25 -26.25]
#  [-26.25 -26.25]]
```

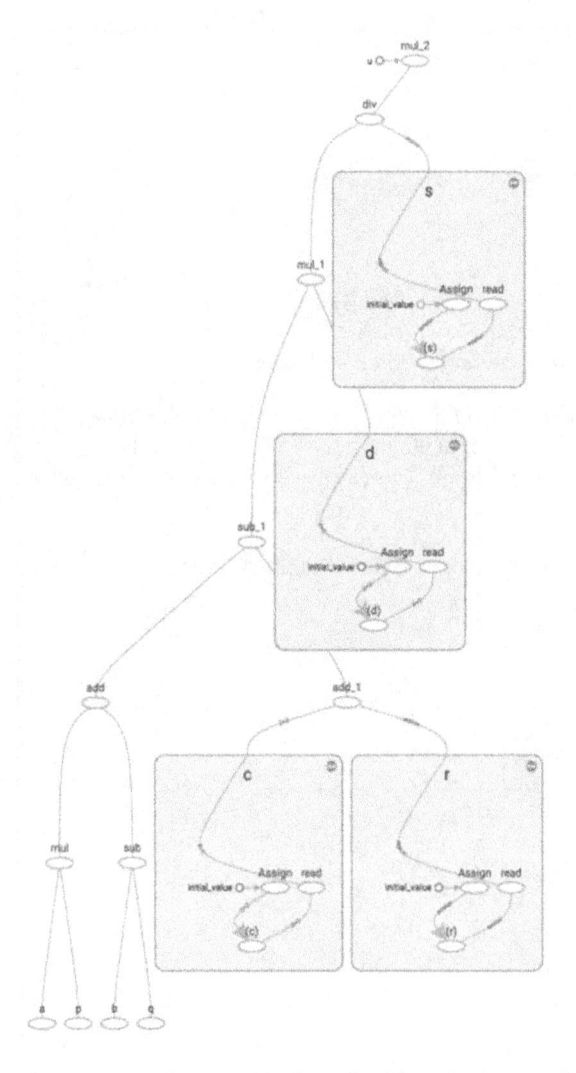

Figure 11-9. Computational graph with scalar/vector placeholders, variables, and constants

CHAPTER 11 ■ INTRODUCTION TO TENSORFLOW

Let us now consider a variety of tensor operations (refer to Listing 11-10 for the source code and Figure 11-10 for the computational graph). The source code listing illustrates addition, subtraction, multiplication, transpose, determinant, inverse, Cholensky decomposition, and computing Eigen values and vectors. All these operations are the basis for defining deep learning models.

Listing 11-10. Computational Graph with Vector/Matrix Operations

```python
import numpy as np
import tensorflow as tf

# Construct from diagonal
a = tf.diag([1.0,1.0,1.0], name="a")

# Random Normalised Matrix
b = tf.truncated_normal([3,3], name = "b")

# Simple Fill
c = tf.fill([3,4], -1.0, name = "c")

# Uniform Random
d = tf.random_uniform([3,3], name = "d")

# From Numpy
e = tf.convert_to_tensor(np.array([[1.0, 2.0, 3.0], [4.0, 5.0, 6.0], [7., 8.0, 9.0]]), name="e")

# Addition
f = tf.add(a,b, name="f")

# Subtraction
g = tf.subtract(a,b, name="g")

# Multiplcation
h = tf.matmul(a,b, name="h")

# Transpose
i = tf.transpose(a, name="i")

# Determinant
j = tf.matrix_determinant(d, name = "j")

# Inverse
k = tf.matrix_inverse(e, name = "k")

# Cholesky Decomposition
l = tf.cholesky(a, name = "l")

# Eigen Values and Vectors
m = tf.self_adjoint_eig(a, name = "m")

sess = tf.Session()
writer = tf.summary.FileWriter("./temp")
writer.add_graph(sess.graph)
```

173

CHAPTER 11 ■ INTRODUCTION TO TENSORFLOW

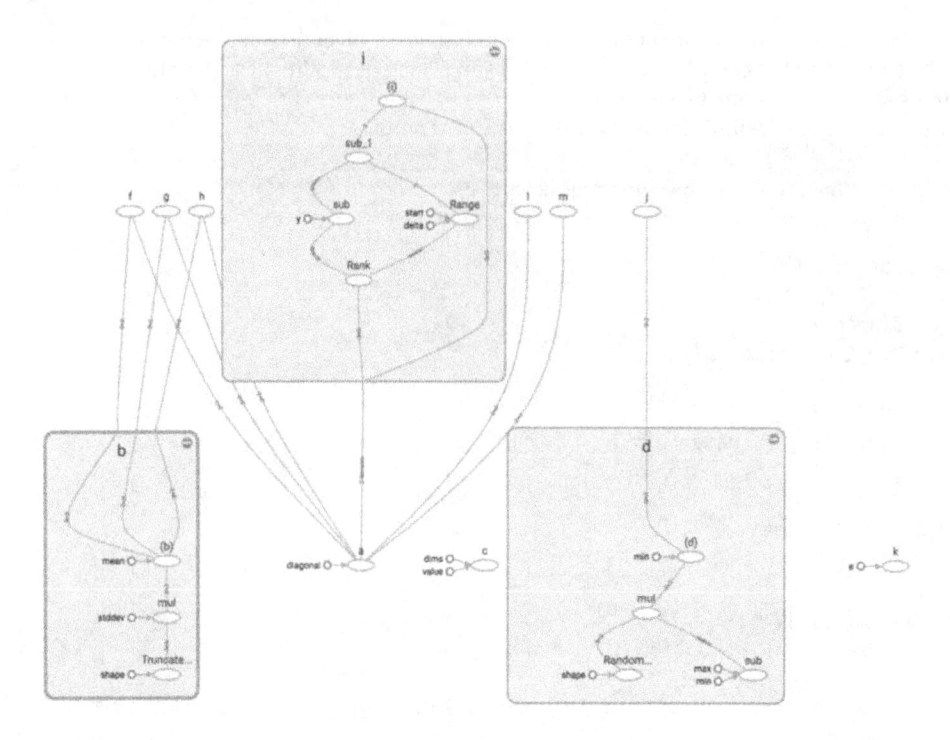

Figure 11-10. *Computational graph with vector/matrix operations*

Let us now consider a variety of tensor initialization operations (refer to Listing 11-11 for the source code and Figure 11-11 for the computational graph). The source code listing illustrates creating tensors of ones/zeros; creating variables based on dimensions;, fill-based initialization; initialization of constants, linear, logarithmic, and stepped initialization; and, finally, random initialization. All these operations are the basis for defining Deep Learning models.

Listing 11-11. Creation and Initialization Operations

```
import tensorflow as tf

# Creating a tensor
t1 = tf.zeros([1,20], name="t1")

# Creating variables
v1 = tf.Variable(t1, name="v1")
v2 = tf.Variable(t1, name="v2")
```

```python
# Creating variables based on given dimensions
r = 4
c = 5
t2 = tf.zeros([r,c], name="t2")
t3 = tf.ones([r,c], name="t3")
v3 = tf.Variable(t2, name="v3")
v4 = tf.Variable(t3, name="v4")

# Using the shape of a previously defined variable
v5 = tf.Variable(tf.zeros_like(v3), name="v5")
v6 = tf.Variable(tf.ones_like(v4), name="v6")

# Fill Initialization
v7 = tf.Variable(tf.fill([r, c], -42), name="v7")

# Constant Initialization
v8 = tf.Variable(tf.constant([1,2,3,4,5,6,7,8]), name="v8")

# Constant Initialization
v9 = tf.Variable(tf.constant(42, shape=[r, c]), name="v9")

# Linearly spaced Initialization
v10 = tf.Variable(tf.linspace(start=-10.0, stop=10.0, num=100), name="v10")

# Range Initialization
v11 = tf.Variable(tf.range(start=-1.0, limit=1, delta=0.1), name="v11")

# Random Normal Initialization
v12 = tf.random_normal([r, c], mean=0.0, stddev=1.0, name="v12")

# Add the graph for visualization on TensorBoard
sess = tf.Session()
writer = tf.summary.FileWriter("./temp")
writer.add_graph(sess.graph)
```

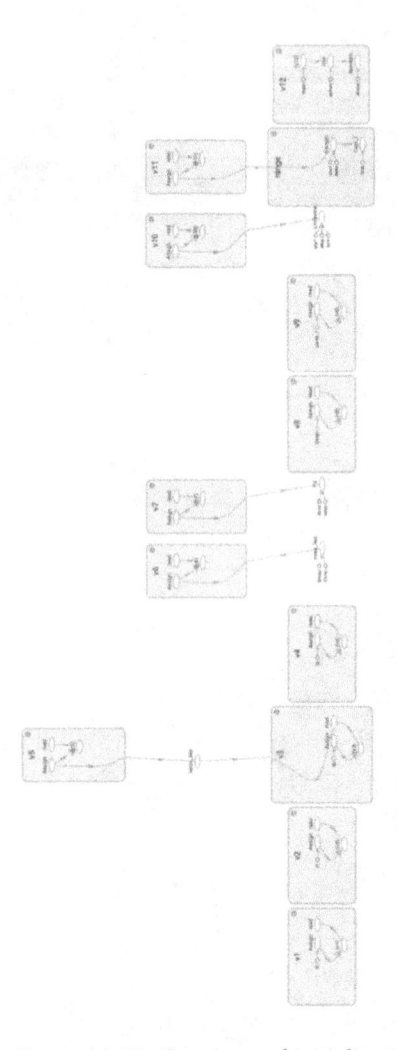

Figure 11-11. Creation and initialization operations

Let us now consider an end-to-end example involving training a linear regression model (refer to Listing 11-12 for the source code and Figures 11-12 and 11-13 for the computational graph). The reader is advised to carefully observe the dimensionality as indicated on the edges of the computational graph. This example builds upon the concepts introduced earlier in this chapter. The following points are to be noted:

1. The linear regression model is defined with the input and output being placeholders and the weight and the bias term being variables.

2. The weight and bias are initialized using random_normal (introduced earlier).

3. We use the GradientDescentOptimizer object to minimize the loss function of interest as defined by squared_loss.

4. The train_step is invoked for a said number of epochs wherein gradients are computed and the weight vectors are updated.

5. Data is passed on via the feed_dict for each invocation of train_step.

CHAPTER 11 ■ INTRODUCTION TO TENSORFLOW

Listing 11-12. Linear Regression

```python
import numpy as np
import tensorflow as tf

# Generate Random Data
examples = 1000
features = 100
x_data = np.random.randn(examples, features)
y_data = np.random.randn(examples,1)

# Define the Linear Regression Model
X = tf.placeholder(tf.float32, shape=[None, features], name = "X")
y = tf.placeholder(tf.float32, shape=[None, 1], name = "y")
w = tf.Variable(tf.random_normal(shape=[features,1]), name= "w")
b = tf.Variable(tf.random_normal(shape=[1,1]), name="b")
y_hat = tf.add(tf.matmul(X,w),b, name="y_hat")

# Define the loss
squared_loss = tf.reduce_sum(tf.pow(y - y_hat,2), name="squared_loss")/examples

# Set up the gradient descent
learning_rate = 0.05
optimiser = tf.train.GradientDescentOptimizer(learning_rate)
train_step = optimiser.minimize(squared_loss)

sess = tf.Session()
writer = tf.summary.FileWriter("./temp")
writer.add_graph(sess.graph)
sess.run(tf.global_variables_initializer())

epochs = 5000
batch_size = 5

# Before Training
curr_loss = sess.run(squared_loss, feed_dict={X:x_data, y:y_data})
print "Loss before training:", curr_loss

for i in range(epochs):
    rand_index = np.random.choice(examples, size=batch_size)
    sess.run(train_step, feed_dict={X:x_data[rand_index], y:y_data[rand_index]})

# After Training
curr_loss = sess.run(squared_loss, feed_dict={X:x_data, y:y_data})
print "Loss before training:", curr_loss

# Loss before training: 95.5248
# Loss before training: 2.13263
```

177

CHAPTER 11 ■ INTRODUCTION TO TENSORFLOW

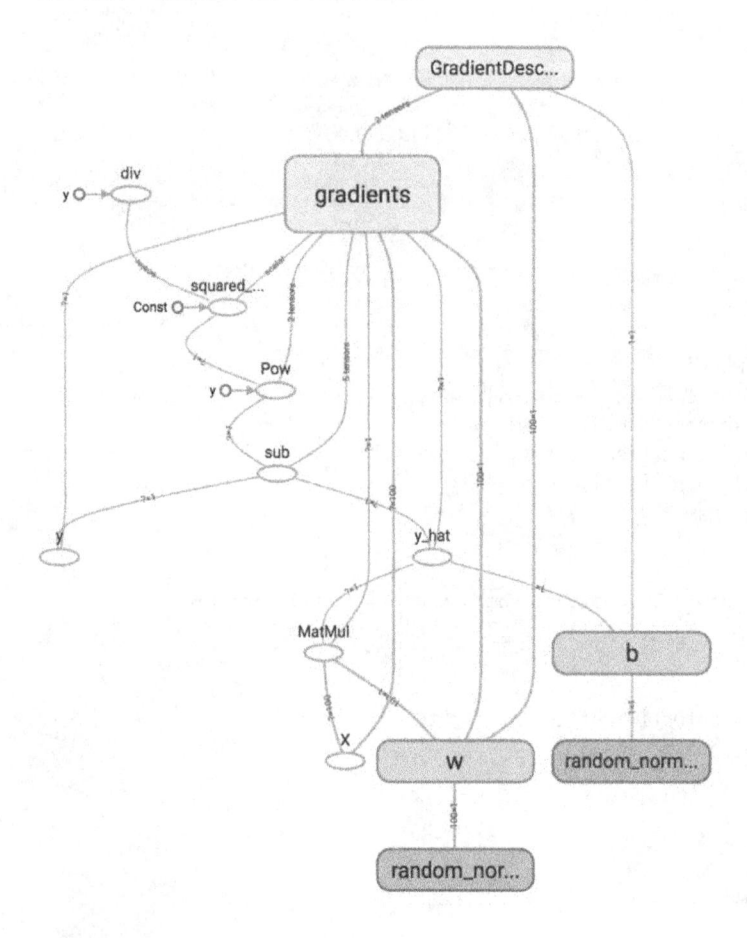

Figure 11-12. Linear regression

CHAPTER 11 ■ INTRODUCTION TO TENSORFLOW

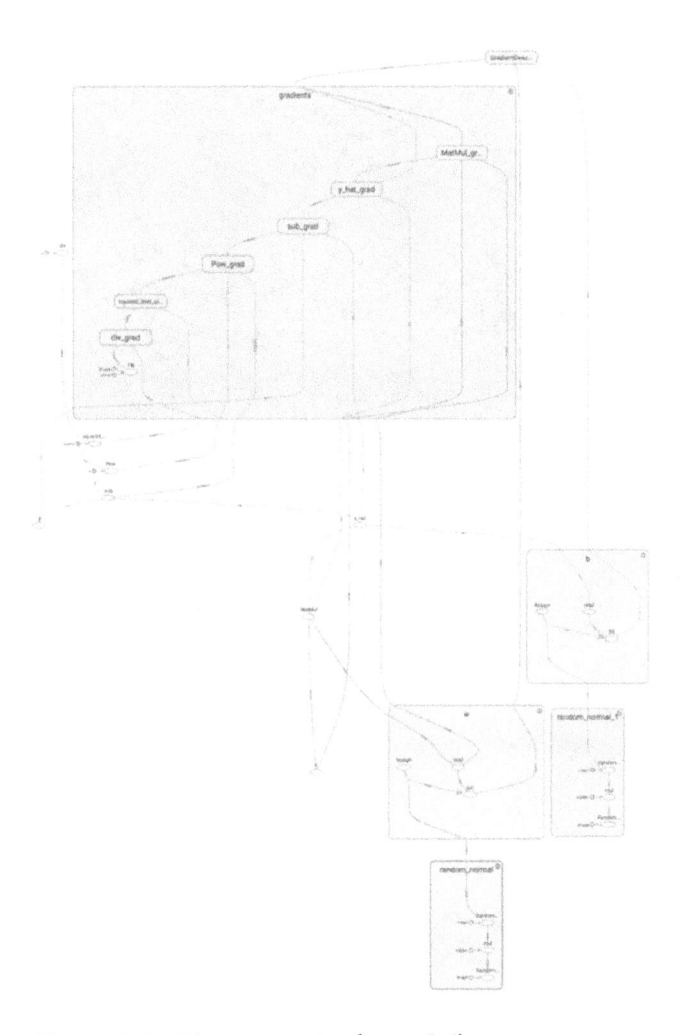

Figure 11-13. Linear regression (expanded)

Let us now consider an end-to-end example involving training a logistic regression model (refer to Listing 11-13 for the source code and Figures 11-14 and 11-15 for the computational graph). The reader is advised to carefully observe the dimensionality as indicated on the edges of the computational graph. This example builds upon the concepts introduced earlier in this chapter. The following points are to be noted:

1. The logistic regression model is defined with the input and output being placeholders and the weight and the bias term being variables.

2. The weight and bias are initialized using random_normal (introduced earlier).

3. We use the GradientDescentOptimizer object to minimize the loss function of interest (logistic loss). The sigmoid_cross_entropy_with_logits function is computing the logits and then the cross entropy over the labels as a single convenience function.

4. The train_step is invoked for a said number of epochs wherein gradients are computed and the weight vectors are updated.

5. Data is passed on via the feed_dict for each invocation of train_step.

CHAPTER 11 ■ INTRODUCTION TO TENSORFLOW

Listing 11-13. Logistic Regression

```
import numpy as np
import tensorflow as tf

# Generate Random Data
examples = 1000
features = 100
x_data = np.random.randn(examples, features)
y_data = np.random.randint(size=(examples, 1),low=0, high=2)

# Define the Logistic Regression Model
X = tf.placeholder(tf.float32, shape=[None, features], name = "X")
y = tf.placeholder(tf.float32, shape=[None, 1], name = "y")
w = tf.Variable(tf.random_normal(shape=[features,1]), name= "w")
b = tf.Variable(tf.random_normal(shape=[1,1]), name="b")

# Loss
temp = tf.add(tf.matmul(X, w),b, name="temp")
loss = tf.reduce_mean(tf.nn.sigmoid_cross_entropy_with_logits(logits=temp, labels=y),
name="loss")

# Set up the gradient descent
learning_rate = 0.05
optimiser = tf.train.GradientDescentOptimizer(learning_rate)
train_step = optimiser.minimize(loss)

sess = tf.Session()
writer = tf.summary.FileWriter("./temp")
writer.add_graph(sess.graph)
sess.run(tf.global_variables_initializer())

epochs = 5000
batch_size = 5

# Before Training
curr_loss = sess.run(loss, feed_dict={X:x_data, y:y_data})
print "Loss before training:", curr_loss

for i in range(epochs):
    rand_index = np.random.choice(examples, size=batch_size)
    sess.run(train_step, feed_dict={X:x_data[rand_index], y:y_data[rand_index]})

# After Training
curr_loss = sess.run(loss, feed_dict={X:x_data, y:y_data})
print "Loss before training:", curr_loss

# Loss before training: 3.50893
# Loss before training: 0.704702
```

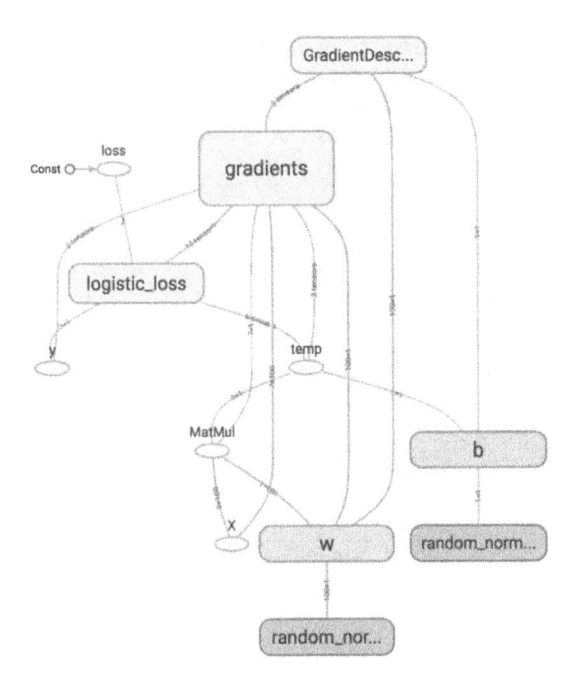

Figure 11-14. Logistic regression

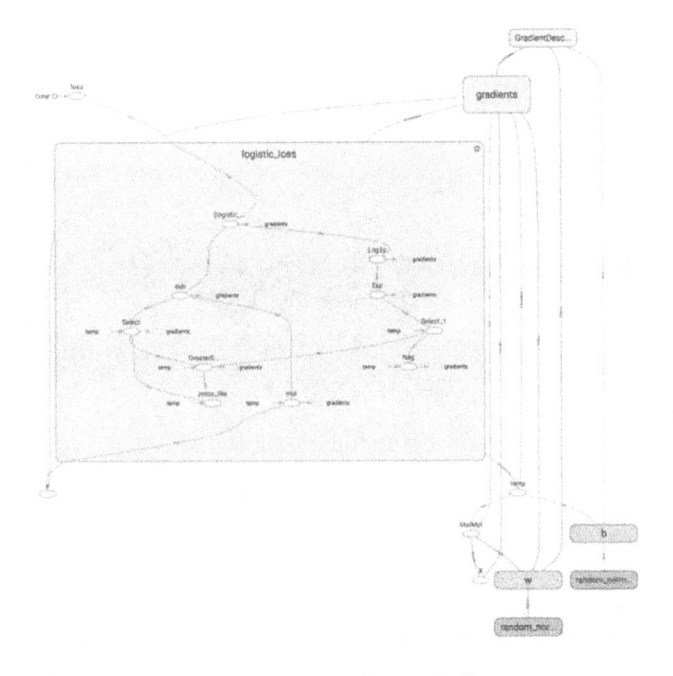

Figure 11-15. Logistic regression (expanded)

CHAPTER 11 ■ INTRODUCTION TO TENSORFLOW

Let us now consider an end-to-end example involving training a two-layer neural network (refer to Listing 11-14 for the source code and Figure 11-16 for the computational graph). The reader is advised to carefully observe the dimensionality as indicated on the edges of the computational graph. This example builds upon the concepts introduced earlier in this chapter. The following points are to be noted:

1. We use a ReLU activation and squared loss.
2. The neural network model is defined with the input and output being placeholders and the weight and the bias term being variables.
3. The weights and bias terms are initialized using random_normal (introduced earlier).
4. We use the GradientDescentOptimizer object to minimize the loss function of interest
5. The train_step is invoked for a said number of epochs wherein gradients are computed and the weight vectors are updated.
6. Data is passed on via the feed_dict for each invocation of train_step.

Listing 11-14. Neural Network

```python
import numpy as np
import tensorflow as tf

# Generate Random Data
examples = 1000
features = 100
x_data = np.random.randn(examples, features)
y_data = np.random.randn(examples,1)

# Define the Neural Network Model
hidden_layer_nodes = 10
X = tf.placeholder(tf.float32, shape=[None, features], name = "X")
y = tf.placeholder(tf.float32, shape=[None, 1], name = "y")

# Layer 1
w1 = tf.Variable(tf.random_normal(shape=[features,hidden_layer_nodes]), name="w1")
b1 = tf.Variable(tf.random_normal(shape=[hidden_layer_nodes]), name="b1")

# Layer 2
w2 = tf.Variable(tf.random_normal(shape=[hidden_layer_nodes,1]), name="w2")
b2 = tf.Variable(tf.random_normal(shape=[1,1]), name="b2")
hidden_output = tf.nn.relu(tf.add(tf.matmul(X, w1), b1), name="hidden_output")
y_hat = tf.nn.relu(tf.add(tf.matmul(hidden_output, w2), b2), name="y_hat")
loss = tf.reduce_mean(tf.square(y_hat - y), name="loss")

# Set up the gradient descent
learning_rate = 0.05
optimiser = tf.train.GradientDescentOptimizer(learning_rate)
train_step = optimiser.minimize(loss)

sess = tf.Session()
writer = tf.summary.FileWriter("./temp")
writer.add_graph(sess.graph)
sess.run(tf.global_variables_initializer())
```

CHAPTER 11 ■ INTRODUCTION TO TENSORFLOW

```
epochs = 5000
batch_size = 5

# Before Training
curr_loss = sess.run(loss, feed_dict={X:x_data, y:y_data})
print "Loss before training:", curr_loss

for i in range(epochs):
    rand_index = np.random.choice(examples, size=batch_size)
    sess.run(train_step, feed_dict={X:x_data[rand_index], y:y_data[rand_index]})

# After Training
curr_loss = sess.run(loss, feed_dict={X:x_data, y:y_data})
print "Loss before training:", curr_loss

# Loss before training: 42.431
# Loss before training: 0.976375
```

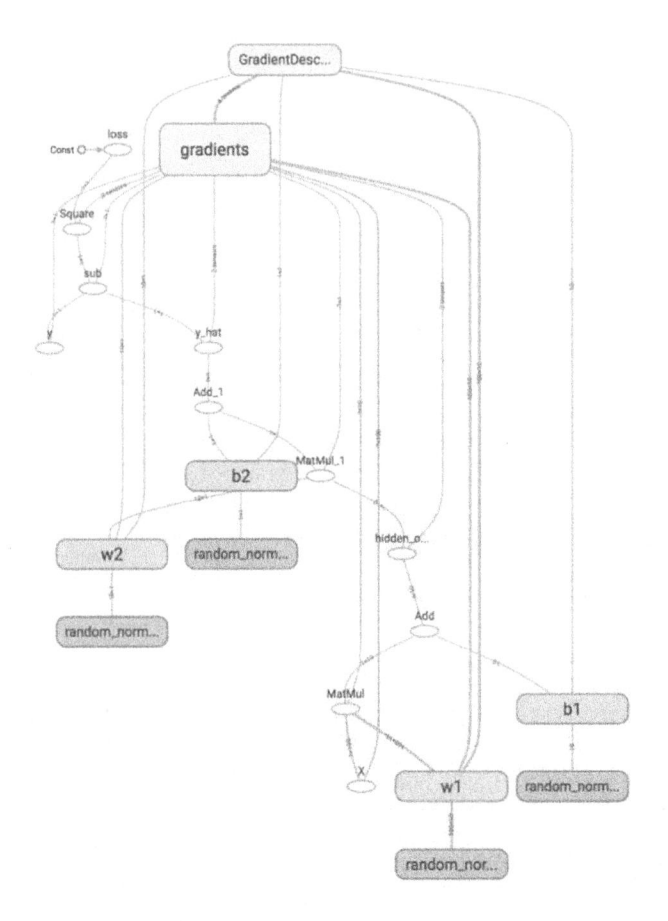

Figure 11-16. Neural network

CHAPTER 11 ■ INTRODUCTION TO TENSORFLOW

Let us now consider a significantly large end-to-end example involving training a convolution neural network (refer to Listing 11-15 for the source code and Figures 11-17, 11-18, 11-19, and 11-20 for the computational graphs).

Instead of using the convenient high-level functions provided by Tensorflow (such as convolution and pooling) we will be implementing the convolution neural network from scratch, or better put using only the basic/primitive functionality. While this implementation is not highly optimized it will give the reader an in-depth view of how complex deep networks can be built using Tensorflow.

The data set we will be using is MNIST, which is a commonly used benchmark data set for Deep Learning. The data set consists of handwritten digits (60,000 training examples and 10,000 test examples). The task at hand is to predict the digit given the image, so this is a multiclassification problem with ten classes.

The reader is encouraged to view the code listing in conjunction with the computational graph and to reference Chapter 5 as required.

The following points are to be noted:

1. The key functions which are implemented from scratch are ReLU, convolution, max pooling, cross entropy loss, and accuracy.

2. A key helper function is flatten_out. This function basically converts a tensor to a form such that convolution and pooling can be implemented using matmul and reduce_max.

3. The construct name_scope is used so that the computational graph is properly labeled.

Listing 11-15. CNN from Scratch

```
import tensorflow as tf
from tensorflow.examples.tutorials.mnist import input_data

# Helper function to flatten a tensor for convolution and pooling operations
def flatten_out(X, height, width, channels,
                convolution_output_height_dim,
                convolution_output_width_dim,
                stride, padding):

    # Pad zeros
    X_padded = tf.pad(X, [[0,0], [padding, padding], [padding, padding], [0,0]])

    # Simulate the sliding of the convolution weights (filter) as a window over the images
    slices = []
    for i in range(convolution_output_height_dim):
        for j in range(convolution_output_width_dim):
            window = tf.slice(X_padded, [0, i*stride, j*stride, 0], [-1, height, width, -1])
            slices.append(window)

    # Combine, reshape and return result
    stacked = tf.stack(slices)
    return tf.reshape(stacked, [-1, channels * width * height])
```

```python
# Convolution Operation
def convolution(X, conv_weights,
                conv_bias, padding,
                stride, name="convolution"):

    with tf.name_scope(name):

        # Extract dimensions of input (X)
        # and convolution weights
        X_filter_count_dim, \
        X_height_dim, \
        X_width_dim, \
        X_channels_dim = [d.value for d in X.get_shape()]

        cw_height_dim, \
        cw_width_dim, \
        cw_channels_dim, \
        cw_filter_count_dim = [d.value for d in conv_weights.get_shape()]

        # Compute the output dimensions of the
        # of the convolution operation on
        # X and conv_weights
        convolution_output_height_dim =\
            (X_height_dim + 2*padding - cw_height_dim)//stride + 1

        convolution_output_width_dim =\
            (X_width_dim + 2*padding - cw_width_dim)//stride + 1

        # Flatten X and conv_weights so that a
        # matrix mutiplication will lead
        # to a convolution operation
        X_flattened = flatten_out(X, cw_height_dim,
                                  cw_width_dim, cw_channels_dim,
                                  convolution_output_height_dim,
                                  convolution_output_width_dim,
                                  stride, padding)

        cw_flattened = tf.reshape(conv_weights, [cw_height_dim *
                                                 cw_width_dim *
                                                 cw_channels_dim,
                                                 cw_filter_count_dim])

        # Multiply the flattened matrices
        z = tf.matmul(X_flattened, cw_flattened) + conv_bias

        # Unflatten/reorganise and return result
        return tf.transpose(tf.reshape(z, [convolution_output_height_dim,
                                           convolution_output_width_dim,
                                           X_filter_count_dim,
                                           cw_filter_count_dim]),
                            [2, 0, 1, 3])
```

```python
# ReLU operation
def relu(X, name = "relu"):
    with tf.name_scope(name):
        return tf.maximum(X, tf.zeros_like(X))

# Max Pooling Operation
def max_pooling(X, pooling_height, pooling_width,
                padding, stride, name ="pooling"):
    with tf.name_scope(name):
        # Get dimensions of input (X)
        X_filter_count_dim, \
        X_height_dim, \
        X_width_dim, \
        X_channels_dim = [d.value for d in X.get_shape()]

        # Compute the output dimensions of the result
        # of the convolution operation on
        # X and conv_weights
        convolution_output_height_dim = (X_height_dim + 2 * padding - pooling_height)
        // stride + 1
        convolution_output_width_dim = (X_width_dim + 2 * padding - pooling_width)
        // stride + 1

        # Flatten for max operation
        X_flattened = flatten_out(X, pooling_height, pooling_width,
                                  X_channels_dim,
                                  convolution_output_height_dim,
                                  convolution_output_width_dim, stride, padding)
        # Max Pooling
        pool = tf.reduce_max(tf.reshape(X_flattened,

                                        [convolution_output_height_dim,
                                         convolution_output_width_dim,
                                         X_filter_count_dim,
                                         pooling_height *
                                         pooling_width,
                                         X_channels_dim]),
                             axis=3)
        # Reorg and return result
        return tf.transpose(pool, [2, 0, 1, 3])

# Fully connected layer
def fully_connected(X, W, b, name="fully-connected"):
    with tf.name_scope(name):
        n = X.get_shape()[0].value
        X_flat = tf.reshape(X, [n, -1])
        return tf.matmul(X_flat, W) + b

# Softmax
def softmax(X, name="softmax"):
    with tf.name_scope(name):
        X_centered = X - tf.reduce_max(X)
```

```
        X_exp = tf.exp(X_centered)
        exp_sum = tf.reduce_sum(X_exp, axis=1)
        return tf.transpose(tf.transpose(X_exp) / exp_sum)

# Cross Entropy (Loss function for training)
def cross_entropy(y, t, name="cross-entropy"):
    with tf.name_scope(name):
        return -tf.reduce_mean(tf.log(tf.reduce_sum(y * t, axis=1)))

# Accuracy (for evalution)
def accuracy(network, t, name="accuracy"):
    with tf.name_scope(name):
        t_predict = tf.argmax(network, axis=1)
        t_actual = tf.argmax(t, axis=1)
        return tf.reduce_mean(tf.cast(tf.equal(t_predict, t_actual), tf.float32))

# Read the input
mnist = input_data.read_data_sets("./temp", one_hot=True, reshape=False)

# Parameters describing the input data
batch_size = 1000
image_height = 28
image_width = 28
image_channels = 1 # monochromatic images
categories = 10

# Placeholders for input and output
X = tf.placeholder(tf.float32, shape=[batch_size, image_height, image_width,
image_channels], name = "X")
y = tf.placeholder(tf.float32, shape=[batch_size, categories], name = "y")

# Convolution weight parameters
conv_height = 7
conv_width = 7
conv_channels = 1
conv_filter_count = 20

# Convolution weight and bias
convolution_weights = tf.Variable(tf.random_normal([conv_height, conv_width, conv_channels,
conv_filter_count], stddev=0.01),
                                   name="convolution_weights")
convolution_bias = tf.Variable(tf.zeros([conv_filter_count]), name="convolution_bias")

# Convolution Layer
conv_layer = convolution(X, convolution_weights, convolution_bias, padding=2, stride=1,
name="Convolution")

# Convolution Layer Activation
conv_activation_layer = relu(conv_layer,name="convolution_actiavation_relu")
```

CHAPTER 11 ■ INTRODUCTION TO TENSORFLOW

```python
# Pooling Layer
pooling_layer = max_pooling(conv_activation_layer, pooling_height=2, pooling_width=2,
padding=0, stride=2, name ="Pooling")

# Fully Connected Layer-1 (Hidden Layer)
hidden_size = 150
batch_size, pool_output_h, pool_output_w, conv_filter_count = [d.value for d in pooling_
layer.get_shape()]
weights1 = tf.Variable(tf.random_normal([pool_output_h * pool_output_w * conv_filter_count,
hidden_size], stddev=0.01),
                        name="weights1")
bias1 = tf.Variable(tf.zeros([hidden_size]), name="bias1")
fully_connected1 = fully_connected(pooling_layer, weights1, bias1, name="Fully-Connected-1")
fully_connected1_activation = relu(fully_connected1, name="fully_connected1_activation_
relu")

# Fully Connected Layer-2 (Output Layer)
output_size = 10
weights2 = tf.Variable(tf.random_normal([hidden_size, output_size], stddev=0.01),
name="weights2")
bias2 = tf.Variable(tf.zeros([output_size]), name="bias2")
fully_connected2 = fully_connected(fully_connected1_activation, weights2, bias2,
name="Fully-Connected-2")

# Softmax
softmax_layer = softmax(fully_connected2, name="Softmax")

# Cross Entropy Loss
loss = cross_entropy(softmax_layer, y, name ="Cross-Entropy")

# Training and Evaluation
learning_rate = 0.1
train_step = tf.train.GradientDescentOptimizer(learning_rate).minimize(loss)

# Before Training
test_x = mnist.test.images[:batch_size]
test_y = mnist.test.labels[:batch_size]

sess = tf.Session()
writer = tf.summary.FileWriter("./temp")
writer.add_graph(sess.graph)
sess.run(tf.global_variables_initializer())

print "Accuracy before training:", sess.run(accuracy(softmax_layer, y), feed_dict={X:test_x,
y:test_y})
batches = int(mnist.train.num_examples/batch_size)
steps = 5
```

```
for i in xrange(steps):
    for j in xrange(batches):
        x_data, y_data = mnist.train.next_batch(batch_size)
        sess.run(train_step, feed_dict={X:x_data, y:y_data})
print "Accuracy after training:", sess.run(accuracy(softmax_layer, y), feed_dict={X:test_x,
y:test_y})

# Accuracy before training: 0.124
# Accuracy after training: 0.894
```

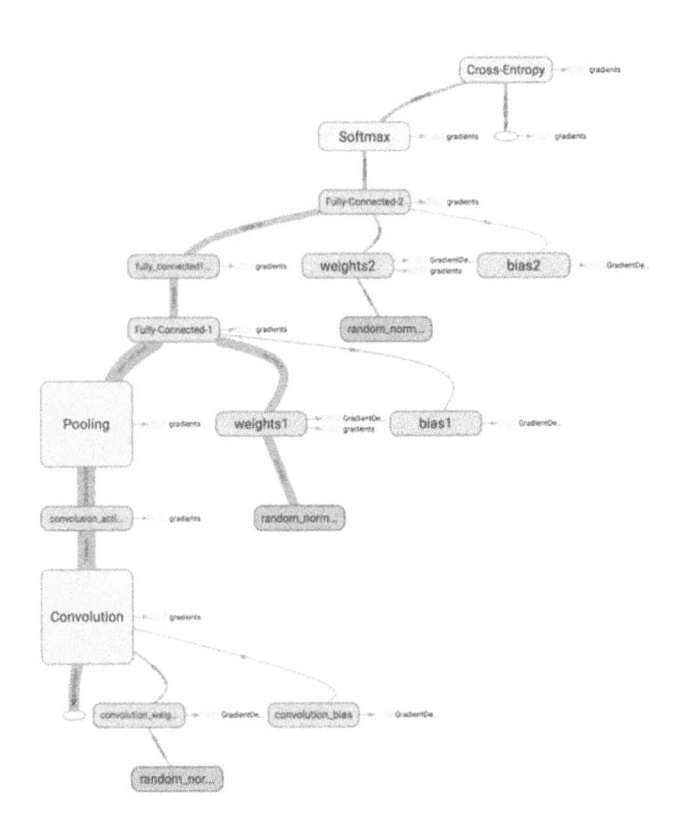

Figure 11-17. Computational graph for Convolutional Neural Networks (CNN)

CHAPTER 11 ■ INTRODUCTION TO TENSORFLOW

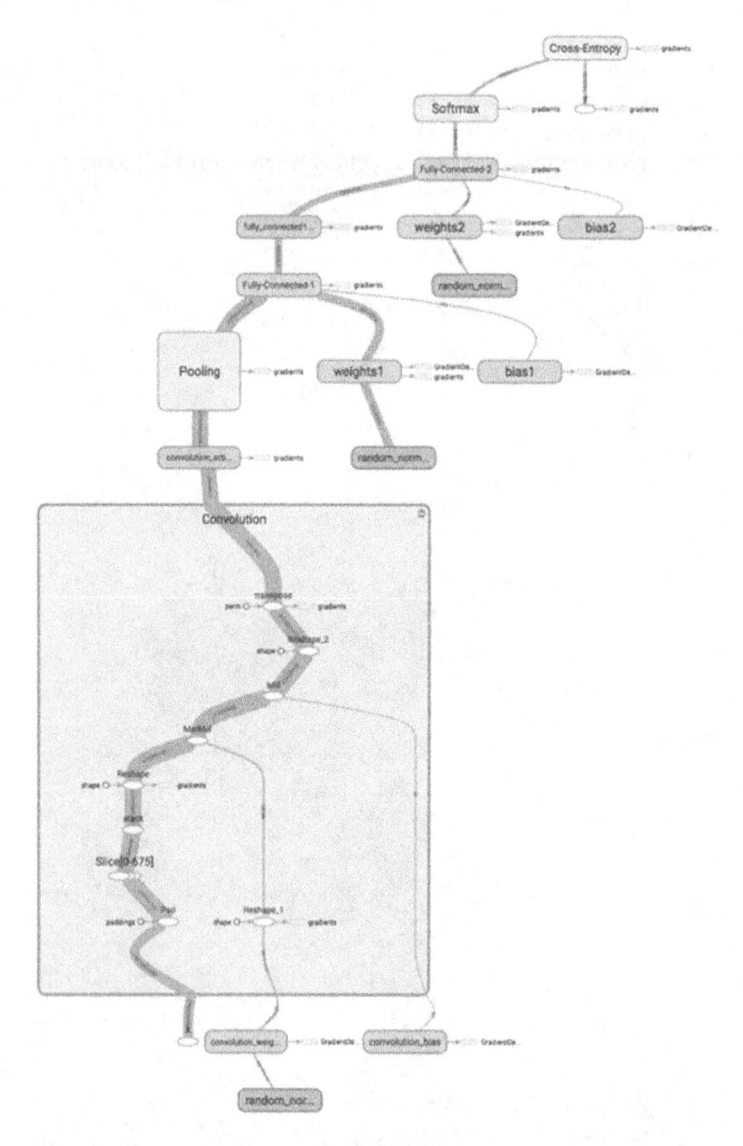

Figure 11-18. Computational graph for CNN (convolution expanded)

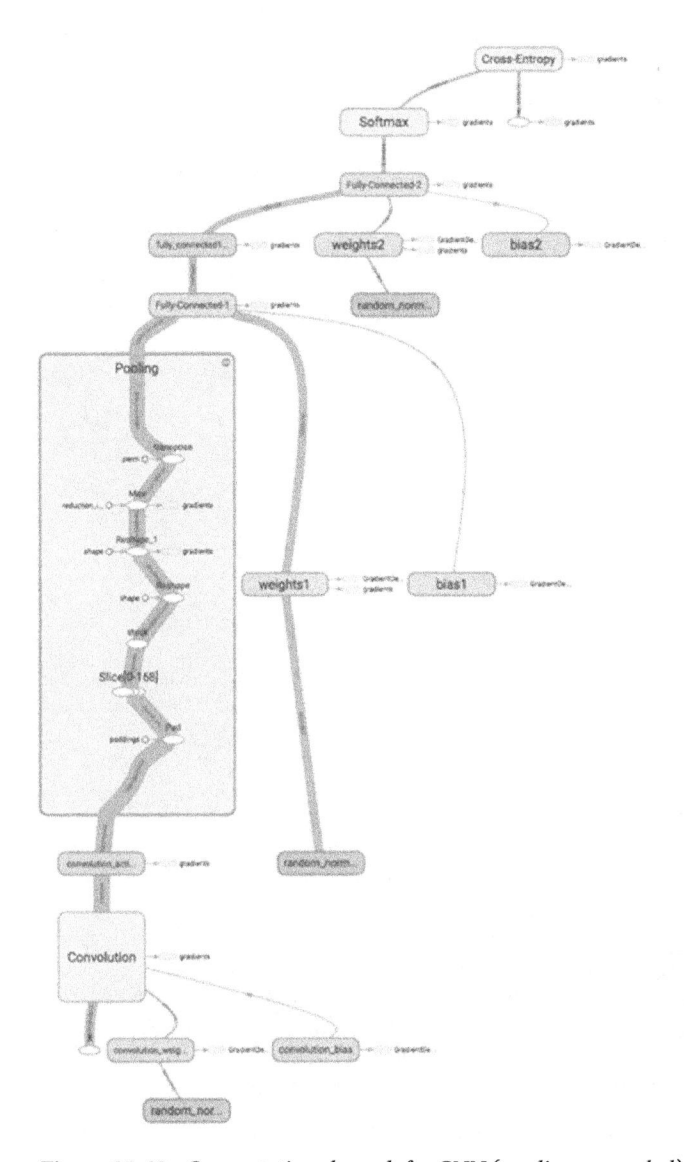

Figure 11-19. Computational graph for CNN (pooling expanded)

CHAPTER 11 ■ INTRODUCTION TO TENSORFLOW

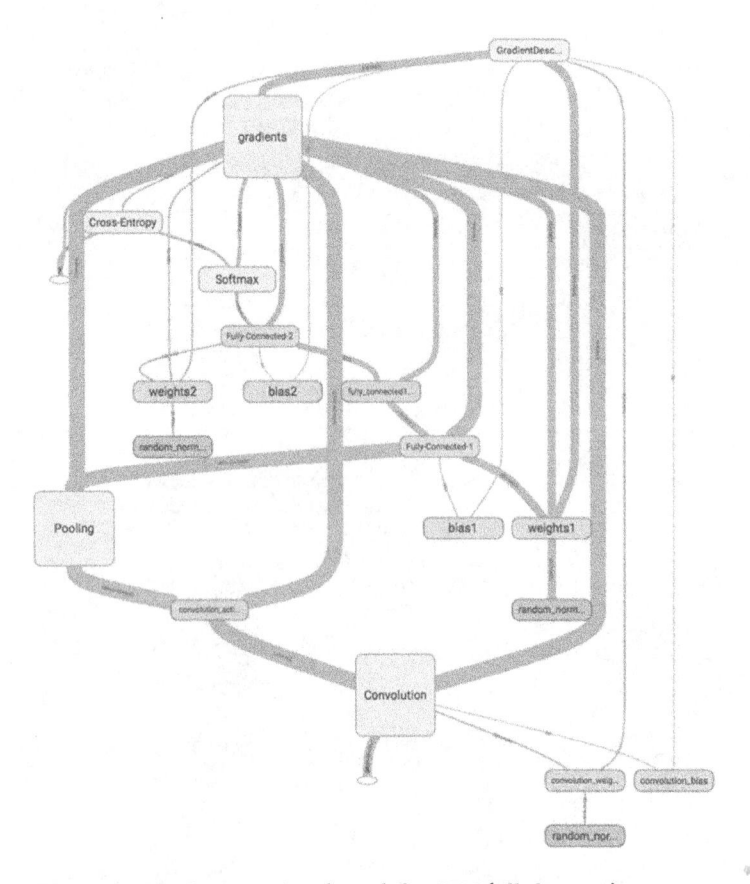

Figure 11-20. Computational graph for CNN (all elements)

In all our examples so far we have generated visualizations of the computational graph using Tensorboard. Tensorboard also allows users to visualize plots over scalars and histograms over weights/biases to understand and tune models using a construct called summaries. Let us now consider an example that generates such summaries (refer to Listing 11-16 for the source code and Figures 11-21 and 11-22 for the visualizations of scalars and histograms, respectively). The following points are to be noted:

1. We use the summary.scalar function to create a scalar summary of the loss function.

2. We use the summary.histogram function to create a histogram summary of the weight and bias term.

3. Summaries are collected and merged via the summary.merge_all function.

4. The merged summary returned as a part of the session.run is passed on to the writer object.

Listing 11-16. Using Summaries

```
import tensorflow as tf

W = tf.Variable([.3], tf.float32, name="W")
b = tf.Variable([-.3], tf.float32, name = "b")
x = tf.placeholder(tf.float32, name="x")
with tf.name_scope("linear_model"):
    linear_model = W * x + b

    # Tensorboard Histogram Summary of W and b
    tf.summary.histogram("W", W)
    tf.summary.histogram("b", b)

y = tf.placeholder(tf.float32, name="y")
with tf.name_scope("loss_computation"):
    loss = tf.reduce_sum(tf.square(linear_model - y))

    # Tensorboard Scalar Summaries for Loss
    tf.summary.scalar("loss", loss)

optimizer = tf.train.GradientDescentOptimizer(0.01)
train = optimizer.minimize(loss)
x_train = [1,2,3,4]
y_train = [0,-1,-2,-3]
init = tf.global_variables_initializer()

# Merge Summaries
merged_summary = tf.summary.merge_all()

sess = tf.Session()
sess.run(init)

# Graph Summary
writer = tf.summary.FileWriter("./temp")
writer.add_graph(sess.graph)

for i in range(1000):
  train_result, summary_result = sess.run([train,merged_summary], {x:x_train, y:y_train})
  writer.add_summary(summary_result, i)

curr_W, curr_b, curr_loss  = sess.run([W, b, loss], {x:x_train, y:y_train})
print("W: %s b: %s loss: %s"%(curr_W, curr_b, curr_loss))

# W: [-0.9999969] b: [ 0.99999082] loss: 5.69997e-11
```

CHAPTER 11   INTRODUCTION TO TENSORFLOW

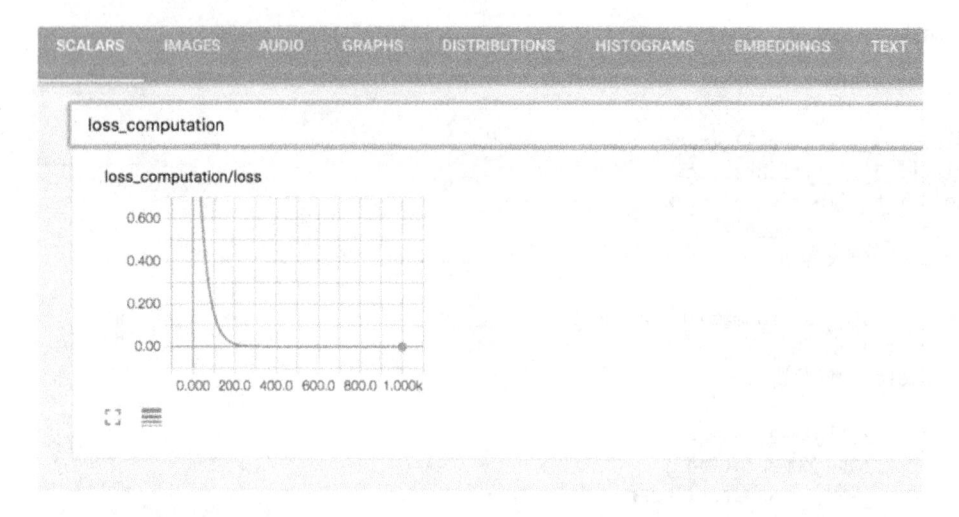

Figure 11-21. Using summaries (scalars)

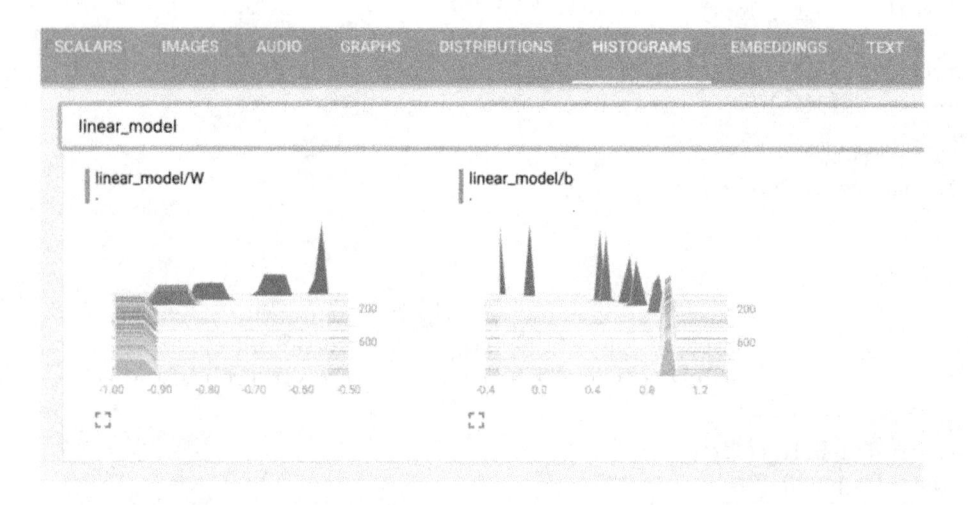

Figure 11-22. Using summaries (histograms)

Summary

In this chapter, we covered Tensorflow in great detail. At its essence, Tensorflow allows users to define mathematical functions on tensors (hence the name) using computational graphs and to compute their gradients. Tensorflow supports training of large models in a multiple GPU, distributed setting and provides capabilities for visualizing computational graphs and other metrics of interest via Tensorboard.

CHAPTER 12

Introduction to PyTorch

In this chapter, we will cover PyTorch which is a more recent addition to the ecosystem of the Deep Learning framework. PyTorch can be seen as a Python front end to the Torch engine (which initially only had Lua bindings) which at its heart provides the ability to define mathematical functions and compute their gradients. PyTorch has fairly good Graphical Processing Unit (GPU) support and is a fast-maturing framework.

There is a significant difference between PyTorch and other frameworks like Theano or Tensorflow from a programming paradigm point of view. Frameworks such as Theano or Tensorflow provide constructs with which a user can express a computational graph representing a mathematical expression, which is then processed (or compiled) to compute the expression or the gradient. Theano or Tensorflow basically follows a define-compile-run paradigm. PyTorch is a dynamic, define-by-run framework in the sense that there is no compilation step. The user can define mathematical expressions and directly evoke an operator to compute the gradient of a particular expression.

PyTorch is very well suited for research purposes as it makes developing and experimenting with new deep learning architectures relatively easy. Source code written in PyTorch seems much more intuitive with a tighter correspondence to the mathematical expressions describing the network as compared to Theano/Tensorflow. Debugging with PyTorch is much easier due to its dynamic nature. When using Theano or Tensorflow, debugging requires cutting through two abstractions, the Python code, which wires up the construction of the computational graph, and the actual computational graph that gets executed after compilation. However, it must be noted that the define-compile-run paradigm does give more room to optimize the underlying computation.

Let us start looking at PyTorch by going over a few examples. Like Tensorflow, all mathematical functions are defined on the basis of tensors. Listing 12-1 illustrates tensor creation. Specific snippets of code illustrate creating a tensor of a given size, random tensors, normalized tensors, tensors from diagonals, linearly and logarithmically spaced tensors, ones and zeros, permutations, and creating tensors over a range (and step).

Listing 12-1. Tensor Creation

```
import torch
import numpy

# Create a Tensor
a1 = torch.Tensor(4,3)
print a1
# 1.00000e-35 *
#    0.0000   0.0000   0.0000
#    0.0000   0.0004   0.0000
#    0.0104   0.0000   0.0156
#    0.0000   1.5086   0.0000
# [torch.FloatTensor of size 4x3]
```

```python
# Create a Tensor populated with random values
a2 = torch.rand(4,3)
print a2
#  0.6553  0.7280  0.5829
#  0.5965  0.1383  0.8214
#  0.7690  0.7348  0.2798
#  0.6695  0.4295  0.2672
# [torch.FloatTensor of size 4x3]

# Normalised (0 mean, unit (1) variance)
a3 = torch.randn(5)
print a3
# -0.9593
# -2.2416
#  0.5279
# -0.4319
#  1.4821
# [torch.FloatTensor of size 5]

# Diagonal Matrices
a4 = torch.eye(3)
print a4
#  1  0  0
#  0  1  0
#  0  0  1
# [torch.FloatTensor of size 3x3]

# From Numpy
a5 = torch.from_numpy(numpy.array([1,2,3]))
print a5
#  1
#  2
#  3
# [torch.LongTensor of size 3]

# Linearly spaced
a6 = torch.linspace(0,1,steps=5)
print a6
#  0.0000
#  0.2500
#  0.5000
#  0.7500
#  1.0000
# [torch.FloatTensor of size 5]
```

```
# Logarithmically spaced
a7 = torch.logspace(1,3,steps=3)
print a7
#     10
#    100
#   1000
# [torch.FloatTensor of size 3]

# Ones and Zeros
a8 = torch.ones(5)
print a8
#  1
#  1
#  1
#  1
#  1
# [torch.FloatTensor of size 5]

a9 = torch.zeros(5)
print a9
#  0
#  0
#  0
#  0
#  0
# [torch.FloatTensor of size 5]

# Random Permutation of numbers from 0 to n-1
a10 = torch.randperm(5)
print a10
#  3
#  1
#  2
#  4
#  0
# [torch.LongTensor of size 5]

# Range from start to end with given step
a11 = torch.arange(1,10,step=2)
print a11
#  1
#  3
#  5
#  7
#  9
# [torch.FloatTensor of size 5]
```

CHAPTER 12 ■ INTRODUCTION TO PYTORCH

PyTorch has good integration with Numpy. Listing 12-2 illustrates conversion of Numpy data structures to PyTorch data structures and vice versa.

Listing 12-2. Conversion from/to Numpy

```
import torch
import numpy

# Converting Torch tensors to Numpy
a1 = torch.ones(5)
print a1.numpy()
# [ 1.  1.  1.  1.  1.]

na1 = numpy.array([1,2,3,4,5])
a2 = torch.from_numpy(na1)
print a2
#  1
#  2
#  3
#  4
#  5
# [torch.LongTensor of size 5]
```

Our next example covers tensor operations in PyTorch. Refer to Listing 12-3, which illustrates operations like concatenation, chunking, indexing, selection, splitting, adding/removing dummy dimension, and stacking.

Listing 12-3. Tensor Operations

```
import torch

# Concatenation operation along given axis (starting from 0)
a = torch.rand(1,2)
print torch.cat((a,a,a,a),0).size() # (4L, 2L)
print torch.cat((a,a,a,a),1).size() # (1L, 8L)

# Break apart a tensor into parts along
a = torch.rand(10,1)
b = torch.chunk(a,10,0) # 10 parts, axis 0
print len(b) # 10
print b[0].size() # (1L, 1L)

# Get values along an axis given indices (using gather)
t = torch.Tensor([[1,2],[3,4],[5,6]])
print torch.gather(t, 0, torch.LongTensor([[0,0]])) # 1 2
print torch.gather(t, 0, torch.LongTensor([[1,1]])) # 3 4
print torch.gather(t, 0, torch.LongTensor([[2,2]])) # 5 6
print torch.gather(t, 1, torch.LongTensor([[0],[0],[0]])) # 1 3 5
print torch.gather(t, 1, torch.LongTensor([[1],[1],[1]])) # 2 4 6
```

```
# Get values along an axis given an indices vector (using index_select)
t = torch.Tensor([[1,2],[3,4],[5,6]])
index = torch.LongTensor([0,0])
print torch.index_select(t, 0, index)
#  1   2
#  1   2
print torch.index_select(t, 1, index)
#  1   1
#  3   3
#  5   5

# Masked Select
t = torch.Tensor([[1,2],[3,4],[5,6]])
mask = t.ge(3) # Greater than
print torch.masked_select(t,mask)
#  3
#  4
#  5
#  6

# Get Indices of Non-Zero elements
print torch.nonzero(torch.Tensor([1, 0, 1, 1, 1]))
#  0
#  2
#  3
#  4
# [torch.LongTensor of size 4x1]

# Split tensor into given size chunks, last one will be smaller
# if dimension of tensor is not not exact multiple of split size
print torch.split(torch.ones(5), split_size=2)
# (
#  1
#  1
# [torch.FloatTensor of size 2]
# ,
#  1
#  1
# [torch.FloatTensor of size 2]
# ,
#  1
# [torch.FloatTensor of size 1]
# )

# Remove dimensions that are of size 1 (essentially dummy)
a = torch.ones(1,3,1,3,1)
print a.size()
# (1L, 3L, 1L, 3L, 1L)
print torch.squeeze(a).size()
# (3L, 3L)
```

```
# Remove only the specified dimension
print torch.squeeze(a, dim=0).size()
#(3L, 1L, 3L, 1L)

# Stacking tensors along a dimension
a = torch.rand(1,2)
print torch.stack((a,a,a,a),0).size()
# (4L, 1L, 2L)
print torch.stack((a,a,a,a),1).size()
# (1L, 4L, 2L)
print torch.stack((a,a,a,a),2).size()
# (1L, 2L, 4L)

# Transpose a 2D matrix
a = torch.ones(3,4)
print a.size() # (3L, 4L)
print torch.t(a).size() # (4L, 3L)

# Transpose a matrix
a = torch.ones(3,4,5)
print a.size() # (3L, 4L, 5L)
print torch.transpose(a,0,1).size() # (4L, 3L, 5L)
print torch.transpose(a,0,2).size() # (5L, 4L, 3L)
print torch.transpose(a,1,2).size() # (3L, 5L, 4L)

# Transpose a matrix
a = torch.ones(3,4,5)
print [i.size() for i in torch.unbind(a,0)]
# [(4L, 5L), (4L, 5L), (4L, 5L)]
print [i.size() for i in torch.unbind(a,1)]
# [(3L, 5L), (3L, 5L), (3L, 5L), (3L, 5L)]
print [i.size() for i in torch.unbind(a,2)]
# [(3L, 4L), (3L, 4L), (3L, 4L), (3L, 4L), (3L, 4L)]

# Add a dimension (dummy)
a = torch.ones(3)
print a.size() # (3L,)
print torch.unsqueeze(a, 0).size() # (1L, 3L)
print torch.unsqueeze(a, 1).size() # (3L, 1L)
```

Let us start looking at computing gradients with PyTorch. Listing 12-4 defines a simple mathematical function and computes its gradient using the backward method. Note that this method can be invoked on Variables and it is essential to define the requires_grad parameter.

Listing 12-4. Computing Gradients

```
import torch
from torch.autograd import Variable

def f(x, y, w, b):
    y_hat = torch.tanh(torch.dot(x,w) + b)
    return torch.sqrt((y_hat - y) * (y_hat - y))
```

```
x = Variable(torch.rand(5), requires_grad=False)
y = Variable(torch.rand(1,1), requires_grad=False)
w = Variable(torch.rand(5), requires_grad=True)
b = Variable(torch.ones(1,1),requires_grad=True)
result = f(x, y, w, b)
result.backward()
print w.grad
# Variable containing:
# 1.00000e-02 *
#   5.7800
#   2.4759
#   1.8131
#   3.8120
#   0.5258
# [torch.FloatTensor of size 5]
print b.grad
# Variable containing:
# 1.00000e-02 *
#   6.6010
# [torch.FloatTensor of size 1x1]
```

Let us now look at a complete example using PyTorch for linear regression. Refer to Listing 12-5. The following points are to be noted:

1. We define a class called linear regression that inherits from nn.module.

2. We define a forward method that computes the forward pass via the network.

3. We use RMSE (root mean squared error) as the loss function.

4. The model is trained over the training data but computing gradients and implementing gradient descent.

Listing 12-5. Linear Regression

```
import torch
from torch.autograd import Variable
import torch.nn as nn
import random

# Define the Linear Regression Model
class LinearRegression(nn.Module):
    def __init__(self, input_size):
        super(LinearRegression, self).__init__()
        self.w = Variable(torch.rand(1,1), requires_grad = True)
        self.b = Variable(torch.rand(1,1), requires_grad = True)
    def forward(self, x):
        return (x * self.w) + self.b
```

```
def rmse(lr_model, x, y):
    y_hat = []
    for i in x:
        y_hat.append(lr_model(i))
    Y = torch.stack(y, 1)
    Y_hat = torch.stack(y_hat, 1)
    diff = Y - Y_hat
    return torch.sqrt(torch.mean(diff * diff))

# Prepare Dataset
dataset_size = 100
x_data = []
y_data = []
for i in xrange(0,100):
    x = Variable(torch.rand(1,1))
    y = Variable(torch.rand(1,1))
    x_data.append(x)
    y_data.append(y)

lr = LinearRegression(1)

loss_func = torch.nn.MSELoss()
print "RMSE before training ", rmse(lr, x_data, y_data).data.numpy()

# Training
steps = 1000
learning_rate = 0.0001
for i in xrange(steps):
    index = random.randint(0, dataset_size-1)
    lr.w.data.zero_()
    lr.b.data.zero_()
    loss = loss_func(lr(x_data[index]), y_data[index])
    loss.backward()
    lr.w.data -= learning_rate * lr.w.grad.data
    lr.b.data -= learning_rate * lr.b.grad.data

print "RMSE after training ", rmse(lr, x_data, y_data).data.numpy()

# RMSE before training   [ 0.73697698]
# RMSE after training    [ 0.49001607]
```

PyTorch provides a number of optimizers that the user can use instead of implementing gradient descent and its variants by hand. We illustrate this in Listing 12-6. The following points are to be noted:

1. We use the SGD (Stochastic Gradient Descent) optimizer that takes the parameters to optimize, the learning rate and the momentum.

2. We compute the gradients via invoking the backward method on the variable corresponding to the loss and then invoke the optimiser.step

Listing 12-6. Using Optimizers

```
import torch
from torch.autograd import Variable
import torch.nn as nn
import random
import torch.optim as optim

# Define the Linear Regression Model
class LinearRegression(nn.Module):
    def __init__(self, input_size):
        super(LinearRegression, self).__init__()
        self.linear = torch.nn.Linear(input_size, 1)
    def forward(self, x):
        return self.linear(x)

def rmse(lr_model, x, y):
    y_hat = []
    for i in x:
        y_hat.append(lr_model(i))
    Y = torch.stack(y, 1)
    Y_hat = torch.stack(y_hat, 1)
    diff = Y - Y_hat
    return torch.sqrt(torch.mean(diff * diff))

# Prepare Dataset
dataset_size = 100
x_data = []
y_data = []
for i in xrange(0,100):
    x = Variable(torch.rand(1,1))
    y = Variable(torch.rand(1,1))
    x_data.append(x)
    y_data.append(y)

lr = LinearRegression(1)

loss_func = torch.nn.MSELoss()
optimizer = optim.SGD(lr.parameters(), lr = 0.01, momentum=0.9)

print "RMSE before training ", rmse(lr, x_data, y_data).data.numpy()

# Training
steps = 5000
for i in xrange(steps):
    index = random.randint(0, dataset_size-1)
    lr.zero_grad()
    loss = loss_func(lr(x_data[index]), y_data[index])
    loss.backward()
    optimizer.step()
```

CHAPTER 12 ■ INTRODUCTION TO PYTORCH

```
print "RMSE after training ", rmse(lr, x_data, y_data).data.numpy()

# RMSE before training   [ 0.57391912]
# RMSE after training    [ 0.31023207]
```

Let us now look at a complete example using PyTorch for a neural network. Refer to Listing 12-7. We build upon all the constructs introduced so far and also use the linear construct, which basically implements a single layer, rather than implementing this by having a weight vector and bias terms. The linear construct does the same for us under the hood.

Listing 12-7. Neural Network Model

```
import torch
from torch.autograd import Variable
import torch.nn as nn
import random
import torch.optim as optim
import torch.nn.functional as F

# Define NN Model
class NNModel(nn.Module):
    def __init__(self, input_size, hidden_size):
        super(NNModel, self).__init__()
        self.linear1 = torch.nn.Linear(input_size, hidden_size)
        self.linear2 = torch.nn.Linear(hidden_size, 2)
    def forward(self, x):
        temp = self.linear1(x)
        temp = F.relu(temp)
        temp = self.linear2(temp)
        temp = F.softmax(temp)
        return temp

def accuracy(nn_model, x_data, y_data):
    correct = 0.0
    for x, y in zip(x_data, y_data):
        output = nn_model(x)
        pred = output.data.max(1)[1]
        temp = pred.eq(y.data)
        curr_correct = temp.sum()
        correct += curr_correct
    return correct/len(y_data)

# Prepare Dataset
dataset_size = 100
x_data = []
y_data = []
for i in xrange(0,dataset_size):
    x = Variable(torch.rand(1,5))
    if random.random() > 0.5:
        y = Variable(torch.LongTensor([0]))
    else:
```

```
        y = Variable(torch.LongTensor([1]))
    x_data.append(x)
    y_data.append(y)

nnet = NNModel(5,20)

loss_func = torch.nn.CrossEntropyLoss()
optimizer = optim.SGD(nnet.parameters(), lr = 0.01)

print "Accuracy before training ", accuracy(nnet, x_data, y_data)

# Training
steps = 10000
for i in xrange(steps):
    index = random.randint(0, dataset_size-1)
    nnet.zero_grad()
    loss = loss_func(nnet(x_data[index]), y_data[index])
    loss.backward()
    optimizer.step()

print "Accuracy after training ", accuracy(nnet, x_data, y_data)

# Accuracy before training   0.455
# Accuracy after training    0.62
```

Let us now look at a complete example using PyTorch for a convolutional neural network. We will be using the MNIST data set, which is a commonly used benchmark data set for Deep Learning. The data set consists of handwritten digits (60,000 training examples and 10,000 test examples). The task at hand is to predict the digit given the image, so this is a multiclassification problem with ten classes. Refer to Listing 12-8. We build upon all the constructs introduced so far and also use constructs like Conv2D, ReLU, and log_softmax. We also use the dropout regularization technique which is covered in Chapter 13.

Listing 12-8. Convolution Neural Network

```
import torch
import torch.nn as nn
from torchvision import datasets, transforms
import torch.nn.functional as F
import torch.optim as optim
from torch.autograd import Variable

class Net(nn.Module):
    def __init__(self):
        super(Net, self).__init__()
        self.convolution1 = nn.Conv2d(1, 10, kernel_size=5)
        self.convolution2 = nn.Conv2d(10, 20, kernel_size=5)
        self.dropout = nn.Dropout2d()
        self.fc1 = nn.Linear(320, 50)
        self.fc2 = nn.Linear(50, 10)
```

CHAPTER 12 ■ INTRODUCTION TO PYTORCH

```
    def forward(self, x):
        x = F.relu(F.max_pool2d(self.convolution1(x), 2))
        x = F.relu(F.max_pool2d(self.dropout(self.convolution2(x)), 2))
        x = x.view(-1, 320)
        x = F.relu(self.fc1(x))
        x = F.dropout(x, training=self.training)
        x = self.fc2(x)
        return F.log_softmax(x)

def accuracy():
    correct = 0.0
    for data, target in test_loader:
        data, target = Variable(data, volatile=True), Variable(target)
        output = model(data)
        pred = output.data.max(1)[1]
        correct += pred.eq(target.data).cpu().sum()
    return correct/len(test_loader.dataset)

model = Net()
batch_size = 100
train_loader = torch.utils.data.DataLoader(datasets.MNIST('./temp', train=True, download=True,
transform=transforms.Compose([transforms.ToTensor()])),
batch_size=batch_size)
test_loader = torch.utils.data.DataLoader(datasets.MNIST('./temp', train=False, download=True,
transform=transforms.Compose([transforms.ToTensor()])),
batch_size=batch_size)

optimizer = optim.SGD(model.parameters(), lr = 0.01, momentum=0.9)

print "Accuracy before training:", accuracy()
for batch_idx, (data, target) in enumerate(train_loader):
        data, target = Variable(data), Variable(target)
        optimizer.zero_grad()
        output = model(data)
        loss = F.nll_loss(output, target)
        loss.backward()
        optimizer.step()
print "Accuracy after training: ", accuracy()

# Accuracy before training:   0.1005
# Accuracy after training:    0.8738
```

Let us now look at a complete example using PyTorch for a recurrent neural network (refer to Listing 12-9). We will be using dummy sequence data which needs to be classified into two categories. The example uses the constructs mentioned earlier, and the reader is advised to review chapter 6.

Listing 12-9. Recurrent Neural Network

```
import torch
import random
import torch.nn as nn
from torch.autograd import Variable
import torch.nn.functional as F
import torch.optim as optim
import random

# Generate training data
data_x = []
data_y = []
max_sequence_len = 10
min_sequence_len = 3
for i in xrange(0,50):
    curr_seq_len = random.randint(min_sequence_len, max_sequence_len)
    # Positive Examples
    data_x.append(torch.ones(curr_seq_len))
    data_y.append(torch.LongTensor([1]))
    # Negative Examples
    temp = torch.ones(curr_seq_len)
    pos = random.randint(0,curr_seq_len-1)
    temp[pos] = 0
    data_x.append(temp)
    data_y.append(torch.LongTensor([0]))

class RNN(nn.Module):
    def __init__(self, input_size, hidden_size, output_size):
        super(RNN, self).__init__()
        self.hidden_size = hidden_size
        self.inputToHidden = nn.Linear(input_size + hidden_size, hidden_size)
        self.input2output = nn.Linear(input_size + hidden_size, output_size)
        self.softmax = nn.LogSoftmax()

    def forward(self, input, hidden):
        combined = torch.cat((input, hidden), 1)
        hidden = self.inputToHidden(combined)
        output = self.input2output(combined)
        output = self.softmax(output)
        return output, hidden

    def initHidden(self):
        return Variable(torch.zeros(1, self.hidden_size))
```

```python
def accuracy(rnn, data_x, data_y):
    correct = 0.0
    for x, y in zip(data_x, data_y):
        X = Variable(x)
        expected = Variable(y)
        hidden = rnn.initHidden()
        for j in range(len(x)):
            output, hidden = rnn(torch.unsqueeze(X[j],0), hidden)
        pred = output.data.max(1)[1]
        correct += pred.eq(expected.data).sum()
    return correct/len(data_y)

rnn = RNN(1, 1, 2)
hidden = rnn.initHidden()
index = random.randint(0,99)
learning_rate = 0.1
optimizer = torch.optim.SGD(rnn.parameters(), lr = learning_rate)

print "Accuracy before training: ", accuracy(rnn,data_x, data_y)

for i in xrange(500):
    index = random.randint(0,99)
    X = Variable(data_x[index])
    expected = Variable(data_y[index])
    rnn.zero_grad()
    hidden = rnn.initHidden()
    for j in range(len(data_x[index])):
        output, hidden = rnn(torch.unsqueeze(X[j],0), hidden)
    loss = F.cross_entropy(output, expected)
    loss.backward()
    optimizer.step()

print "Accuracy after training: ", accuracy(rnn, data_x, data_y)

# Accuracy before training:  0.5
# Accuracy after training:   0.7
```

Summary

In this chapter we covered PyTorch, which allows users to define mathematical functions and compute their gradients, dynamically. PyTorch is very well suited for research purposes as it makes developing and experimenting with new deep learning architectures relatively easy. PyTorch has fairly good GPU support and is a fast-maturing framework.

CHAPTER 13

Regularization Techniques

In this chapter we will cover three regularization techniques commonly used in Deep Learning, namely, early stopping, norm penalties, and dropout. The reader is advised to refer to Chapter 2 introducing the basics of machine learning, specifically to revisit the notions of model capacity, overfitting, and underfitting.

Model Capacity, Overfitting, and Underfitting

Let us briefly revisit the notions of model capacity, overfitting, and underfitting. We will use the previous example (from Chapter 2) of fitting a regression model. We have data of the form $D = \{(x_1, y_1), (x_2, y_2), \ldots (x_n, y_n)\}$ where $x \in \mathbb{R}^n$ and $y \in \mathbb{R}$ and our task is to generate a computational procedure that implements the function $f : x \to y$. We measure performance over this task as the root mean squared error (RMSE) over unseen data,

$$E(f, D, U) = \left(\frac{\sum_{(x_i, y_i) \in U} (y_i - f(x_i))^2}{|U|} \right)^{\frac{1}{2}}.$$

Given a data set of the form $D = \{(x_1, y_1), (x_2, y_2), \ldots (x_n, y_n)\}$ where $x \in \mathbb{R}^n$ and $y \in \mathbb{R}$, we use the least squares model which takes the form $y = \beta x$ where β is a vector such that $\|X\beta - y\|_2^2$ is minimized. Here X is a matrix where each row is an x. The value of β can be derived using the closed form $\beta = (X^T X)^{-1} X^T y$.

We can transform x to be a vector of values $[x^0, x^1, x^2]$. That is, if $x = 2$, it will be transformed to $[1, 2, 4]$. Post this transformation, we can generate a least squares model β using the formula described above. What is happening under the hood is that we are approximating the given data with a second-order polynomial (degree = 2) equation, and, the least squares algorithm is simply curve fitting or generating the coefficients for each of $[x^0, x^1, x^2]$.

Similarly, we can generate another model with least squares algorithm but we will transform x to $[x^0, x^1, x^2, x^3, x^4, x^5, x^6, x^7, x^8]$. That is, we are approximating the given data with a polynomial with degree = 8.

By increasing the degree of the polynomial we can fit arbitrary data. It is easy to see that if we have n data points, a polynomial of degree n can perfectly fit the data. It is also easy to see that such a model is simply memorizing the data. We can use this example to develop perspective on model capacity, overfitting, and underfitting. The degree of the polynomial we use to fit the data is basically a proxy for the capacity of the model. The more the degree, the higher the capacity of the model.

© Nikhil Ketkar 2017
N. Ketkar, *Deep Learning with Python*, DOI 10.1007/978-1-4842-2766-4_13

CHAPTER 13 REGULARIZATION TECHNIQUES

Let us assume that the data was generated using a polynomial of degree 5 with some noise. Also, note that while fitting the data we do not know anything about the process that generated the data. We have to produce a model that best fits the data. Essentially, we do not know how much of the data is the *pattern* and how much of the data is *noise*.

On such a data set, if we use models with high enough capacity (degree of the polynomial greater than 5, in the worst case equal to the number of data points), we can get a perfect model when evaluated on the training data, but this model will do very poorly on unseen data because it has essentially fit the *noise*. This is overfitting. If we use a model with low capacity (less than 5), it will not fit either the training or the unseen data well. This is underfitting.

Regularizing the Model

From the previous example, it is easy to see that while fitting models, a central problem is getting the capacity of the model exactly right so that one neither overfits nor underfits the data. Regularization can be simply seen as any modification to the model (or its training process) that intends to improve the error on the unseen data (at the cost of the error on the training data) by systematically limiting the capacity of the model. This process systematically limiting or regulating the capacity of the model is guided by a portion of the labeled data that is not used in training. This data is commonly referred to as the validation set.

In our running example, a regularized version of least squares takes the form $y = \beta x$ where β is a vector such that $\|X\beta - y\|_2^2 + \lambda \|\beta\|_2^2$ is minimized, and λ is a user-defined parameter that controls the complexity. Here by introducing the term $\lambda \|\beta\|_2^2$ we are penalizing models with extra capacity. To see why this is the case, consider fitting a least squares model using a polynomial of degree 10, but the values in the vector β have 8 zeros and 2 non-zeros. Against this, consider the case where all values in the vector β are non-zeros. For all practical purposes, the former model is a model with degree = 2 and has a lower value of $\lambda \|\beta\|_2^2$. The λ term allows us to balance accuracy over the training data with the complexity of the model. Lower values of λ imply a model with lower capacity.

One natural question to ask is, Why don't we simply use the validation set as a guide and simply increase the degree of the polynomial in the previous example? Since the degree of the polynomial is a proxy for the capacity of the model why can't we just use that to tune the model capacity? Why do we need to introduce the change in the model ($\|X\beta - y\|_2^2 + \lambda \|\beta\|_2^2$ instead of $\|X\beta - y\|_2^2$ previously)? The answer is that we want to systematically limit the capacity of the model for which we need a fine-grained control. Changing the model capacity by varying the degree of the model is a very course-grained, discrete knob while varying λ is very fine grained.

Early Stopping

One of the simplest techniques for regularization in deep learning is early stopping. Given a training set and a validation set and a network with sufficient capacity, we observe that with increasing training steps, first the error on both the training set and the validation set decreases, and then the error of the training set continues to decrease while the error in validation increases (refer to Figure 13-1).

The key idea with early stopping is to keep track of the model parameters/weights that give the best performance over the validation set and then to stop the training after this *best performance so far over the validation set* does not improve over a predefined number of training steps.

CHAPTER 13 REGULARIZATION TECHNIQUES

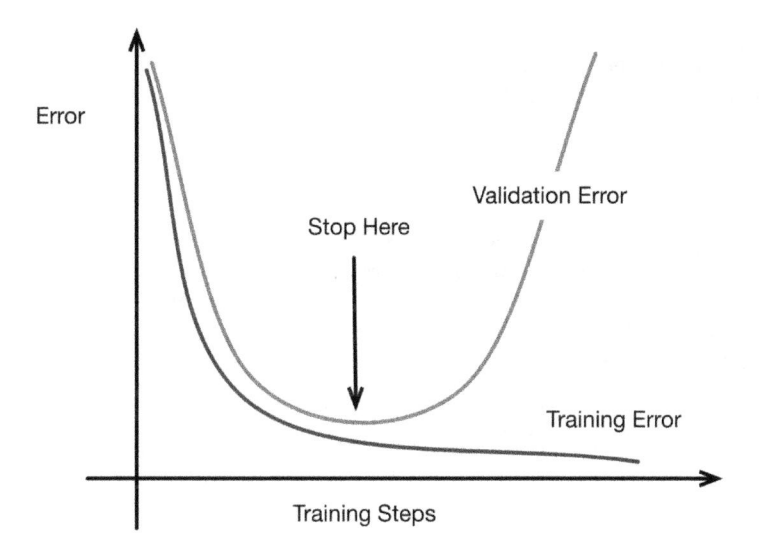

Figure 13-1. Early stopping

Early stopping acts as a regularizer by restricting the values that the parameters/weights of the model can take. Early stopping limits w to a neighborhood around the starting values (around w_0) (see Figure 13-2). So, if we stop at w_s, the values of w_{s+1} are not possible. This essentially restricts the capacity of the model.

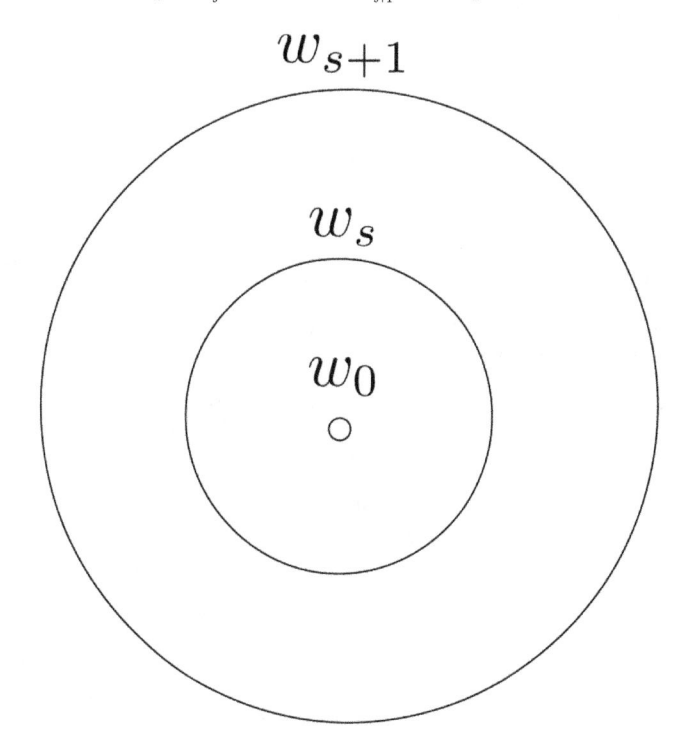

Figure 13-2. Early stopping restricts w

211

CHAPTER 13 REGULARIZATION TECHNIQUES

Early stopping is quite non-invasive in the sense that it does not require any changes to the model. It is also cheap as it only requires storing the parameters of the model (best so far on the validation set). It can also be combined with other regularization techniques easily.

Norm Penalties

Norm penalties are a common form of regularization in deep learning (and machine learning in general). The idea is simply to add a term $r(\theta)$ to the loss function of a neural network (refer to Chapter 5) where r typically represents either the L^1 norm or the L^2 norm and θ represents the parameters/weights of the network. Thus, the regularized loss function becomes $l(f_{NN}(x,\theta),y)+\alpha \cdot r(\theta)$ instead of just $l(f_{NN}(x,\theta),y)$. Note that the α term is the regularization parameter.

Note In general, an L_p norm is defined as $\|x\|_p = \left(\sum_i |x_i|^p\right)^{1/p}$. Accordingly, the L_1 norm is defined as $\|x\|_1 = \left(\sum_i |x_i|^1\right)^{1/1} = \sum_i |x_i|$. Similarly, the L_2 norm is defined as $\|x\|_2 = \left(\sum_i |x_i|^2\right)^{1/2} = \left(\sum_i (x_i)^2\right)^{1/2}$.

Let us now dive deeper into the regularized loss function $l(f_{NN}(x,\theta),y)+\alpha \cdot r(\theta)$. The following points are to be noted:

1. As we attempt to minimize the overall loss function $l(f_{NN}(x,\theta),y)+\alpha \cdot r(\theta)$ we attempt to reduce the contribution of the $l(f_{NN}(x,\theta),y)$ term as well as the regularization term given by $\alpha \cdot r(\theta)$.

2. It follows that for two sets of parameters θ_a and θ_b if $l(f_{NN}(x,\theta_a),y)=l(f_{NN}(x,\theta_b),y)$ then the optimization algorithm will choose θ_a if $r(\theta_a)<r(\theta_b)$ and θ_b if $r(\theta_a)>r(\theta_b)$.

3. Thus, the role of the regularization term is to direct the optimization in the direction of the θ which lowers $r(\theta)$.

4. It is easy to see that lower values of $r(\theta)$ when r corresponds to L^1 regularization will lead to a sparser θ, hence reducing the effective capacity.

5. It is easy to see that lower values of $r(\theta)$ when r corresponds to L^2 regularization will lead to a θ closer to 0, hence reducing the effective capacity (refer to Figure 13-3).

6. The α term is used to control how much emphasis we place on $l(f_{NN}(x,\theta),y)$ versus $r(\theta)$. Higher values of α means more emphasis placed on regularization.

CHAPTER 13 REGULARIZATION TECHNIQUES

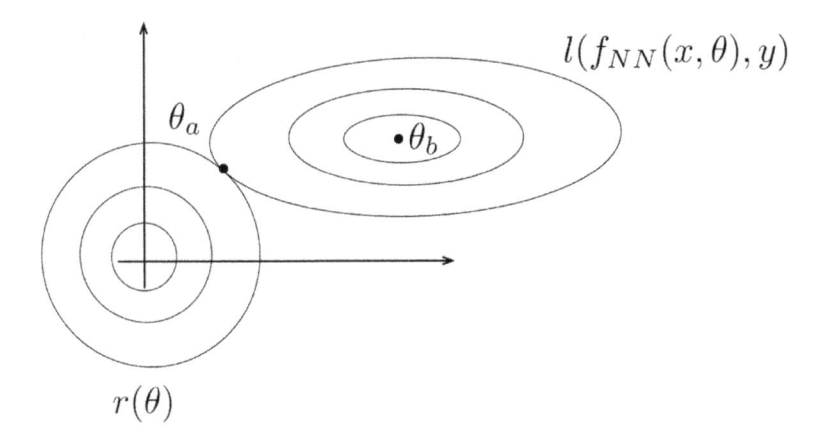

Figure 13-3. *L^2 norm leads to θ closer to zero, θ_a is picked by the optimization algorithms because of regularization; without it, θ_b would be picked.*

It must be noted that norm penalties are applied to the weight vectors, not to the bias terms. The reasoning behind this that that any regularization is a trade-off between overfitting and underfitting and regularizing the bias term leads to a bad trade-off due to too much underfitting.

While training deep learning networks different values of α can be used for different layers and the appropriate value of α is determined via an experiment using the validation set as a guide.

Dropout

Dropout is essentially a computational cheap form of a model ensemble/averaging. Let us first consider the key concept of model ensemble/averaging. While individual models with sufficient capacity can overfit, if we average or take majority voting on the predictions of multiple models (trained over subsets of data, or different weight initializations or different hyper-parameters) we can address overfitting. Model ensemble/averaging is an extremely useful form of regularization which helps us deal with overfitting; however, it is quite computationally expensive given that we have to train multiple models and make predictions on multiple models (and then combine them via voting or averaging). This computational expense is particularly high with deep learning models with multiple layers. Dropout provides a cheap alternative.

The key idea of dropout is to drop units and their connections randomly while training the network with probability p and then to multiply the learned weights with p at prediction time (refer to Figure 13-4).

Let us make this idea precise in the form of mathematical expressions. A standard neural network layer can be expressed as $y = f(w \cdot x + b)$ where y is the output, x is the input, f is the activation function, and w and b are the weight vector and bias terms, respectively. A dropout layer at training time can be expressed as $y = f(w(x \odot r) + b)$ where $r \sim Bernoulli(p)$ and the symbol $\odot$ denotes point-wise multiplication of two vectors (if $a = [1,1,2]$ and $b = [0.5,0.5,0.5]$ then $a \odot b = [0.5,0.5,1]$. At prediction time the dropout layer can be represented as $y = f((p \cdot w \cdot x) + b)$.

It is easy to see that the dropout layer, while training, actually trains multiple networks, as for every distinct r we have a different network. It is also easy to see that at prediction time we are averaging over the multiple networks as $y = f((p \cdot w \cdot x) + b)$.

213

CHAPTER 13 ■ REGULARIZATION TECHNIQUES

While training with dropout with batch stochastic gradient, a single value of *r* is used over the entire batch. In relevant literature, the recommended values for *p* are 0.8 for input units and 0.5 for hidden units. A norm regularization found useful with dropout is max norm regularization where *w* is constrained as $\|w\|_2 < c$, where *c* is a user-defined parameter.

At training time present with probability p

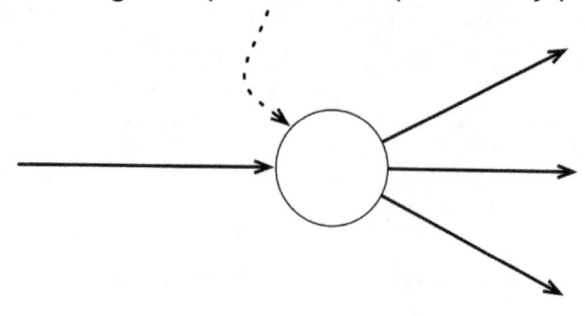

At prediction time always present

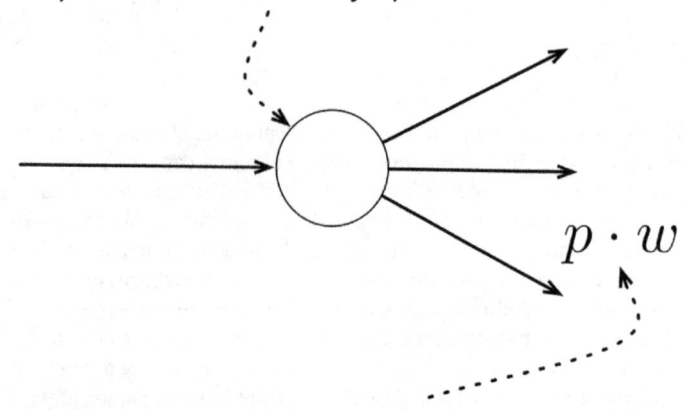

$p \cdot w$

At prediction time, multiple learned weights with p

Figure 13-4. Dropout

Summary

In this chapter we covered three regularization techniques commonly used in Deep Learning, namely, early stopping, norm penalties, and dropout. There are several other advanced/domain-specific techniques found in the literature that must be mentioned. Parameter tying and sharing in the convolution layer of a convolution neural network can be thought of as a regularization technique as it reduces the capacity as compared with a fully connected layer (refer to Chapter 5). Data set augmentation where artificial data is introduced by making invariant transformations to the real data can be thought of as a regularization technique. Noise ingestion in the data and labels can also be thought of as a regularization technique. The reader is also advised to look at literature on semisupervised learning and unsupervised pre-training which are fairly advanced techniques.

CHAPTER 14

Training Deep Learning Models

Throughout the book we have covered the theoretical aspects of models and introduced the reader to a number of frameworks for Deep Learning. In this chapter we will cover the process of training deep learning models.

Performance Metrics

The model development process typically starts by formulating a crisp problem definition. This basically involves defining the input and the output of the model and the impact (usefulness) such a model can deliver. An example of such a problem definition is the classification of product images into product categories, the input to such a model being product images and the output being product categories. Such a model might aid the automated categorization of products in an e-commerce or online marketplace setting.

Having crisply defined the problem definition, the next task is to define the performance metrics. The key purpose of performance metrics is to tell us how well our model is doing. A simple metric of performance may be accuracy (or equivalently the error), which simply measures the disagreements between the expected output and the output produced by the model. However, there are cases where accuracy is a poor measure of performance.

The two main reasons for this are class imbalance and unequal misclassification cost. Let us understand the class imbalance problem with an example. As a sub-problem of the problem in our previous example of product classification, consider the case of distinguishing between mobile phones and their accessories. The number of examples for a class of mobile phones is a lot smaller than the class of mobile phone accessories. In the case where, say, 95% of the examples are mobile phone accessories and 5% are mobile phones, an accuracy of 95% can be simply acquired by predicting the majority class. Thus, accuracy will be a poor choice of a metric in this example.

Let us now understand the problem of unequal misclassification costs, again by considering an example related to the problem of product classification. Consider the error associated with categorizing food products that are allergen-free (not containing the eight top allergens, namely, milk, eggs, fish, crustacean shellfish, tree nuts, peanuts, wheat, and soybean) versus the rest (non-allergen-free). From a buyer's point of view, as well as a business point of view, the error associated with categorizing a non-allergen-free product as an allergen-free product is significantly more as compared to categorizing an allergen-free product as a non-allergen-free product. Accuracy does not capture this and hence would be a poor choice in this case.

An alternative set of metrics is precision and recall, which measure the fraction of predictions in the predicted class that were correctly recovered and the fraction of the predicted class that were reported, respectively (refer to Figure 14-1). Precision and recall together are robust with respect to class imbalance.

CHAPTER 14 ■ TRAINING DEEP LEARNING MODELS

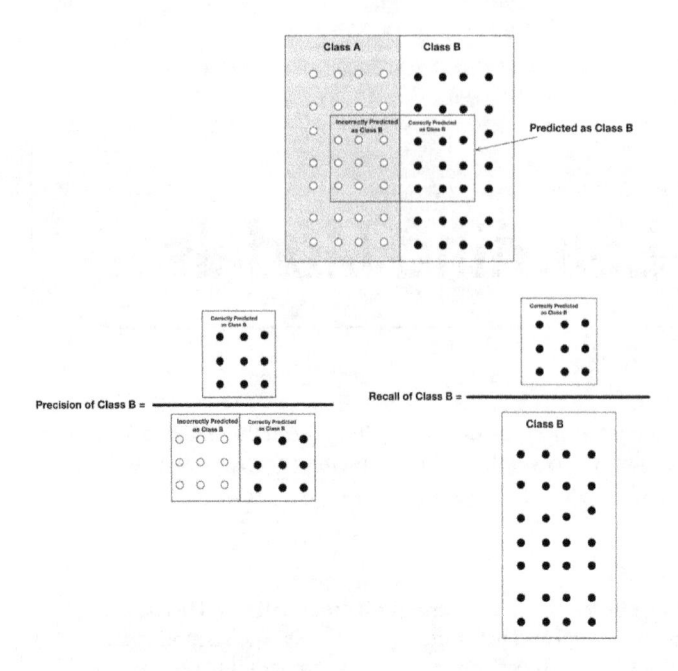

Figure 14-1. Precision and recall

Precision and recall are often visualized using a PR curve (refer to Figure 14-2), which plots precision on the Y axis and recall on the X axis. Different values of precision and recall can be obtained by varying the decision threshold on the score or the probability the model produces (for instance, 0 implying class A and 1 implying class B, a higher value on one side indicating a particular class). This curve can be used to trade off precision for recall by varying the threshold.

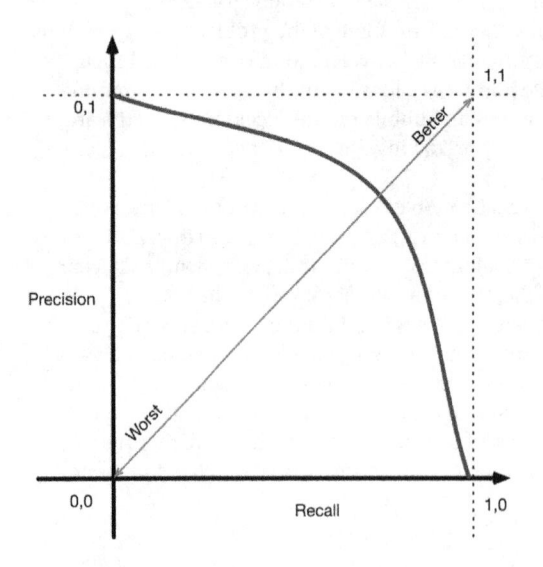

Figure 14-2. PR curve

216

CHAPTER 14 ■ TRAINING DEEP LEARNING MODELS

The F-score defined as $\frac{2pr}{p+r}$ where p denotes precision and r denotes recall can be used to summarize the PR curve.

The Receiver Operating Characteristics (ROC) curve is also useful in cases of class imbalance and unequal misclassification cost. In this setting examples are said to belong to two classes: positive and negative.

The true positive rate measures the fraction of true positives with respect to the actual positives and the true negative rate measures the fraction of true negatives with respect to the actual negatives (refer to Figure 14-3). The ROC curve plots the true positive rate on the X axis and the false positive rate on the Y axis (refer to Figure 14-4). The Area Under the Curve (AUC) is used to summarize the ROC curve.

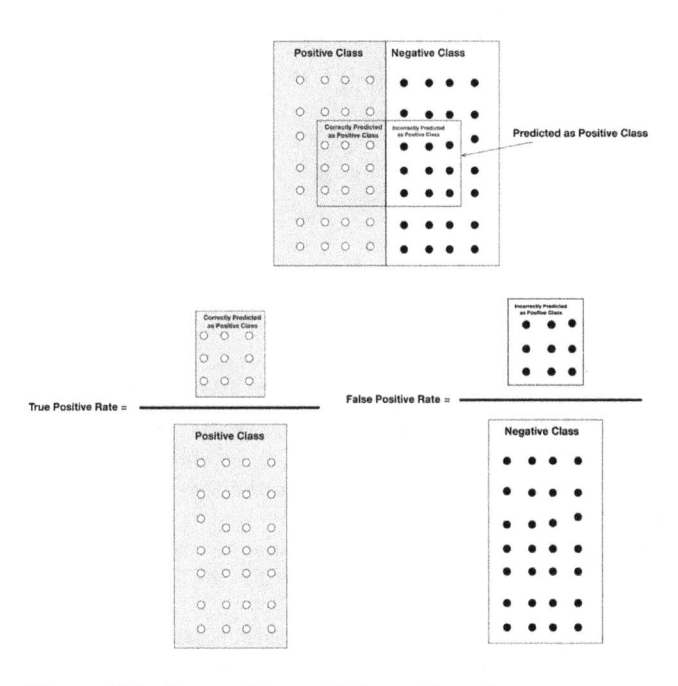

Figure 14-3. True positive and false positive rates

CHAPTER 14 ■ TRAINING DEEP LEARNING MODELS

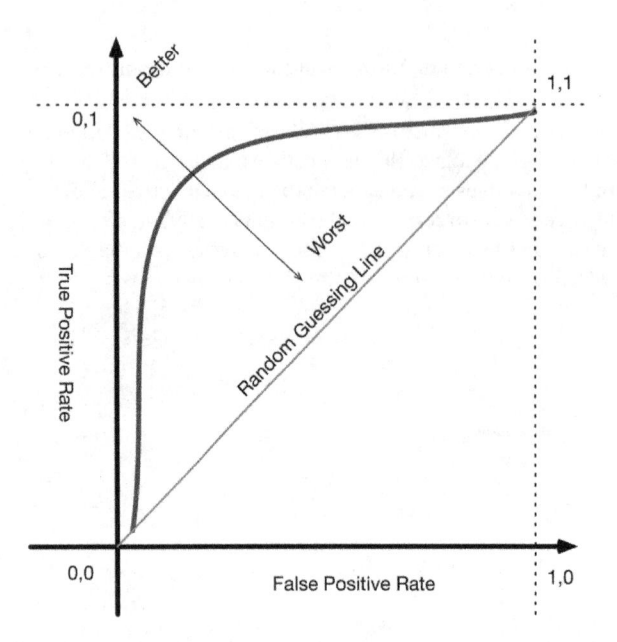

Figure 14-4. ROC curve

In many cases, standard metrics like accuracy, precision/recall, and so on do not allow us to truly capture model performance for the given business use case at hand. In such cases, metrics appropriate to the business use cases need to be formulated keeping in mind the nature of the problem, the class imbalance, and the misclassification cost. For instance, in our running example of product categorization, we may choose not to use predictions with low confidence and have them categorized manually. There is a cost associated with having examples manually categorized and there is a different cost associated with showing wrong products in the wrong category on an e-commerce site. The cost of misclassifying a popular product is also different (typically higher) than the cost of misclassifying a rarely bought product. In such a case, we might choose to use only the high confidence predictions from the model. A possible choice of metrics to use would be the number of examples misclassified (with high confidence) and the coverage (the number of examples covered with high confidence). One may also factor in the misclassification cost in this setting by taking a weighted average of the two (appropriate weights may be chosen based on the misclassification costs).

Metric definition is a very critical step of the model building process in an industry setting. It is recommended that practitioners deeply analyze the business domain to understand the misclassification cost and the data to understand the class distributions and design performance metrics accordingly. A badly defined metric can lead a project down an incorrect path.

Data Procurement

Data procurement is the process of collecting data for building a model according to a problem statement. Data procurement can involve collecting old (already generated) data from production systems, collecting live data from production systems, and in many cases collecting data labeled by human operators (crowd sourcing or internal operations teams). In our running example of product categorization, product titles, images, descriptions, and so on would need to be collected from a company catalogue, and labeled data may be generated using crowd sourcing. We might also want to collect click data and sales to determine the popular products (misclassification in these cases would be costly).

Data procurement typically happens in conjunction with the problem state definition and metrics; thus it is imperative that a practitioner play an active role in the data procurement process. Typically, in an industry setting the data procurement is a fairly time-consuming and painful process. Subtle errors in data procurement can derail a project at a later stage.

Splitting Data for Training/Validation/Test

Once the data for building the model has been procured, one needs to split the data into data used for training, parameter tuning, and go-live testing. Conceptually, the available data is to be used for three distinct purposes. The first purpose is to train the model; that is, the model will try to fit this data. The second purpose is to determine if the model is overfitting the data. This data will not be used for training but will drive the decision making on parameter tuning, regularization techniques, and so on (referred to as the validation set). The third purpose of the data is to determine if the model is really good enough to take to production/go-live (referred to as the test set).

The first key concept to internalize is that data cannot be shared for these three purposes, a distinct portion of the data is required for each purpose. If a certain portion of the data has been used to train the model, it cannot be used to tune the parameters of the model or to serve as the final performance gate (production/go-live). Similarly, if a certain portion of the data has been used for tuning parameters, it cannot serve as the test data for production/go-live. Thus, a practitioner needs to split data into three parts, training, parameter tuning, and go-live. While the idea that training data should be distinct from data used for parameter tuning is intuitive, the reasoning behind having a distinct go-live set is not. The key point to internalize is that if the model has seen the data or the modeler has seen the data, then this data has fundamentally driven some decision making around the model and it cannot be used for final go-live test if we need the test to be truly blind. Truly blind implies never looking at the data (and the labels) or never using it for making any decision that goes into building the model. One must not tune the model any further by looking at the results on the go-live testing set.

The second key point to internalize is that each of the three sets, training, parameter tuning, and go-live testing, needs to be a true representative of the underlying population of data. Splitting the data sets should take this into consideration; for instance, distribution of examples across the classes should be the same as the underlying population. If the data is not a true representative (i.e., if the data is biased in any way), the performance of the model will not be achieved once the model goes to production.

The third key point to internalize is that more data is always better for any of the three purposes (mentioned previously) and since the data sets cannot overlap and since the overall data set is limited, a practitioner, needs to carefully choose the fraction of the data used for each purpose. A 50/25/25 split or a 60/20/20 split across training, validation, and test is a reasonable choice.

Establishing Achievable Limits on the Error Rate

Having defined the problem and performance metrics and having procured and split data into training, parameter tuning, and go-live test sets, the next step is to establish the achievable limit on the error rate. Conceptually, this is the error rate one can hope to achieve given an infinite supply of data and is referred to as the Bayes error. Establishing the limit on the error rate in Artificial Intelligence (AI) tasks is typically done via a proxy like human labeling or variations on the theme appropriate to the business use case. Variations may include using an expert on the subject to label the data, a panel of human beings, or a panel of experts. Establishing this limit is quite valuable and well worth the expenditure of human/expert help if required. First, this establishes the best possible results that can be achieved, and in certain cases, this is not good enough to satisfy the business use case at hand (in which case the problem formulation needs to be rethought). Second, it tells us how far our current model is from the best achievable results.

Establishing the Baseline with Standard Choices

The best place to start the modeling process is with a baseline model with standard choices (based on literature or part experience) of architecture and algorithms—for instance, using CNNs (Convolutional Neural Networks) for images or LSTM (Long Short Term Memory) for sequences. Using ReLU as activation units and batch-SGD (Stochastic Gradient Descent) are also good choices to start with. The baseline model basically establishes a straw man on which to improve based on analysis of the shortcomings.

Building an Automated, End-to-End Pipeline

Having decided upon a baseline model, it is of critical importance to build an end-to-end, fully automated pipeline which includes training the model on the training set, making predictions on the parameter tuning set, and computing the metrics on both sets. Automation is extremely important as it allows the practitioner to iterate quickly on new models by tweaking the model architecture and hyper-parameters.

Orchestration for Visibility

While building the end-to-end pipeline, it's also a good idea to put in the orchestration to visualize histograms of activations, gradients, metrics on training and validation sets, and so on. Tools like Tensorboard (refer to Chapter 11) make it quite easy to do this. Visibility into the model training, weights, and performance can be quite useful when it comes to debugging unexpected behavior.

The key point to internalize is that building the automation and orchestration for visibility to begin with will save a lot of time and energy in the future.

Analysis of Overfitting and Underfitting

The ideal end goal of the iterative cycle of model improvement is to develop a model where the performance over the training and validation sets is nearly equal to the established performance limit (proxy for Bayes error). Figure 14-5 illustrates this final destination of the model improvement process. However, while iteratively developing new models, the practitioner will encounter underfitting and overfitting. Underfitting is the case where the model's performance over the training and validation sets is nearly equal and this is lower than the performance limit (which is desired). Overfitting is the case where the model performance over the validation set is significantly lower than its performance over the training set. Underfitting and overfitting are not mutually exclusive.

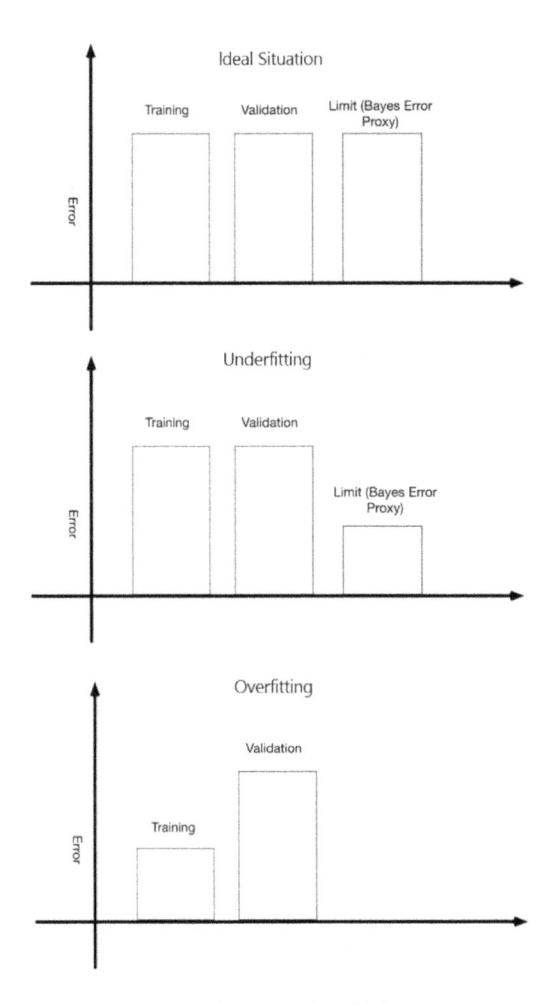

Figure 14-5. Overfitting and underfitting

Detecting whether the model is overfitting or underfitting is the first step after a new model is trained. In the case of underfitting, the key step to take is to increase the effective capacity of the model, which is typically done by modifying the architecture (increasing layers, widths, etc.). In the case of overfitting, the key steps to take are either regularization methods (refer to Chapter 13) or increasing the data set size. An important visualization is learning curves which plot performance metrics on the Y axis and the training data made available to the model. This is quite useful in determining if it makes sense to invest in procuring more labeled data.

Hyper-Parameter Tuning

Tuning hyper-parameters of the model (like learning rate or momentum) can be done manually, via grid search (where in a grid is defined over a small set of values) or random search (wherein values of hyper-parameters are drawn at random from a distribution defined by the user).

Summary

In this chapter we covered the process of model training. We also described a number of critical steps and an analysis that should be systematically performed in order to improve the model. The reader is advised to work with a data set like MNIST (introduced in Chapter 5) to systematically build and improve models to internalize the key concepts introduced in this chapter.

Index

A

Activation functions, 27–29, 31–33
Adadelta, 123
Adagrad algorithm, 122
Adam, 123
Adjointmode. *See* Reverse mode
Artificial Intelligence (AI), 1
Autograd, 33, 145–146, 148
Automatic differentiation
    fundamentals, 135
        forward mode, 136–140
        implementation, 143
        operator overloading, 144
        reverse mode, 140–141, 143
        source code transformation, 143–144
    hands-on with Autograd, 145–146, 148
    numerical differentiation, 133–134
    symbolic differentiation, 134–135

B

Backward difference method, 133
Bernoulli distribution, 25, 28
Bidirectional RNN, 91–92
Binary classification, 7–8
Binary cross entropy, 25–27

C

Central difference approach, 134
Composite functions, 135
Computational graph, 137–140
Computationally heavy code, 150
Compute-intensive code, 150
Constant error carousal, 95
Convolution-detector-pooling block, 72–75
Convolution Neural Networks (CNNs), 184–191, 205–206, 220
    convolution-detector-pooling block, 72–75
    intuition, 77–78
    operation, 63
        fully connected layers, 68
        intuition, 64, 66
        one dimension, 65
        sparse interactions in layer, 69
        tied weights, 70
        two dimensions, 66–67
    pooling operation, 70–71
    variants, 76–77
Cost functions
    computation of, 22
    using Maximum Likelihood
        binary cross entropy, 25
        cross entropy, 25–26
        squared error, 26
Cotangent linearmode. *See* Reverse mode
Cross-correlation, 63, 66
Cross entropy, 25–27

D

Data procurement, 218
Deep learning, 3
Depth of network, 20
Device memory, 155
Digital Signal Processors (DSPs), 150
Downpour, 127

E

End-to-end pipeline, 220
Equilibrated SGD, 124
Exploding gradient, 92–93

F

Feedforward neural networks
    function, 17
    hands-on with Autograd, 33
    for regression, 31–32
    structure, 19–20

INDEX

Feedforward neural networks (*cont.*)
    training, 23–24
    units, 17, 19
        hyperbolic tangent, 30
        linear, 28
        ReLU, 29
        sigmoid unit, 28
        softmax layer, 29
    vector form, 20–21
Field Programmable Gate Arrays (FPGAs), 150
Forward mode, 136–140
Fully connected layer, 68, 75, 77

G

Generalization, 9, 14
    actual and predicted values, 12–13
    dataset for regression, 11
    least squares, 11
    model capacity, 14
    RMSE metric, 12
    vs. rote learning, 9–10
Global indexing space, 155
Global memory, 153
Go-live testing set, 219
Gradient-based methods, 27
Graphics Processing Unit (GPU), 159
    computationally heavy code, 150
    compute-intensive code, 150
    key elements, 150
    sequential code, 150
    SIMD, 149

H

Hidden layers, 19
Hogwild, 126
Hyperbolic tangent, 30
Hyper-parameter tuning, 221–222

I, J

Intermediate symbolic forms, 135

K

Keras
    activation function, 99–106
    adadelta, 109
    building blocks, 97
    computational graph, 97
    convolution neural networks, 106–109
    dropout layers, 109
    flatten layers, 109
    functionality, 97
    IMDB, 111
    IMDB, 111
    input and output dimensionality, 97, 99–100
    loss function, 97, 99
    LSTM, 97, 109, 111
    multiclass classification, 101–102
    optimisers, 104–105
    optimization algorithm, 97
    pooling operation, 109
    regression, 102–104
    Sequential construct, 97, 99–100, 102
    single layer neural network, 98
    softmax, 109
    softmax activation, 100
    Theano, 97
    two convolution-detector, 109
    two layer neural network, 99

L

Linear regression model, 176, 178–179
Linear unit, 28
Logistic regression model, 148, 179–182
Long Short Term Memory (LSTM), 95
Loss function, 22–27

M

Machine learning
    algorithm, 2
    binary classification, 7–8
    generalization, 9–14
    intuition, 7
    regression, 8–9
    regularization, 14–16
Matrix multiplication, 157–158
Maximum Likelihood, cost functions, 24
    binary cross entropy, 25
    cross entropy, 25–26
    squared error, 26
Model capacity, 209
Multinomial distribution, 25

N

Nesterov accelerated gradient (NAS), 121
Neural network model, 182–183
Numerical differentiation, 133–134
Numpy Library, 145

O

OpenCL, 150
    command queues, 152
    defined, 150

device memory, 153
global memory, 153
GPUs, 155–156
heterogeneous, 151
kernel, 152
private memory, 154
system logical view, 152
system physical view, 151
two-dimensional NDRange index space, 154
work group, 154, 155
Operator overloading, 144
Overfitting, 209, 220–221

P, Q

Pooling operation, 70, 78
Private memory, 154
PyTorch
    computing gradients, 200–201
    convolution neural network, 205–206
    linear regression, 201–202
    neural network model, 204–205
    Numpy data structures, 198
    optimizers, 202–203
    recurrent neural network, 207–208
    tensor creation, 195–197
    tensor operations, 198–200

R

RandomStreams, 49
Random variation, 9
Receiver Operating Characteristics (ROC) curve, 217
Rectified Linear Unit (ReLU), 29
Recurrent Neural Networks (RNNs)
    basics, 79–82, 84
    bidirectional, 91–92
    equations, 79–80, 82
    gradient clipping, 93–94
    gradient explosion, 92–93
    LSTM, 95
    notation, 79
    points to be remembered, 84
    recurrence using output, 81
    tanh activation function, 80, 82, 91
    teacher forcing, 90–91
    training, 84–88, 90
    unrolling, 85–89
    vanishing gradients, 92–94
Regression, 8–9
Regularization techniques
    dropout, 213–214
    early stopping, 210–211
    norm penalties, 212–213

Resilient Backpropagation, 124
Reverse mode, 140–143
RMSProp algorithm, 122–123
Root mean squared error (RMSE), 8–9
Rote learning, 14

S

Scipy, 134
Sequential code, 150
Sigmoid unit, 28
Simple function, 136
Single instruction, multiple data (SIMD), 149
Softmax
    activation function, 91
    layer, 29
    units, 27
Source code transformation, 143–144
Split data, 219
Squared error, 26
Stochastic gradient descent (SGD), 113
    algorithmic variations, 120
        Adadelta, 123
        Adagrad algorithm, 122
        Adam, 123
        annealing and learning rate schedules, 122
        Equilibrated SGD, 124
        momentum, 120–121
        NAS, 121
        Resilient Backpropagation, 124
        RMSProp, 122–123
    batch *vs.* stochastic, 116
    challenges, 116
        local minima, 117
        saddle points, 117–118
        selecting learning rate, 118–119
        slow progress in narrow valleys, 120
    with Downhill, 128–129
        generating data, 128
        loss function, 129
        training and validation, 131
        variants, 132
    method of steepest descent, 114–115
    optimization problems, 113–114
    stochastic mini-batch, 116
    stochastic single example, 116
    tricks and tips
        activation function, choice of, 125
        batch normalization, 125
        Downpour, 127
        early stopping, 126
        gradient noise, 126
        Hogwild, 126
        initializing parameters, 125
        parallel and distributed, 126

Stochastic gradient descent (SGD) (*cont.*)
    preprocessing input data, 124
    preprocessing target value, 125
    shuffling data, 125
Symbolic differentiation, 134–135
SymPy, 135

T

Tangent linearmode. *See* Forward mode
Tensorboard, 159
Tensorflow, 97
    characteristic, 159
    CNN, 184–191
    constant scalars and scalar placeholders, 163–164
    initialization operations, 174–176
    landscape, 159
    linear regression model, 176–179
    logistic regression model, 179–182
    matrix operations, 173–174
    neural network, 182–183
    overall flow, 159
    placeholder, 161
    placeholders, variables, and constants, 171–172
    scalar constants, 160–161
    scalar placeholder, 162
    scalar variables and scalar placeholders, 164, 166
    summaries, 192, 194
    vector constants, 166–167
        placeholders, 169–170
        variables and placeholders, 170–171
    vector placeholders, 167–169
Theano, 97, 145, 159
    definition, 35
    hands-on, 36
        activiation functions, 39, 41
        computing gradients, 44
        functions with scalars, 36–37
        functions with scalars and vectors, 38–39
        functions with vectors, 37–38
        gradients, 43
        hinge implemented using max, 57
        linear regression, 53–54
        logistic regression, 51–52
        loss functions, 44–45
        neural network, 55–56
        random streams, 49–50
        regularization, 47–48
        shared variable, 42–43
        switch/if-else, 56
    workflow for using, 35
Training deep learning models
    baseline model, standard choices, 220
    data procurement, 218
    end-to-end pipeline, 220
    error rate, 219
    overfitting and underfitting, 220
    performance metrics
        class imbalance, 215
        PR curve, 216
        precision and recall, 216
        ROC curve, 218
        true positive and false positive rates, 217
        unequal misclassification cost, 215
Tuning hyper-parameters, 222

U

Underfitting, 209–210, 220–221
Unrolling process, 85–89

V

Vanishing gradients, 92–95
Vector addition, 156–157
Vector form, 20–21

W, X, Y, Z

Width of layer, 19
Work groups, 154, 155

Get the eBook for only $5!

Why limit yourself?

With most of our titles available in both PDF and ePUB format, you can access your content wherever and however you wish—on your PC, phone, tablet, or reader.

Since you've purchased this print book, we are happy to offer you the eBook for just $5.

To learn more, go to http://www.apress.com/companion or contact support@apress.com.

Apress®

All Apress eBooks are subject to copyright. All rights are reserved by the Publisher, whether the whole or part of the material is concerned, specifically the rights of translation, reprinting, reuse of illustrations, recitation, broadcasting, reproduction on microfilms or in any other physical way, and transmission or information storage and retrieval, electronic adaptation, computer software, or by similar or dissimilar methodology now known or hereafter developed. Exempted from this legal reservation are brief excerpts in connection with reviews or scholarly analysis or material supplied specifically for the purpose of being entered and executed on a computer system, for exclusive use by the purchaser of the work. Duplication of this publication or parts thereof is permitted only under the provisions of the Copyright Law of the Publisher's location, in its current version, and permission for use must always be obtained from Springer. Permissions for use may be obtained through RightsLink at the Copyright Clearance Center. Violations are liable to prosecution under the respective Copyright Law.

CPSIA information can be obtained
at www.ICGtesting.com
Printed in the USA
LVHW051527190319
611158LV00010B/530/P